imate

UTY

D K

The Ultimate
BEAUTY
BOOK

The complete professional guide to skin-care, make-up,
haircare, hairstyling, fitness, body toning, diet, health and vitality

SALLY NORTON • KATE SHAPLAND • JACKI WADESON

HERMES
HOUSE

This edition published in 2002 by
Hermes House

© 1996 Anness Publishing Limited

Hermes House is an imprint of
Anness Publishing Limited
Hermes House
88–89 Blackfriars Road
London SE1 8HA

Publisher: Joanna Lorenz
Project Editors: Sylvie Wooton and Casey Horton
Photography: Nick Cole, Alistair Hughes and Simon Bottomley
Designers: Patrick Mcleavey, Ruth Prentice and Blackjacks
Make-up: Debbi Finlow, Vanessa Haines, Liz Kitchiner and Paul Miller
Additional make-up: Bettina Graham
Hair: Debbie Finlow and Kathleen Bray
Assisted by Wendy M B Cook
Exercise advisor: Dean Hodgkin
Exercise and Diet Consultant: Dr Naomi Lewis
Illustrator: Cherril Parris
Models: Amanda, Christiana, Carley, Laura Emily, Frieda, Hannah, Juliet, Sarah,
Zonna, Cheryl, Jane, Joanna and Stacey
Production Controller: Don Campaniello

Printed and bound in China

ACKNOWLEDGEMENTS
With many thanks to the following companies. Beauty products from The Body Shop, Boots, Bourjois,
Crabtree & Evelyn, Cutex, Elancyl, L'Oreal, Rimmel and Sensiq. Hair products from Aveda, Bain de Terre,
The Body Shop, Citre, Clynol, Daniel Gavin, Dome, Goldwell, John Frieda, Joico, KMS, Lamaur, Lazartigue,
L'Oreal, Matrix Essentials, Neal's Yard Remedies, Nicky Clarke, Ore-an, Paul Mitchell, Phytologie, Poly,
Redken, Revlon, Schwarzkopf, Silvikrin, St Ives, Trevor Sorbie, Wella, Vidal Sassoon, Zotos. Electrical styling
products from Babyliss, Braun, Clairol, Carmen, Hair Tools, Philips, Rowenta, Vidal Sassoon. Clothing and
accessories from Adrian Mann, Bhs, Debenhams, Descamps, Empire, Fenwicks, Freemans, French
Connection, Knickerbox, Marks & Spencer, Whistles.

CONTENTS

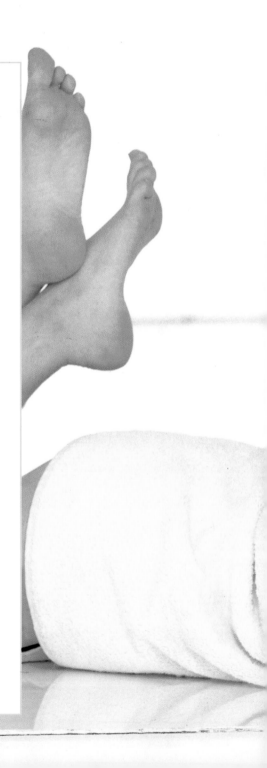

SKIN-CARE

AND

MAKE-UP

It is not only Supermodels and Hollywood stars who can look wonderful. Every woman can make the most of her looks by learning the tricks of the trade, overcoming particular beauty problems and perfecting a look that really suits her.

This section peels away the mystique surrounding the world of skin-care, make-up and beauty products and shows you how to identify your special beauty needs to create tailormade regimes and a make-up look to suit you. Every woman is different, but by analysing what works for you, you'll save yourself time, money and effort while looking better than you ever have before.

WHAT IS SKIN?

The dermis

The dermis is the layer that lies underneath the epidermis, and it is composed entirely of living cells. It consists of bundles of tough fibres which give your skin its elasticity, firmness and strength. There are also blood vessels, which feed vital nutrients to these areas.

Whereas the epidermis can usually repair itself and make itself as good as new, the dermis will be permanently damaged by injury.

The dermis also contains the following specialized organs:

Sebaceous glands are tiny organs which usually open into hair follicles on the surface of your skin. They produce an oily secretion, called sebum, which is your skin's natural lubricant.

The sebaceous glands are most concentrated on the scalp and face – particularly around the nose, cheeks, chin and forehead, which is why these are usually the most oily areas of your skin.

Left: Understanding your skin the way a beauty therapist would allows you to give it the care it deserves and to appreciate why certain factors are good for it – and others are not.
Below: Young or old, everyone's skin has the same basic structure.

Skin is your body's largest organ, covering every single surface of your body. Every woman can have beautiful skin no matter what her age, race or colouring. The secret is to understand how your skin functions, and how to treat it correctly.

TAKING A CLOSER LOOK

Your skin is made up of two main layers, called the epidermis and the dermis.

The epidermis

This is the top layer of skin and the one you can actually see. It protects your body from invasion and infection and helps to seal in moisture. It's built up of several layers of living cells which are then topped by sheets of dead cells. It's constantly growing, with new cells being produced at its base. They quickly die, and are pushed up to the surface by the arrival of new ones. These dead cells eventually flake away, which means that every new layer of skin is another chance to have a soft, glowing complexion.

The lower levels of living cells are fed by the blood supply from underneath, whereas the upper dead cells only need water to ensure they're kept plump and smooth.

The epidermis is responsible for your colouring, as it holds the skin's pigment. Its thickness varies, from area to area. For instance, it's much thicker on the soles of your feet than on your eyelids.

Above: Your skin is a sensor of pain, touch and temperature, offering protection and a means of eliminating waste.

Above: Your skin can cleanse, heal and even renew itself. How effectively it does these things is partly governed by you.

Above: Skin is a barometer of your emotions. It becomes red when you're embarrassed and quickly shows the signs of stress.

Sweat glands are all over your body. There are millions of them and their main function is to regulate your body temperature. When sweat evaporates on the skin's surface, the temperature of your skin drops.

Hairs grow from the hair follicles. They can help keep your body warm by trapping air underneath them. There are no hairs on the soles of your feet and palms of your hands.

THE MAIN FUNCTIONS OF YOUR SKIN

1 It acts as a thermostat, retaining heat or cooling you down with sweat.

2 It offers protection from potentially harmful things.

3 It acts as a waste disposal. Certain waste is expelled from your body 24 hours a day through your skin.

4 It provides you with a sense of touch, to help you communicate with the outside world.

Right: The condition of your skin is an overall sign of your health. It reveals stress, a poor diet and a lack of sleep. Taking care of your health will benefit your skin.

WHAT'S YOUR SKIN-TYPE?

There's no point spending a fortune on expensive skin-care products if you buy the wrong ones for your skin-type and collect yourself an assortment of discarded bottles. The key to developing a skin-care regime that works for you is to analyze your skin-type first.

SKIN-CARE QUIZ
To develop a better understanding of your skin and what will suit it best, start by answering the questions here. Then add up your score and check the list at the end to discover which of the skin-types you fit into.

1 How does your skin feel if you cleanse it with facial wash and water?
A Tight, as though it's too small for your face.
B Smooth and comfortable.
C Dry and itchy in places.
D Fine – quite comfortable.
E Dry in some areas and smooth in others.

2 How does your skin feel if you cleanse it with cream cleanser?
A Relatively comfortable.
B Smooth and comfortable.
C Sometimes comfortable, sometimes itchy.
D Quite oily.
E Oily in some areas and smooth in others.

3 How does your skin usually look by midday?
A Flaky patches appearing.
B Fresh and clean.
C Flaky patches and some redness.
D Shiny.
E Shiny in the T-zone.

4 How often do you break out in spots?
A Hardly ever.
B Occasionally, perhaps before or during your period.
C Occasionally.
D Often.
E Often – in the T-zone.

5 How does your skin react when you use facial toner?
A It stings.
B No problems.
C Stings and itches.
D Feels fresher.
E Feels fresher in some areas but stings in others.

6 How does your skin react to a rich night cream?
A It feels very comfortable.
B Comfortable.
C Sometimes feels comfortable, other times feels irritated.
D Makes my skin feel very oily.
E Oily in the T-zone, and comfortable on the cheeks.

Above: You know best how your skin reacts to different things so check your skin-type before you buy lots of skin-care products. Even if you you've been told what your skin-type is at some stage it is a good idea to run through this quiz now as you skin will change over a period of time.

Now add up your A's, B's, C's, D's and E's. Your skin-type is the one which has the majority of answers.
Mostly A's: Your skin is DRY.
Mostly B's: Your skin is NORMAL.
Mostly C's: Your skin is SENSITIVE.
Mostly D's: Your skin is OILY.
Mostly E's: Your skin is COMBINATION.

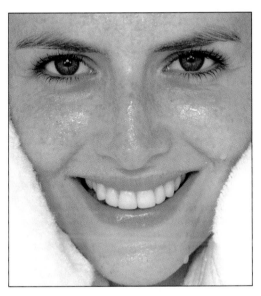

Is traditional soap and water cleansing for you?

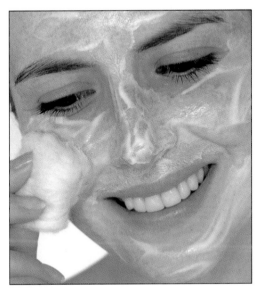

Or is the gentle touch a softer option?

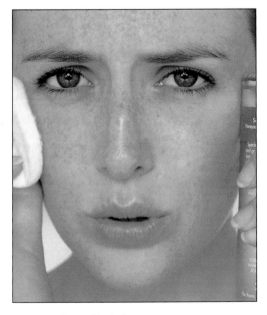

Do toners make your skin sting?

Are your face creams an embarrassment of riches?

THE TOP 10 SKIN-CARE PRODUCTS

Before you can devise the best regime for yourself and give your skin some special care, you need to understand what the main skin-care products are designed to do.

THE KEY TREATMENTS

From a basic soap and water cleansing routine, today's skin-care ranges have evolved into a sophisticated selection.

Facial washes

These liquids are designed to be lathered up with water to dissolve grime, dirt and stale make-up from the skin's surface.

Cleansing bars

Ordinary soap is too drying for most skins. However, now you can foam up with these special bars which will cleanse your skin without stripping it of moisture. They're refreshing for oilier skin-types, and help keep pores clear and prevent pimples and blackheads.

Cream cleansers

These are a wonderful way to cleanse drier complexions. They generally have quite a light, fluid consistency to make them easy to spread onto the skin. They contain oils to dissolve surface dirt and make-up, so they can be easily swept from

your skin with cottonwool (cotton). Use damp cottonwool (cotton) if you prefer a fresher finish.

Toners and astringents

Designed to refresh and cool your skin, they quickly evaporate after being applied to the skin with cottonwool (cotton). They can also remove excess oil from the surface layers of your skin. The word "astringent" on the bottle means it has a higher alcohol content, and is only suitable for oily skins. The words "tonic" and "toner" mean that they're useful for normal or combination skins as they are gentler. Those with dry and sensitive skins should usually avoid these products as they can be too drying. Generally, if the product stings your face, move onto a gentler formulation or weaken it by adding a few drops of distilled water (available from a pharmacist).

Moisturizers

The key function of a moisturizer is to form a barrier film on the surface of your skin and prevent moisture loss from the top layers. This makes the skin feel softer and smoother. Generally, the drier your skin the thicker the moisturizer you should choose. All skin types need a moisturizer.

Moisturizers today also contain a myriad of other ingredients to treat your skin. The most valuable one to look for is a UV filter. With this your moisturizer will give your skin year-round protection from the ageing and burning rays of the sun.

Eye make-up removers

Ordinary cleansers aren't usually sufficient to remove stubborn eye make-up, which is why these products are so useful. If you wear waterproof mascara check that the product you use is designed to remove it.

SPECIAL TREATMENTS

In addition to a basic wardrobe of skin-care products, you can add a few extras.

Face masks

These are intensive treatments, designed either to deep cleanse your skin or dramatically boost its moisture levels.

Facial scrubs and exfoliaters

These creams or gels contain hundreds of tiny abrasive particles. When massaged into damp skin, these particles dislodge dead surface skin cells, revealing the younger, fresher cells underneath.

Eye creams

The delicate skin around your eyes is usually the first to show the signs of ageing. These gels and creams contain special ingredients to plump out fine lines, and keep this skin soft. They can also help reduce puffiness and under eye shadows.

Night creams

These are intensive creams, designed to give your skin extra pampering while you sleep. They can afford to have a thicker consistency because you won't need to apply make-up over the top.

Above: Put some zing into your skin-care regime with a refreshing toner or astringent.

Above: Creamy cleansers should be a top priority for drier complexions, as they cleanse and nourish at the same time.

Right: Before you tailormake a skin-care regime for yourself, you need to know the key benefits of each product.

THE FRESH APPROACH TO OILY SKIN

This skin-type usually has open pores and an oily surface, with a tendency towards pimples, blackheads and a sallow appearance. This is due to the over-production of the oily substance called sebum by the oil glands in the lower layers of the skin. Unfortunately, this skin-type is the one most prone to acne. The good news is that this oiliness will make your skin stay younger-looking for longer – so there are some benefits!

SPECIAL CARE FOR YOUR SKIN

It's important not to treat oily skin too harshly, although this can be tempting when you're faced with a fresh outbreak of pimples. Over-enthusiastic treatment can encourage the oil glands to produce even more sebum, whilst it will leave the surface layers dry and dehydrated.

The best care way to care for oily skin is to use products that gently cleanse away oils from the surface and unblock pores, without drying out and damaging it. The visible part of your skin actually needs water, not oil, to stay soft and supple.

ACNE ALERT

Anyone who has acne knows what a distressing condition it is. It usually appears in our lives at the one time when we're already feeling insecure – adolescence. As well as being a problem that runs in families, it's thought to be triggered by a change in hormones, which results in more sebum being produced by your skin. It can also be aggravated by stress, poor lifestyle and poor skin-care.

Careful skin-care will help keep acne under control. Avoid picking at pimples, as this can lead to scarring. Try over-the-counter blemish treatments. Today's formulations contain ingredients that are very successful at treating this problem. Products containing tea tree oil can be very effective. If these aren't successful, consult your doctor who may be able to provide treatment, or can refer you to a dermatologist.

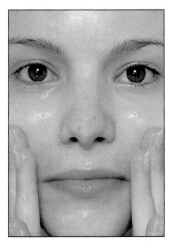

1 Even though the remainder of your face is prone to oiliness, always remember that the skin around your eyes is very delicate, so don't drag at it when removing your eye make-up. Soak a cottonwool (cotton) pad with a non-oily remover and hold over your eyes for a few seconds to give it time to dissolve the make-up. Then lightly stroke away the mascara and make-up from the eyelids, and your upper and lower lashes.

2 Lather up with a gentle foaming facial wash. This is a better choice than ordinary soap, as it won't strip away moisture from your skin, but it will remove grime, dirt and oil. Massage gently over damp skin with your fingertips, then rinse away the soapy suds with lots of warm water.

3 Soak a cottonwool (cotton) ball with a refreshing astringent lotion. Sweep it over your skin to refresh and cool it. This liquid should not irritate or sting your skin – if it does, swap to a product with a gentler formulation or water your existing one down with some distilled water from the pharmacist. Continue until the cottonwool (cotton) comes up completely clean.

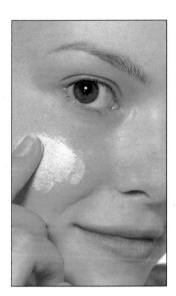

4 Even oily skins need moisturizer, because a moisturizer helps seal water into the top layers to keep the skin soft and supple. However, don't load the skin down with a very heavy formulation. Instead, choose a light, watery fluid as this will be enough for you.

Below: Boosting your skin's moisture levels and controlling excess oiliness will ensure a beautifully clear complexion.

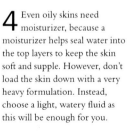

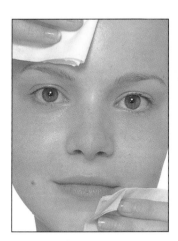

5 Allow the moisturizer to sink into your skin for a few minutes, then press a clean tissue over your face to absorb the excess, and to prevent a shiny complexion.

NOURISHING CARE FOR DRY SKIN

If your skin tends to feel one size too small, it's a fair bet you've got a dry complexion. It's caused by too little sebum in the lower levels of skin, and too little moisture in the upper levels. At its best, it can feel tight and itchy after washing. At its worse it can be flaky, with little patches of dandruff in your eyebrows, and a tendency to premature ageing with the emergence of fine lines and wrinkles. It requires soothing care to look its best.

SPECIAL CARE FOR YOUR SKIN

The condition of dry skin can be aggravated by over-use of soap, detergents and toners. It is also affected by exposure to hot sun, cold winds and central heating. Opt for the gentle approach, concentrating on boosting the skin's moisture level to plump out fine lines and make it soft and supple.

Below: Nourish dry skin to keep it as soft and supple as possible.

1 Pour a little oil-based eye make-up remover onto a cottonwool (cotton) pad and sweep it over the eye area. This oily product will also help soothe away dryness in the delicate eye area, but a little goes a long way. If you overload the skin here with an oily product it can cause puffiness and irritation.

2 Clean up stubborn flecks with a cotton bud (swab) dipped in the eye make-up remover. Be careful not to get the remover in your eyes but work as closely as you can to the eyelashes to remove all signs of make-up.

3 Choose a creamy cleanser which will melt away dirt and make-up from the surface of your skin. It's essential to ensure your skin is really clean. Leave the cleanser on for a few moments for it to work, before sweeping it away with a cottonwool (cotton) pad. Use gentle upward movements to prevent stretching the skin and encouraging lines.

4 One of the main complaints from women with dry skin is that they miss the feeling of water on their skin. However, you can splash your face with cool water to remove excess cleanser and to refresh your skin. This will also help boost the circulation, which means a brighter complexion.

5 This is the most important step of all for dry skins - a nour-ishing cream to seal moisture into the upper levels of your skin. Opt for a thick cream, rather than a runny lotion, as this contains more oil than water, and will help seal in more mois-ture. Give the moisturizer a few minutes to sink into your skin before applying make-up.

BALANCED CARE FOR COMBINATION SKIN

Combination skin needs careful care because it has a blend of oily and dry patches. The centre panel, or T-zone, across the forehead and down the nose and chin tends to be oily, and needs to be treated like oily skin. However, the other areas are prone to dryness and flakiness due to lack of moisture, and need to be treated like dry skin. Having said this, some combination skins don't follow the T-zone pattern and can have patches of dry and oily skin in other arrangements. If you're unsure of your skin's oily and dry areas, press a tissue to your face an hour after washing it. Any greasy patches on the tissue signify oily areas.

SPECIAL CARE FOR YOUR SKIN

Because your skin-type has a combination of dry and oily patches, you need a twin approach to skin-care. Treating your entire complexion like oily skin will leave the dry areas even drier and tighter than

before. In the same way, treating it only like dry skin can provoke excess oiliness and even an outbreak of blemishes. This means you need to deal with the different areas of skin individually with products to suit. This isn't as complicated and difficult as it sounds, and the result will be a softer, smoother and clearer complexion than before!

Left: A twin approach to skin-care will double the benefits for combination skin, and it needn't be terribly time-consuming.

1 Choose an oil-based eye make-up remover to clear away every trace of eye make-up from this delicate area which is prone to dryness. Use a cotton bud (swab) to remove any stubborn traces. Splash with cool water afterwards to rinse away any excess oil.

2 Use a foaming facial wash in the morning to cleanse your skin. This will ensure the oily areas are clean, and that the pores on your nose are kept clear to prevent blackheads and blemishes. Massage a little onto damp skin, concentrating on the oily areas. Leave for a few seconds to dissolve the dirt, then splash with cool water to remove the cleanser.

3 In the evening, switch to a cream cleanser, to ensure the dry areas of skin are kept clean and soothed on a daily basis. This will give you a balance between excess oiliness or excess dryness in your complexion. Massage well into your skin, concentrating on the drier areas, then gently remove with cotton-wool (cotton) pads.

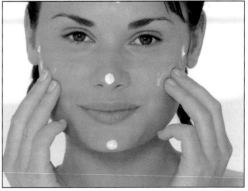

4 To freshen your skin, you need to buy two different strengths of toners to deal with the differing areas of skin. Choose a stronger astringent for the oily areas, and a mild skin freshener for the drier ones. This isn't as expensive as you think, because you'll only need to use a little of each. Sweep over your skin with cottonwool (cotton) pads.

5 Smooth moisturizer onto your entire skin, concentrating on the drier areas. Then blot off any excess from the oily areas with a tissue. This will give all your skin the nourishment it needs.

MAINTAINING NORMAL SKIN

This is the perfect, balanced skin-type! It has a healthy glow, with a fine texture and no open pores. It rarely develops spots or shiny areas. In fact, it's quite rare to find a normal skin, especially as all skins tend to become slightly drier as you get older.

SPECIAL CARE FOR YOUR SKIN

Your main concern is to keep normal skin functioning well, and as a result of this let it continue the good job it's already doing! It naturally has a good balance of oil and moisture levels. Your routine should include gently cleansing your skin to ensure surface grime and stale make-up are removed, and to prevent a build-up of sebum. Then you should boost moisture levels with moisturizer, to protect and pamper your skin.

1 Eye make-up should always be removed carefully. Going to bed with mascara on can lead to sore, puffy eyes. Applying new make-up on the top of stale make-up is positively unhygienic, too! Choose your product according to whether you're wearing ordinary or waterproof mascara.

2 Splash your face with water, then massage in a gentle facial wash and work it up to a lather for about 30 seconds. Take the opportunity to lightly massage your skin, as this will boost the supply of blood to the surface of your skin – which means a rosier complexion.

3 Rinse away with clear water until every soapy trace has been removed from your skin. Then pat your face with a soft towel to absorb residual water from the surface of your skin. Don't rub at your skin, especially around the eyes, as this can encourage wrinkling.

4 Cool your skin with a freshening toner. Again, avoid the delicate eye area as this can become more prone to dryness.

5 Smooth your skin with moisturizing lotion. Dot onto your face, then massage in with your fingertips using light upwards strokes. This will leave a protective film on the skin, allowing make-up to be easily applied and ensuring there's a balanced moisture content.

Below: Follow a regular skin-care regime to
keep normal skin as fresh as a daisy!

SOOTHING CARE FOR SENSITIVE SKIN

Sensitive skin is usually quite fine in texture, with a tendency to be rosier than usual. Easily irritated by products and external factors, it's also prone to redness and allergy, and may have fine broken veins across the cheeks and nose. There are varying levels of sensitivity. If you feel you can't use any products on your skin without irritating it, cleanse with whole milk and moisturize with a solution of glycerin and rosewater. These should soothe it.

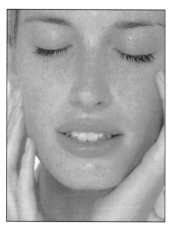

SPECIAL CARE FOR YOUR SKIN

Your skin needs extra-gentle products to keep it healthy. Choose from hypo-allergenic ranges that are specially formulated to protect sensitive skin. They're screened for common irritants, such as fragrance, that can cause dryness, itchiness or even an allergic reaction.

2 Steer clear of facial washes and soaps on your skin, as these are likely to strip your skin of oil and moisture which can increase its sensitivity even more. So, instead, choose a light, hypo-allergenic cleansing lotion.

3 Even the mildest skin freshener ca break down the natural protection your delicate skin needs against the elements. So freshen it by simply splashing with a warm water instead. This will al remove the final traces of cleanser and eye make-up remover from your skin.

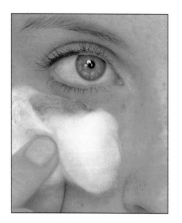

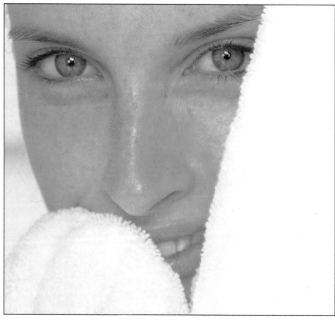

1 Make sure the make-up you use is hypo-allergenic, too, and remove it thoroughly. First use a soothing eye make-up remover. Apply with a cotton-wool (cotton) ball, then remove every last trace with a clean cotton bud (swab).

4 Lightly pat your face dry with a soft towel, taking care not to rub the skin as this could irritate it. (Right)

Below: Careful skin-care will take the sting out of sensitive skin.

5 It's essential to keep your skin well moisturized to strengthen it and provide a barrier against irritants that can lead to sensitivity. Dryness can make sensitive skin even more uncomfortable and irritated, so don't forget to choose an unperfumed moisturizer.

MIRACULOUS MASKS

If there's one skin-care item that can work immediate miracles, it's a face mask! But, like any other skin-care product, you can't just reach for the first one and hope for the best. You should choose carefully to pick the perfect product for you.

MASK IT!

Choose from the wonderful selection of face masks on the market.

Moisturizing masks

These are ideal for dry complexions as they'll boost the moisture levels of your skin. This means they can help banish dry patches, flakiness and even fine lines. They work quickly like an intensive moisturizer, and are usually left on the skin for 5–10 minutes before being removed with a tissue. The slight residue left on your skin will continue to work until you next cleanse your skin. They're a great treat, particularly after sunbathing, or when your skin feels "tight".

Clay and mud masks

These are great for oily skins as they'll absorb excess grease and impurities from your skin, leaving it looking cleaner and fresher. They're an ideal way to "shrink" open pores, blot out shininess and clear away troublesome blemishes. They dry on your skin over a period of 5–15 minutes, then you simply wash them away with warm water, rinsing dead skin cells, dirt and grime away at the same time. They're a great pick-me-up for skin.

Exfoliating masks

Masks with a light exfoliating action can keep your skin in tip-top condition. Even normal skins sometimes suffer from the build-up of dead skin cells, which can create a dull look and lead to future problems such as blackheads. Masks that cleanse and exfoliate are the perfect solution. They smooth on like a clay mask, and are left to dry. When you rinse them away, their tiny abrasive particles slough away the skin's surface debris.

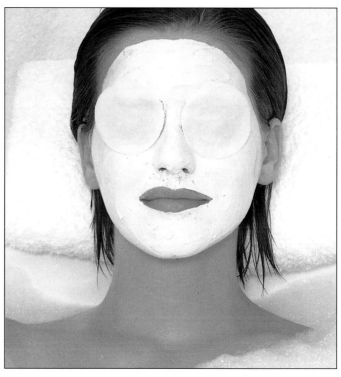

Above: Clay and mud masks: they dry on your skin over a period of 5–15 minutes.

> **TIP**
> If you have combination skin, take this tip from the beauty salons and use two masks – one suitable for oily skin and one for dry skin. Just apply each one to the relevant area that needs it.

Peel-off masks

These are great for all skin-types, and fun to use. You smooth on the gel, leave it to dry, then peel it away. The light formulation will help refresh oily areas, by clearing clogged pores, as well as lightly nourishing drier skins.

Gel masks

These are suitable for sensitive skins, as well as oily complexions, as they have a wonderfully soothing and cooling effect. You simply apply the gel, lie back, then tissue off the excess after 5–10 minutes. They're wonderful after too much sun, or when your skin feels irritated.

POINTS TO REMEMBER

● Your skin can change with the seasons. For instance, skin that becomes oily in the hot summer months can become drier in winter and in central heating. So take your skin's own particular quirks into account when choosing your mask.

● Cleanse your face before applying your chosen mask. Afterwards, rinse with warm water, then apply moisturizer.

● Most masks should be left on the skin for between 3–10 minutes. For the best results, read the instructions carefully.

FACIAL SCRUBS – GRAINS OF TRUTH

Brighten up your complexion in an instant with this skin-care treat! If you don't include a facial scrub in your weekly skin-care regime, then you've been missing out! Technically known as exfoliation, it's a simple method that whisks away dead surface cells from the top of your skin, revealing the plumper, younger ones underneath. It also encourages your skin to speed up cell production, which means that the cells that reach the surface are younger and better-looking. The result is, a brighter, smoother complexion - no matter what your age.

ACTION TACTICS

Use an exfoliater on dry or normal skin once or twice a week. Oily or combination skins can be exfoliated every other day. As a rule, avoid this treatment on sensitive skin, or if you have bad acne. However, you can gently exfoliate pimple-prone skin once a week to help keep pores clear and prevent break-outs.

GETTING TO THE NITTY-GRITTY

• Apply a blob of facial scrub cream to damp skin, massage gently, then rinse away with lots of cool water. Opt for an exfoliater that contains gentler, rounded beads, rather than scratchy ones like crushed kernels.
• Try a mini exfoliating pad, lathering up with soap or facial wash.

Above: Get your skin glowing with a quick and easy facial treat.
Left: Instead of using a facial scrub, gently massage your skin with a soft flannel, facial brush, or old, clean shaving brush.

TIP
Whichever method of exfoliation you use, avoid the delicate eye area. This is because the skin is very fine here and can be easily irritated.

DELICATE CARE FOR EYES

The fine skin around your eyes is the first to show the signs of ageing, as well as dark circles and puffiness. Don't be tempted to deal with the problem by slapping on heavy oils and moisturizers - your eyes will benefit more from specially designed eye creams and gels. The delicate skin around your eyes needs extra special care because it's thinner than the skin on the rest of your face, so it's less able to hold in moisture. There are also fewer oil glands in this area, which adds to the potential dryness, and there's no fatty layer underneath the skin to act as a shock absorber. The result is that this skin quickly loses its elasticity.

Below: Moisturizing the very delicate skin surrounding the eyes calls for special products.

CHOOSING AN EYE TREATMENT

Face creams and oils are too heavy for the eye area. They can block tear ducts, causing puffiness, so you should choose a specific eye treatment that won't aggravate your skin. There are hundreds of products to choose from. Gel-based ones are great for young or oily skins, and are refreshing to use. However, most women find light eye creams and balms more suitable.

Use a tiny amount of the eye treatment, as you don't want to overload this area. It's better to apply it regularly in small quantities than apply lots only occasionally. Apply with your ring finger, as this is the weakest one on your hand and won't stretch the delicate skin. This will help keep your skin more supple, and prevent premature wrinkling in this area.

PREVENTING PUFFY EYES

This is one of the most common beauty problems. These ideas can help:

● Gently tap your skin with your ring finger when you're applying eye cream to encourage the excess fluid to drain away.

● Store creams in the refrigerator, as the coldness will also help reduce puffiness.

● Place strips of grated potato under your eyes to help reduce swelling. Strawberries and cucumber can also help.

● Fill a small bowl with iced water or ice-cold milk. Soak a cottonwool (cotton) pad with the liquid and lie down with the dampened pads over your eyes. Replace the pads as soon as they become warm. Continue for 15 minutes. As well as reducing puffiness, this treatment will brighten the whites of your eyes.

GOOD NIGHT CREAMS

Going to bed with night cream on your face can benefit your skin while you sleep. The main difference between night creams and ordinary daily moisturizers is that most night creams have added ingredients such as vitamins and anti-ageing components. They can be thicker and more intensive than day creams because you don't need to wear make-up on top of them.

Your skin's cell renewal is more active during the night, and night creams are designed to make the most of these hours. Using a night cream gives your skin the chance to repair the daily wear and tear caused by pollution, make-up and ultra-violet light.

Above: Applying night cream before bed means waking up to a softer complexion.
Left: Dry areas, like cheeks, will absorb the extra moisture a night cream can give.

WHO NEEDS NIGHT CREAMS?

While very young skins don't really need the extra nourishing properties of night creams, most women will benefit from using one. Dry and very dry skins respond particularly well. You don't have to choose very rich formulations, as there are lighter alternatives that contain the same special ingredients. Choose the formulation on the basis of how dry your skin is – it shouldn't feel overloaded.

Applying night cream to slightly damp skin can really boost its performance, as this seals in extra moisture – which means softer, smoother skin in the morning.

BE A FRUITY BEAUTY

Since their launch a couple of years ago, skin-care products that contain alpha-hydroxy acids (AHAs) have grown in popularity. They've become the biggest skin-care invention of the 1990s, and their success looks set to continue. Many women find they dramatically improve the condition and look of their skins.

AHA KNOW-HOW

Alpha-hydroxy acids, also commonly known as fruit acids, are found in natural products. These include citric acid from citrus fruit; lactic acid from sour milk; tartaric acid from wine, and malic acid from apples and other fruits. Incorporated in small amounts, AHAs have recently become a key ingredient in specialized skin-care products.

They work by breaking down the protein bonds that hold together the dead cells on the surface of your skin. They then lift them away and reveal the brighter, plumper cells underneath. This gentle process cleans and clears blocked pores, improves your skin-tone and softens the look of fine lines. Basically, they're the ideal solution to most minor skin-care problems. You should start to see results within a couple of weeks. Many women report that they see an improvement after only a few days.

Without even realizing it, women have used AHAs for centuries and have reaped the benefits on their skins. For example Cleopatra is said to have bathed in asses' sour milk and ladies of the French court applied wine to their faces to keep their skin smooth, supple and blemish free — both these ancient beauty aids are now known to contain AHAs.

AHA products are best used under your ordinary everyday moisturizer as a treatment cream. You should avoid applying them to the delicate eye and lip areas. If you have very sensitive skin, you may find they're not suitable for you, but some women experience a slight tingling sensation at first anyway, as the product gets to work.

The great news is that AHA products are now becoming more affordable, and not just the preserve of more expensive skin-care companies. Many mid-market companies are including the benefits of AHAs in their products, so everyone can give their skin the high-tech treatment it deserves. You can also find AHA products for the hands and body, so you can reap the benefits from top to toe.

Above: AHAs (otherwise known as fruit acids) are an effective way to put the zing back into your skin. In fact, there's nothing new about AHAs — by bathing in asses' milk Cleopatra was absorbing AHAs into her skin.

SPECIAL SKIN TREATMENTS

You'd be forgiven for thinking you need a PhD in chemistry to choose a skin treatment these days! As well as basic moisturizers, there are a whole host of special treatments, serums and gels that are designed to treat specific problems.

THE KEY TREATMENTS

You'll find that special skin treatments come in all shapes and sizes, and in various formulations.

Serums and gels

These have an ultra-light formulation, a non-greasy texture and a high concentration of active ingredients. They're not usually designed to be used on their own, except on oily skins. They're generally applied under a moisturizer to enhance its benefits and boost the anti-ageing process.

Above: Good things come in small packages – highly effective ingredients often come in tiny ampules.

Ampule treatments

These are very concentrated active ingredients contained in sealed glass phials or ampules, to ensure that they're very fresh. Typical extracts include herbs, wheat germ, vitamins and collagen – used for their intensive and fast-acting results. Vitamin E is another great skin saver. Break open a capsule and smooth the oil onto your face for an immediate skin treat.

Liposome creams

Liposomes are tiny spheres within the cream which contain and carry special ingredients into the skin. Their shells break down once they're absorbed into the upper layers of your skin, releasing the active ingredients.

Above: Just a few drops of a special skin serum will work wonders on your skin.

Below: Choose a cream that contains specialized ingredients to improve your skin.

Skin-firmers

You can lift your skin instantly with creams that are designed to tighten, firm and smooth. They work by forming an ultra-fine film on the skin, which tightens your complexion and reduces the appearance of fine lines. The effects last for a few hours, and make-up can easily be applied on top. These products are a wonderful treat for a special night out or when you're feeling particularly tired.

Skin energizers

These are creams that contain special ingredients designed to speed up the natural production and repair of skin cells. As well as producing a fresher, younger-looking skin, this is also thought to help combat the signs of ageing.

TRY A FABULOUS FACIAL

For deep-down cleansing and a definite improvement in skin-tone, try an at-home facial. Just once a month will make a noticeable difference to your complexion. Follow these steps to re-create the benefits of the beauty salon in the comfort and privacy of your own home.

1 Smooth your skin with cleansing cream. Leave on for 1-2 minutes to give it time to dissolve grime, oils and stale make-up. Then gently smooth away with cottonwool (cotton).

2 Dampen your skin with warm water. Then, gently massage with a blob of facial scrub, avoiding the delicate eye area. This will loosen dead surface skin cells, and leave your skin softer and smoother. It will also prepare your complexion for the beneficial treatments to come. Rinse away with warm water.

3 Fill a bowl or wash basin with a kettleful of boiling water. Then lean over the top, capturing the steam with a towel placed over your head. Stay there for 5 minutes, to allow the steam to warm and soften your skin. If you have any blackheads, you can try to gently remove them with tissue-covered fingers after this treatment. If you suffer from very sensitive skin, or are prone to broken veins, you should avoid this step.

4 Smooth on a face mask. Choose a clay-based one if you have oily skin, or a moisturizing one if you have dry or normal skin. Leave on for 5 minutes, or for as long as specified by the instructions on the product.

5 Rinse away the face mask with warm water. Finish off with a few splashes of cool water to close your pores and freshen your skin, then pat dry with a towel.

6 Soak a cottonwool (cotton) pad with a skin toner lotion, and smooth over oily areas, such as the nose, chin and forehead.

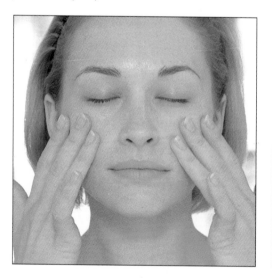

7 Dot your skin with moisturizer and smooth in. Take the opportunity to massage your skin, as this encourages a brighter complexion and can help reduce puffiness.

8 Smooth your undereye areas with a soothing eye cream to reduce fine lines and wrinkles, and make the skin ultra-soft.

EATING FOR BEAUTIFUL SKIN

While lotions and potions can improve your skin from the outside, a healthy diet works from the inside out. A nutritious, balanced diet isn't only a delicious way to eat – it can work wonders for your skin.

YOU ARE WHAT YOU EAT

A diet for a healthy body is the same one as for a healthy, clear complexion. That is, one that contains lots of fresh fruit and vegetables, is high in fibre, low in fat, and low in added sugar and salt. This should provide your body and your skin with all the vitamins and minerals needed to function at their very best.

Healthy skin checklist

These are the essentials your body needs to keep your skin in tip-top condition.
1 The most essential element is water. Although there's water in the foods you eat, you should drink at least two litres (quarts) of water a day to keep your body healthy and your skin clear.

Below: A fresh and fruity diet will keep your complexion looking good.

2 Cellulose carbohydrates, better known as fibre foods, have another less direct effect on the skin. Their action in keeping you regular can help to give you a brighter, clearer complexion.
3 Vitamin A is essential for growth and repair of certain skin tissues. Lack of it causes dryness, itching and loss of skin elasticity. It's found in foods such as carrots, spinach, broccoli and apricots.
4 Vitamin C is needed for collagen production, to help keep your skin firm. It's found in foods such as strawberries, citrus fruits, cabbage, tomatoes and watercress.
5 Vitamin E is an antioxidant vitamin that neutralizes free radicals – highly reactive molecules that can cause ageing. It occurs in foods such as almonds, hazelnuts and wheat germ.
6 Zinc works with vitamin A in the making of collagen and elastin, the fibres that give your skin its strength, elasticity and firmness.

DIET Q & A

A healthy diet and a beautiful complexion go hand in hand together. Check you know the facts.

1 Yo-yo dieting

Q *"Is it true that constantly losing and gaining weight can have a bad effect on your skin?"*

A Yes. Eating too much and becoming overweight thickens the layer of fat under your skin and consequently stretches it. Crash dieting can then result in your skin collapsing, leading to the appearance of lines and wrinkles. What's more, a crash diet will deprive your skin and body of the essential nutrients they need to stay healthy and look good. If you need to lose weight, do it slowly, sensibly and steadily, to give your skin time to acclimatize. It's always advisable to consult your doctor before starting any weight loss programme.

2 Daily diet

Q *"What would be a good typical day's diet for a clearer complexion?"*

A One that follows the rules already outlined. For example, here's a typical day you could follow.
Breakfast: A glass of unsweetened fruit juice; bowl of unsweetened muesli (whole grain cereal), topped with a chopped banana and semi-skimmed (1 per cent or skim) milk; two slices of wholewheat toast with a scraping of low-fat spread.
Lunch: Baked potato, filled with low-fat cottage cheese and plenty of fresh, raw salad; one low-fat yogurt, any flavour.
Evening meal: Grilled fish or chicken, with boiled brown rice, and plenty of steamed vegetables. Fresh fruit salad, topped with natural yogurt and nuts.

3 On the spot

Q *"Does chocolate cause pimples?"*

A There isn't any scientific evidence that links eating chocolate to having breakouts, but as a healthy low-fat, high-fibre diet is known to be good for skin, keep snacks such as chocolate to a minimum and eat them only as an occasional treat.

Below: It's clearly obvious, drinking plenty of
water during the day helps purify your body
– which means a fresher, firmer skin.

10 WAYS TO BEAT WRINKLES

Fine lines and wrinkles aren't inevitable. In fact, skin experts believe that most skin damage can be prevented with a little know-how and some special care. Here are the 10 main points to bear in mind, no matter what your age.

1 Protect your skin from the sun
The single biggest cause of skin ageing is sunlight. You should use a sunscreen every single day of the year. This will help prevent your skin from becoming prematurely aged, as well as guard against burning. The ageing rays of the sun are as prevalent in the cold winter months as in the hot summer ones, so it's a daily safeguard you should take.

2 Stop smoking
Cigarette smoke speeds up the ageing process because it strips your skin of oxygen and slows down the rate at which new cells are regenerated. It's responsible for giving the skin a grey, sluggish look,

and can cause fine lines around the mouth because heavy smokers tend to be constantly pursing their lips to draw on a cigarette.

3 Deep cleanse
Many older women don't cleanse their skin as thoroughly as they should, believing this can lead to dryness and lines. However, it's essential to ensure your skin is clear of dead skin cells, dirt and make-up to give it a youthful, fresh glow.

You don't have to use harsh products to do this – a creamy cleanser removed with cottonwool (cotton) is a good option for most women. If your skin is very dry, try massaging it with an oily cleanser. Leave it on your skin for a few minutes, then rinse away the excess with warm water.

4 Deep moisturize
As well as a daily moisturizer, you can also boost the water levels of your skin on a weekly basis. You can either use a nourishing face mask, or apply a thick layer of your usual moisturizer or night cream. Whichever you choose, leave it on the skin for 5-10 minutes, then remove the excess with tissues. Apply to damp skin for greater effect.

5 Boost the circulation
Buy a gentle facial scrub or exfoliater, and use once a week to keep the surface of your skin soft and smooth. This will also increase the blood flow to the top layers of skin, giving it a rosy glow and help encourage cell renewal. Alternatively, you can get the same effect by lathering up a facial wash on your skin using a clean shaving brush.

6 Disguise lines
Existing lines can be minimized to the naked eye by opting for the latest light-reflecting foundations, concealers and powders. These contain luminescent particles to bounce light away from your skin, making lines less noticeable and giving your skin a wonderful luminosity.

7 Pamper regularly
As well as a regular skin-care regime, remember to treat your skin occasionally to special treatments such as facials, serums and anti-ageing creams. As well as improving the look of your skin, they'll encourage you to give it extra care on a regular basis.

8 Be weather vain
Extremes of cold and hot weather can strip your skin of essential moisture, leaving it dry and more prone to damage. Central heating can have the same effect. For this reason, ensure you moisturize regularly, changing your products according to the seasons.

For instance, you may need a more oily product in the winter, which will keep the cold out and won't freeze on the skin's surface. In hot weather, lighter formulations are more comfortable on the skin, and you can boost their activity by using a few drops of special treatment serum underneath.

9 Be gentle

Be careful you don't drag at your skin when applying skin-care products or make-up. The skin around your eyes is particularly vulnerable to showing the signs of ageing. A heavy touch can cause the skin to stretch and go crepey. So, make sure you always use a light touch instead, and whenever you can, take your strokes upwards, rather than drag the skin down. Also, avoid any products that make your skin itch, sting or feel sensitive. If any product causes this sort of reaction, stop using it at once, and switch to a gentler formulation.

10 Clever make-up

Skin-care benefits aren't just confined to skin-care products these days. In fact, many make-up products now contain UV filters and skin-nourishing ingredients to treat your skin as well as superficially improve it's appearance. So investigate the latest products – it's well worth making use of them for 24-hour day benefits.

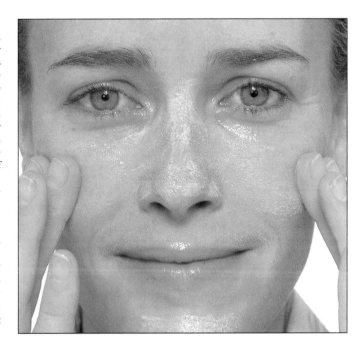

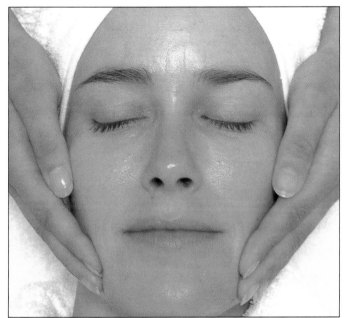

This page (above): Wake up to the benefits of special skin-care treatments.
This page (left): Relax and enjoy a beneficial facial!

Opposite page (left): You won't believe the difference regular cleansing can make.
Opposite page (right): Protect and survive with a good moisturizer.

YOUR TOP 20 SKIN-CARE QUESTIONS ANSWERED

1 Night watch

Q *"My dry skin needs night cream, but I seem to lose most of it onto my pillow. Any solutions?"*

A Put a little night cream into the palm of your hand, then gently rub your hands together. The heat created will help liquefy the cream and make it more easily absorbed. Gently massage it into your skin, and you'll find it sinks in better. Another method is to place the cream in a teaspoon, and heat gently over a low gas flame on the cooker until just warm, before applying as usual. It sounds strange, but really works!

Above: The soft touch of a sponge is a cheap – and effective – option to facial scrub.

2 Polished perfection

Q *"I spend a fortune on skin-care products, but resent paying for an exfoliater. Are there any alternatives?"*

A Yes, here's a good, cheap alternative to facial scrubs! After washing your skin, gently massage with a soft facecloth or natural sponge to ease away the dead surface skin cells which can give your complexion a muddy look. Make sure you avoid ones with scratchy surfaces as they'll be too harsh for your skin. If you have dry skin, massage a little cream cleanser onto damp skin, then rub over the top with

your flannel. Rinse afterwards, then apply moisturizer in the normal way. However, it is essential to wash the facecloth after every couple of uses, and to hang it up to dry in between to prevent the build-up of bacteria.

3 Lip tricks

Q *"How can I stop my lips getting so chapped and flaky in winter?"*

A This three-step action plan will help.
a) Massage dry lips with a generous dollop of petroleum jelly. Allow it to get to work for a couple of minutes to soften your skin. Then, gently rub your lips with a warm, damp facecloth. As the petroleum jelly is removed, the flakes of skin will come with it!
b) Smooth your lips morning and night with a lip balm.
c) Switch to a moisturizing lipstick to prevent your lips from drying out during the daytime.

4 Red nose day

Q *"It's so embarrassing! My nose looks really red in the winter. What's the best way to cover it?"*

A Try smoothing a little green foundation or concealer over the red area before applying your normal foundation and powder. Although it sounds strange, the green works by cancelling out the redness – leaving your skin looking a normal shade again.

5 Winter sun

Q *"Someone told me you should still wear a sunscreen in winter. Is this true?"*

A Yes, if you want to guard against the signs of ageing! Exposure to sunlight is thought to be the main cause of wrinkling, and the ultraviolet A rays that are responsible for this process are around every single day of the year. You don't, however, need to use a suntan lotion – just choose one of the many moisturizers that contain sunscreens.

6 Lighten up

Q *"My skin feels as though it needs a richer cream in the winter months, but I find most of them too heavy. What can you suggest?"*

A Just choose the level of moisturizer that feels right for you. Just because a moisturizer is heavier, it doesn't necessarily mean it's more effective. You can help seal in extra moisture to your skin by spritzing your complexion with water before

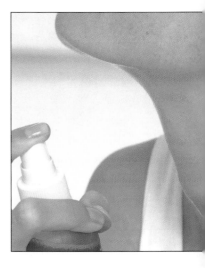

Above: Puttin' on the spritz – boost the moisture in your skin.

applying it. Also, choose a nourishing foundation or tinted moisturizer to ensure your skin stays smooth and soft all day long. You can help counteract the drying effects of central heating by placing a bowl of water near the radiators to replenish moisture levels in the air.

7 Water factor

Q *"I like the feeling of water on my face, but I find soap too drying. Should I switch to a cream cleanser instead?"*

A If you have dry skin, it's generally better to use a creamy cleanser, which you

Left: Cream cleanser will get dry skin deep-down clean.

winds and cold, because this breaks down the natural oily layer which protects your skin. Milder summer weather doesn't tend to be so hard on the skin. The best way to cope is to moisturize regularly with a hypo-allergenic cream that is specially formulated for sensitive skin.

10 Pregnant pause

Q *"I'm pregnant and have developed patches of darker colour on my face, particularly under my eyes and around my mouth. What causes this?"*

A This is called chloasma, or "the mask of pregnancy". It's triggered by a change in hormones at this time, and is made more obvious by sunbathing. Cover up under the sun and wear a sunblock to prevent the patches from becoming denser. It usually fades within a few months of having your baby. Chloasma can also be triggered by birth-control pills, but disappears once you stop taking them.

11 On the spot

Q *I suffer from oily skin, but find blemish creams too drying. What can you suggest?*

A Many women have skin that has dry patches as well as blemishes. The solution is to choose an antibacterial cream that will kill off the cause of your blemishes, while soothing the skin around them. This means you won't be left with dry patches of skin as well as blemishes.

12 Treatment sprays

Q *"I find body lotions too hot and sticky to wear after bathing. Is there anything else I can try?"*

A There's a lovely new trend for body treatment sprays, which combine the moisturizing and toning properties of a body care product with the fragrance of a traditional perfume. This means they'll make you smell beautifully fresh as well as lightly moisturizing your skin. Many of the large perfume companies now offer a choice of these products.

apply with your fingertips and remove with cottonwool (cotton) or soft tissues. This is because it will prevent too much moisture from being lost from the surface of your skin. However, normal and oily skins can still happily use water – but switch to a facial wash or wash-off cleanser instead. They're specially formulated to be non-drying, while still getting your face clean – and you can splash with water as much as you like!

8 Age spots

Q *"I've noticed 'liver spots' appearing on the back of my hands. How are they caused – and how can I get rid of them?"*

A Many people find these light-to-dark brown patches appearing on the back of their hands as they grow older. They can also appear on other areas, such as the forehead and temples. They're caused by an uneven production of the tanning pig-

ment called melanin in the skin. This can be caused by excess sun exposure, or merely highlighted by it.

You can use a cream containing an ingredient called hydroquinone, which works by penetrating the skin tissue to "dissolve" the melanin. Within six to eight weeks, your skin should be back to normal. However, you must ensure you use a safe level of hydroquinone – the recommended amount in a cream is a mere two per cent. Using a sunscreen on your hands on a daily basis can prevent these patches from appearing again.

9 Sensitive issue

Q *"Why does my skin feel more sensitive in winter than summer?"*

A Eighty per cent of women claim to have sensitive skin – which tingles, itches and is prone to dryness. It can be aggravated by harsh winter weather, such as the

13 The throat vote

Q *"The skin on my neck looks grey and dull. Are there any special treats to use?"*

A Necks can quickly show the signs of ageing. This is mainly due to the fact that they have a lack of sebaceous glands. Using a creamy cleanser can help. Massage in, leave to dissolve dirt, and then remove with cottonwool (cotton) pads. Dull grey skin will benefit from regular exfoliation - scrub briskly with a face cloth or soft shaving brush. Grey lines on neck and throat can be bleached away by smoothing plain yogurt over clean skin. Leave on for about half an hour, then rinse away thoroughly with warm water. Boost softness by smoothing on moisturizer. There's no need for a specialized throat cream – your ordinary one will do.

14 Beautiful back

Q *"How can I get rid of the pimples on my back and bottom?"*

A Because backs are covered up, and hard to reach, they're prone to breakouts. Keep yours blemish-free by exfoliating daily with a loofah or body brush to remove dry, flaking skin and superficial blemishes. For more stubborn pimples, try a clay mask to draw out deep-seated impurities. Smooth onto broken-out areas, leave until dry, then rinse away with lots of warm water.

Above: Back to basics with a clay mask for the body.

15 Mole watch

Q *"I understand you need to keep an eye on moles on your skin to guard against the risk of skin cancer. But what exactly should I be looking for?"*

A Moles are clumps of clustered pigment cells that are nearly always darker than freckles. All changes in existing moles should be checked by your doctor. Any that cause concern will be removed and sent off for analysis. You should also check moles yourself once a month. Try the following A.B.C.D. Code: check for A (asymmetry); B (border irregularity); C (colour change); D (change in diameter).

Above: Don't forget your beauty sleep.

16 Shadow sense

Q *"I've got dark shadows under my eyes. What's the best way to deal with them?"*

A Dark shadows can be the result of a variety of causes, including fatigue, anaemia, poor digestion and lack of fresh air. They can also be hereditary. If in doubt, consult your doctor for advice. Take steps to ensure you're cutting out the causes – for instance, getting a good night's sleep, and keeping to a low-fat, high-fibre diet.

For special occasions, you can bathe the area with pads soaked in ice-cold water for 15 minutes. This will help lessen the shadow effect temporarily. Or cover shadows by dotting on some concealer.

17 Brown baby

Q *"Is there anything I can do to hang onto my tan for longer?"*

A Just when you want to show off a golden tan, it begins to peel away. This is because your skin is especially dry after sunbathing, and so it sheds its old cells more quickly. You can prolong the colour for a little while longer by applying lots of body lotion in the morning and evening. Apply it while your skin is still damp to make it extra effective. Apply a little fake tan every few days to keep your colour topped up. Or better still, protect your skin by not tanning at all.

18 Sticky situation

Q *"I exercise a lot, and find body odour a problem. How can I prevent it?"*

A Sweating is your body's natural cooling device. Sweat itself has no odour, but it begins to smell when it comes into contact with bacteria on the skin's surface. Keeping underarms hair-free can help prevent sweat from being trapped.

Opt for an antiperspirant deodorant rather than just an ordinary deodorant alone. The antiperspirants help prevent sweating, while the deodorant helps prevent odour. As a result, a product with the combination of the two is highly effective. Also, try to wear natural fibres next to your skin because they help you to stay fresh for longer.

19 Massage magic

Q *"I had a facial massage in a beauty salon. Is there a way I can give myself one at home?"*

A Yes, just like every other part of your body, your face will look better after a bit of exercise, and a massage is the ideal way to give your complexion a workout. Pour a few drops of vegetable oil into the palms of your hands and smooth it onto your face and neck. Make sure your skin is damp, as this makes the oil go on more easily. Then follow these steps:

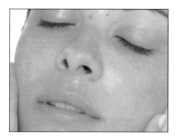

Above: Stroke away the stresses and strains of the day.

- Use the pads of your fingers to stroke upwards from the base of your neck to your chin.
- Continue with long strokes up one side of your face, then the other.
- Now go around your nose and up towards your forehead.
- When you get to your forehead, stroke it across from left to right using one hand. Finish off by gently drawing a circle around each eye using one finger.

20 Stretch marks

Q *"Is there anything I can do to get rid of the stretch marks that have appeared on my tummy, breasts and thighs?"*

A Stretch marks are a sign of your skin's inability to cope with the rapid expansion of flesh underneath. The collagen and elastin fibres underneath actually tear with the sheer strain of it all. They usually make an appearance in times of rapid weight gain, such as puberty and pregnancy. They look quite red when they first appear, although you can take heart that, with time, they fade away to an almost unnoticeable silvery shade.

There's nothing you can do once you've got them, except wait until they start to fade. However, keeping your skin well moisturized can help guard against them. Apply body lotion after a bath or shower, and give it plenty of time to sink in before dressing. Finally, an application of fake tan can be a good disguise for stretch marks that might be on view.

Above: Take time in the bathroom to pamper yourself from top to toe.

BEAUTY BUZZWORDS

If you're confused about the various claims and ingredients in your skin-care products, check out what they mean here in our guide to the most commonly found skin-care jargon.

Allergy-screened

This means that the individual ingredients in the product have gone through exacting tests to ensure that they're safe to use and that there's just the minimum risk of causing allergy.

Aloe vera

The juice from the leaves of this cactus-type plant is often used in skin-care ingredients because of its soothing, protecting and moisturizing qualities.

Anti-oxidants

These work by mopping up and absorbing 'free radicals' from your skin - that is highly reactive molecules that can damage your skin and cause premature ageing. Good anti-oxidants are the ACE vitamins, that is vitamins A, C and E.

Benzoyl peroxide

This is an ingredient commonly used in over-the-counter spot and acne treatments because it gently peels surface skin and unclogs blocked follicles which can cause spots.

Cocoa butter

This comes from the seeds of the cacao tree in tropical climates. Cocoa butter is an excellent moisturizer, especially for dry skin on the body.

Collagen

Collagen is an elastic type of substance in the underlying tissues of your skin that provide support and springiness. Old collagen fibres are less elastic than young collagen, which is one of the main reasons why skin can become less springy as it ages. Collagen is a popular ingredient in skin-care treatments, although it's doubtful if a molecule this size can actually penetrate the skin.

Dermatologically tested

This means the product has been patch tested on a panel of human volunteers to monitor it for any tendency to cause irritation. This means it's usually suitable for sensitive skins.

Exfoliation

Exfoliating means whisking away the top layers of dead surface cells from your skin, making it look brighter and feel smoother. To exfoliate, you massage a gritty exfoliating scrub over damp skin, then rinse away with warm water.

Elastin

These are fibres in the underlying layer of your skin, rather like collagen, which help give it strength and elasticity.

Fruit acids

Also known as AHAs or alpha-hydroxy acids. They're commonly found in natural products, such as fruit, sour milk and wine. AHSs are included in many face creams because they work by breaking down the protein bonds that hold together the dead cells on the skin's surface, to reveal newer, fresher skin underneath.

Below: A pH balanced facial wash will help prevent your skin feeling tight.

Humectants

These ingredients are often found in moisturizers, as they work by attracting moisture to themselves, and so keep the surface layers of your skin well hydrated.

Hypo-allergenic

These products are usually fragrance-free, contain the minimum of colouring agents and no known irritants or sensitizers. This is not a total guarantee that no-one will have an allergic reaction to them. Some people are even allergic to water.

Jojoba oil

Jojoba is a liquid wax obtained from the seeds of a Mexican shrub. It was used for centuries by American Indians. It's a gentle, non-irritant oil which makes an excellent moisturizer as it is easily absorbed into the skin and helps improve the condition of the hair and scalp.

Lanolin free

This means a product doesn't contain the ingredient lanolin – the fat stripped from sheep's wool. At one time it was thought that lanolin was a common skin allergen, although evidence does now seem to show that lanolin is even suitable for sensitive skins.

Liposomes

These are tiny fluid-filled spheres made of the same material that forms cell membranes. Their very small size is said to let them penetrate into the skin's living cells, where they act as delivery parcels that release their active ingredients.

Milia

Another word for whiteheads – small pimples on the skin. Oil produced from the sebaceous glands gathers to form a white plug which is trapped under the skin. You can try to remove these by gently squeezing with tissue-covered fingers or treat them with an antibacterial cream.

Non-comedogenic

A comedo is a blackhead, so this means the product has been screened to eliminate ingredients which can clog the follicles and encourage blackheads and spots. It's particularly useful for oily skins.

Oil of Evening Primrose

The oil taken from the seeds of the evening primrose plant is very useful for helping your skin retain its moisture. It's a wonderful moisturizer, particularly for dry or very dry skins, as it hydrates, protects and soothes. It also improves the skin's overall softness and suppleness. Many sufferers of eczema find it useful.

pH balanced

The pH scale measures the acidity or alkalinity of a solution, with 7 meaning that it is neutral. Any number below that is acidic, and numbers above are alkaline. Healthy skin has a slightly acidic reading, so pH balanced skin-care products are slightly acidic to maintain this natural optimum level.

Retin A

Also known as Retinoic Acid, this is a derivative of vitamin A that has been used for years to treat acne. Now it's available on prescription and to be used under medical supervision, to help reverse the visible signs of ageing on the skin.

Above: Ensure your moisturizer has an effective sunscreen – check the SPFs to be sure.

S.P.F.

These initials stand for Sun Protection Factor. They'll tell you how long the sun cream or moisturizer will protect you from the sun's burning ultraviolet B rays. The higher the number, the more protection it will give you.

T-panel

This is the area across the forehead and down the centre of the face where the oil glands and sweat glands of the face are most concentrated.

Ultraviolet (UV) rays

Ultraviolet light can damage your skin. UVB rays will burn your skin if you sunbathe too long. UVA rays are strong all year round and cause ageing and wrinkling of the skin. Guard against this with a broad-spectrum sun cream, which contains both UVA and UVB filters.

Vitamin E

This is often used in moisturizers because it can help combat dryness and the signs of ageing. It's also useful for helping to heal scars and burns.

Water soluble

Cleansers are described as water-soluble when they contain oils to dissolve grime and make-up from your skin, with the bonus that they can be easily rinsed away.

Below: Try the healing benefits of vitamin E on your skin.

HOW WELL DO YOU CARE FOR YOUR BODY?

BODYWISE MEANS BODY BEAUTIFUL

The secret to a beautifully maintained body is to lavish the same care on it as you do on your complexion and make-up. You need to take into account both general maintenance and any special needs it may have. Whatever beauty boosts your body needs, you'll find the help you need in this section of the book.

Throat

Does skin-care stop at your neck?
Is the skin rough and grey?
Do you indulge yourself with special treats to keep your skin in tip-top condition?

Chest

Do you give your breasts the care they need?
Is your chest prone to breakouts?
Do you protect this area of your skin from the harmful rays of the sun?

Arms

Are your elbows grey and dull in tone?
Is the skin soft and supple, or rough and dry?
Do darker hairs on your lower arms need bleaching?

If you remove hair from your underarms, have you found the best method, the one that suits you for convenience and results? Have you found the solution to underarm freshness?

Hands

Do they suffer from too much housework?
Do they need some moisturizing care?
Are your nails neatly filed and shaped?
Would a lick of polish or a French manicure give them a helping hand?

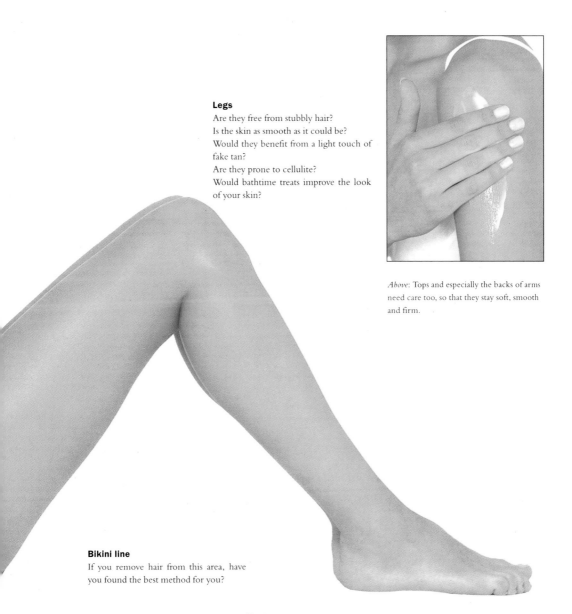

Legs

Are they free from stubbly hair?
Is the skin as smooth as it could be?
Would they benefit from a light touch of
fake tan?
Are they prone to cellulite?
Would bathtime treats improve the look
of your skin?

Above: Tops and especially the backs of arms
need care too, so that they stay soft, smooth
and firm.

Bikini line

If you remove hair from this area, have
you found the best method for you?

Feet

Are they free from hard skin, corns and calluses?
Are your nails neatly trimmed?
Do you smooth a foot cream on them regularly to
ensure that the skin stays soft?

BATHROOM ESSENTIALS

Caring for your body creates endless rewards. So, keep a selection of beauty products on hand to maintain your skin from top to toe on a daily and occasional basis.

BATHING BEAUTY

The time of day and even the time of year will affect what you like using, so why not take the opportunity to try different products, adding the ones you particularly like to those you already know well.

Below: Wonder bars for the body.

Soaps and cleansing bars

These are a cheap and effective way of cleansing your body. If you find them too drying, choose ones that contain moisturizers to minimize these effects. Most people can use ordinary soaps and cleansers without any problem. However, if you have particularly dry or sensitive skin, opt for the pH-balanced variety.

Shower gels and bubble baths

These are mild detergents that help cleanse your body while you soak in the water. There are hundreds of varieties to choose from, including those containing a host of additives, ranging from herbs to essential oils. If you find them too harsh for your skin, look for the ones that offer 2-in-1 benefits – these contain moisturizers as well, to soothe your skin.

Sponges and washcloths

These are useful for lathering up soaps and gels on your skin, and dislodging dirt and grime from your body. Wash your washcloth regularly, and allow it to dry between uses on a wash line or the bathroom window sill. Natural sponges are a more expensive but long-lasting alternative. Squeeze out afterwards in warm clear water and allow to dry naturally. However, don't underestimate the power of your hands for washing yourself; they keep you in touch with your body and will make you aware of any lumps, bumps and changes in texture that occur.

Bath oils

These are a wonderful beauty boon for those with dry skins. They float on the top of the water, and your entire body becomes covered with a fine film when you step out of the bath. Most cosmetic houses produce a bath oil, but if you're not worried about the fragrance, you can use a few drops of any vegetable oil, such as olive, corn or peanut.

Bath salts

Made from sodium carbonate, these are particularly useful for softening hard water, and for preventing your skin from becoming too dry. Combined with warm water, they're a popular way to soothe away aches and pains.

Below: Bubbles, bubbles - soothe away toils and troubles!

Above: Stock your bathroom shelves for top-to-toe freshness.
Right: Grab yourself some bathroom benefits!

BATHROOM TREATMENTS

As well as a chance to cleanse your body, bath- or shower-time is the perfect opportunity to pamper and polish your skin, and indulge in some beauty treats.

SUPER SOFT SKIN
Try some of these effective body treats on a regular basis!

Body lotions and oils
These can seal moisture into your skin, making it soft and smooth. Especially concentrate them on drier areas such as feet, elbows and knees. Oilier and normal skins benefit from lotions, while oils and creams suit drier skins.

Exfoliating scrubs
These help combat the rough patches and blackheads that can appear on your skin. Use once or twice a week in the bath or shower, rinsing away the excess with clear warm water.

Pumice stone
These are made from very porous volcanic rock, and work best if you lather up with soap before rubbing at hardened areas of skin in a circular motion. Don't rub too fiercely or else you'll make the skin sore. A little and often is best.

Loofah or back-brush
Loofahs are useful as exfoliators, and their length makes them great for scrubbing difficult-to-reach areas like the back. They're actually the pod of an Egyptian plant and need a bit of care if they're to last. Rinse and drain them thoroughly after use to stop them going black and mouldy. Avoid rinsing them in vinegar and lemon juice as this can be too harsh for these once-living things. Back-brushes are easier to care for; you simply rinse them in cool water after use and leave them to dry.

Right: Get back to basics with a brush to reach difficult areas.

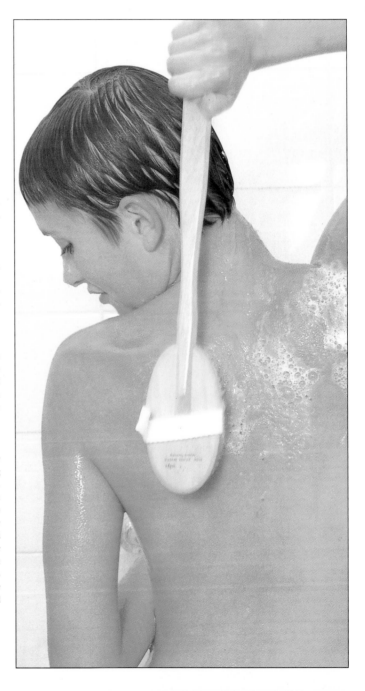

GET FRESH!

From cleaning your teeth to preventing underarm odour, here's the lowdown.

A toothbrush

You need to choose the right toothbrush to get the maximum benefit from it. A nylon brush is best, as bristle splits and loses its shape quickly. Choose one with a small head so you can easily clean your back teeth. A soft or medium brush is best as the harder brushes may damage the tooth enamel and gums. Change your toothbrush regularly, about every month.

Dental floss

Use floss at least once a day to clean between the teeth where the toothbrush can't reach. Waxed floss is best as it's less likely to catch on fillings or uneven edges. To floss, wind a short length around the second finger of each hand. Slide it gently down between two of the teeth, taking care to press it against the side of the tooth. Then gently slide it upwards out of the teeth, removing any food particles with it. Repeat between all of the teeth.

Antiperspirant deodorant

Deodorants don't stop perspiration - they only stop the bacteria from decomposing the sweat. If you perspire heavily, use an antiperspirant or even better an antiperspirant deodorant. The antiperspirant part prevents the production of sweat. Never use on inflamed or broken skin or immediately after shaving.

Talcum powder

Talcum powder is made from finely ground magnesium silicate, usually perfumed. It has been out of fashion in recent years, which is a shame as it makes you smell fresh and helps you slide into your clothes, but it is no substitute for a thorough job with the towel, especially between the toes.

Right: Powder power for fresh, dry skin!

FRESH IDEAS FOR THE SHOWER & BATH

Once you've armed yourself with some bathroom basics, try these water-baby treats to boost your body, beauty and mood.

BATH-TIME TREATS

Soaking in a warm bath has to be one of the most popular ways to relax. You can literally feel your cares disappear as you sink into the soothing water. However you can also use bathtime for a variety of other benefits and beauty boosters.

The sleepy "sitz" bath

The combination of hot and cold temperatures is an effective way of helping you get to sleep. Try a "sitz" bath, which helps you relax by drawing energy away from your head and stopping your mind from racing. Here's how to create your own "sitz" bath:

• Ensure the bathroom is warm, then fill the bath with 7.5-10 cm (3-4 in) of cold water.

• Wrap the top half of your body in a warm sweater or towel, then immerse your hips and bottom in the cold water for 30 seconds.

• Get out of the bath, pat yourself dry, then climb into bed and fall asleep.

Learning to relax

Turn bathtime into an aromatherapy treat by adding relaxing essential oils such as camomile and lavender to the water. Just add a few drops once you've run the bath, then lie back, inhale the vapours and relax. Salts and bubble baths that contain sea minerals and kelp also have a relaxing effect, and purify your skin, too. Bathe by candlelight and listen to soothing music to make it even more of a treat. Put on eye pads and relax for 10 minutes.

Be a natural beauty

You don't have to splash out on expensive bath additives – try making your own:

• Soothe irritated skin by adding a cup of cider vinegar to the running water.

• A cup of powdered milk will soothe rough skin.

Above: Bathtime is more fun if you share it!

• Add a cupful of oatmeal or bran to cleanse, whiten and soothe your skin.

Sleek skin

Smooth your body with body oil before getting into the bath. After soaking for 10 minutes, rub your skin with a soft wash-cloth – you'll be amazed at how much dead skin you remove!

Fabulous fragrance

Add free samples of perfume to a bath. It won't cost you anything and will smell wonderfully luxurious.

SHOWER-TIME TREATS

Showers are a wonderful opportunity to cleanse your body quickly, cheaply and to wake yourself up. Here are some of the other benefits.

Circulation booster

Switch on the cold water before finishing your shower to help boost your circulation. Strangely, it will also make you feel warmer once you get out of the shower! It also works well if you concentrate the blasts of cold water on cellulite-prone areas, as this stimulates the sluggish circulation in these spots.

Boosting benefits

If you pat yourself dry after a bath, it'll help you to unwind, whereas briskly rubbing your skin with a towel will help to invigorate you.

Shower sensation

Add a few drops of essential oils to the floor of the shower itself. As they evaporate you will find that you're surrounded by a sensuous-smelling mist while you wash your body.

BE A SMOOTHIE!

Hair on a woman's body is quite natural, but fashion and cultural practices mean that it's usually removed. Here are the main removal methods.

THE KEY METHODS

There are several different ways to tackle superfluous hair.

Shaving

Shaving works by cutting the hair at the skin surface with a razor blade. It's best for legs and underarms.

Pros: Cheap, quick and painless.
Cons: Regrowth appears again quickly, within a couple of days.

> ### SHAVING TIPS
> • Combine with a moisturizing shave foam or gel for a close shave. Moisturize afterwards to soothe your skin.
>
> • A closer shave means a less frequent one. Let the shaving cream get to work and soften the hair for a few moments before using your razor.

Tweezing

Tweezing plucks out hairs, one at a time. Because it's time-consuming, it's best for small areas like eyebrows, or for removing the odd stray hair missed by waxing.

Pros: Good control for shaping.
Cons: Can be painful and may make skin slightly reddened for a while afterwards. You also need to remember to check the area regularly in a mirror to see that you don't need to re-tweezer.

> ### TWEEZER TIP
> Hold a warm washcloth over the area of hair to dampen and soften it first, and open the pores – this will make tweezing easier. Or, press an ice cube over the area to anaesthetize it first if you find it really painful!

Waxing

This method uproots the hair from below the skin's surface. Either wax is smoothed onto the skin and removed with strips, or pre-prepared wax strips are used. This is a form of hair removal that can be safely used on any part of your body.

Pros: The results last for 2-6 weeks.
Cons: Can be painful and there's the risk of soreness and of ingrowing hairs. Also, hair has to be left to grow until it's long enough to wax, so you have a time when the hairs have grown back. If the hair is too short, it won't come out, or will be removed patchily.

> ### WAXING TIPS
> • After waxing the bikini area, apply an antibacterial cream to prevent infection or a rash.
>
> • Wear loose clothing after waxing.
>
> • Never wax on a sore area.

Depilatory creams

These contain chemicals that weaken the hair at the skin's surface, so hair can be wiped away. Simply apply, leave for about 5-10 minutes, then rinse away. (Check the packaging for exact instructions.) You can use a depilatory cream anywhere, especially as some companies produce different formulations for specific areas.

Do a patch test 24 hours before using the product to make sure it won't cause irritation or an allergy.

Pros: It's cheap, and the results last a bit longer than a razor – up to a week.
Cons: Can be messy, and takes time. The smell of some products can be off-putting although formulations have improved.

Bleaching

Although this isn't technically hair removal, it's a great way to make superfluous hair less noticeable. A solution of hydrogen peroxide solution is used to lighten the hair, which makes it less visible. Bleaching is best for use on your arms, upper lip and face.

Above: Sugaring – the sweeter solution to superfluous hair.
Right: Shaving is the no-fuss option for silky smooth legs.

Pros: Results last between 2-6 weeks, and there's no regrowth.
Cons: Not suitable for coarse hair.

> ### BLEACHING TIP
> If using a new product, do a patch test on your skin first to ensure you don't react to the product's bleaching agents.

Sugaring

Works in a similar way to waxing, but uses a paste made from sugar, lemon and water. It's well known in the Middle East, and is growing in popularity elsewhere.

Pros: Has the same benefits as waxing and can be used anywhere on the body.
Cons: Can be fairly painful and there is a risk of ingrowing hairs.

Electrolysis

A needlelike probe conducts an electric current into the hair follicle, inactivating it. This method is best for small areas such as breasts and face. Go to a qualified practitioner (and ask to see their certificates).

Pros: A permanent solution.
Cons: Expensive and is more painful for some people than others, depending upon your pain threshold. You may find that you are more sensitive to the pain just before or during your period.

INDULGE YOURSELF WITH AROMATHERAPY

Many more of us are waking up to the benefits of aromatherapy these days, and for good reason. It's wonderful to use, the products are easily available, and they can give immediate results. It's no surprise then, that it's one of the most popular therapies around.

Aromatherapy uses essential oils, that are the distilled essences of herbs, plants, flowers and trees. These oils smell wonderful, and are a pleasure to use. It's this smell that usually attracts people to them for treating a variety of physical and mental conditions, from skin infections to stress. There are three main ways to use essential oils.

In your bath

Add 5-10 drops of your chosen oil to your bath, then sink in and relax. Inhaling the wonderful aromas will soothe your mind, and the oils will also have a beneficial effect on your skin and body. Only pour oil into the bath once it's been run, or the oil will evaporate with the heat of the water and you'll lose the therapeutic properties before you even get in!

For massage

Mix 3-4 drops of essential oil into 10 ml (2 teaspoons) of a neutral carrier oil such as sweet almond oil, and use to massage your body – or ask someone else to massage you! Alternatively, choose one of the many pre-blended oils currently on the market. Most aromatherapists believe that you're naturally drawn to the oils that will do you most good at that time – so why not start by experimenting with some of the oils described here.

To perfume your room

Fragrance your room and indulge in the beneficial scent. Clay burners are readily available to diffuse oils into the air. You add the oil to some water in the bowl at the top, then light the night candle underneath. This will prevent the oil from burning and help to create sweet-smelling steam. Alternatively, place 6 drops of your favourite oil in a small bowl

of water and put it in a warm place. There are also ring diffusers you can put on light bulbs, or you can add a few drops of oil to the water in a plant sprayer, and use it to spritz the room whenever you like.

WONDERFUL OILS TO TRY

There are several hundred essential oils to choose from, so it can be confusing knowing which ones to try. These are some useful ones to start with:

Essential oil	Benefits	Use for
Chamomile	calming	headaches and anxiety
Mandarin	calming, refreshing	digestive problems
Eucalyptus	decongestant	colds
Lavender	calming and balancing	stress, colds, headaches, P.M.S.
Peppermint	refreshing	indigestion and sickness
Rose	soothing	depression
Rosemary	antiseptic and stimulating	aches and pains
Sandalwood	relaxing	stress, dry skin-care
Tea tree	anti-bacterial	pimples and cold sores
Ylang ylang	love potion	boosting sex drive

Below: Flower power – treat yourself with fragrant oils from flowers, plants and herbs.

AROMATHERAPY TIPS

1 If you don't want to buy individual essential oils buy them ready-blended, or treat yourself to bath and body products that contain them.

2 Some oils are thought to carry some risk during pregnancy. For this reason, consult a qualified aromatherapist for advice if you are expecting a child and want to use essential oils.

3 Don't try to treat medical conditions with them – always consult your GP.

4 Essential oils can be expensive, but remember that a little goes a long way.

5 Don't apply essential oils to the skin undiluted as they're far too concentrated in this form, and can result in inflammation. The only exception is lavender, which can be used directly on the skin for insect bites and stings. Otherwise essential oils should be mixed with a carrier oil.

6 Don't take essential oils internally. Essential oils are approximately 50 to 100 times more powerful than the plant they were extracted from.

7 Don't apply oils to areas of broken, inflamed or recently scarred skin.

8 Whichever method of aromatherapy you use, shut the door to the room to prevent the aroma from escaping!

9 For immediate results from aromatherapy, try inhaling the steam. Add about 4 drops of your chosen oil to a bowl of hot water, lean over it and cover your head with a towel. Inhale deeply for about 5 minutes.

10 Place a few drops of your favourite oil on a tissue, so you can inhale it whenever you like. Eucalyptus is great if your sinuses are blocked and you have a cold. Alternatively, sprinkle a few drops of chamomile or lavender on your pillow to help you sleep.

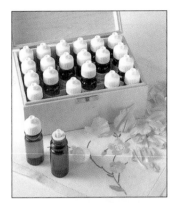

Top left: Special essential oils – for a sensual experience.

Top right: Dilute them in light carrier oil to pamper the body.

Right: Try a soothing aromatherapy bath, and let your cares float away.

BEAT THE CELLULITE PROBLEM

It's not just plumper, older women who suffer from "orange-peel skin" on their thighs, hips, bottom and even tummy – many slim, young women suffer, too. Despite what you may have heard, there is no miracle cure for cellulite, but there are some effective and practical things you can do to see great results.

FACTS ON CELLULITE

Experts differ about what exactly causes cellulite. It seems likely that it's an accumulation of fat, fluid and toxins trapped into the hardened network of elastin and collagen fibres in the deeper levels of your skin. This causes the dimpled effect and feel of cellulite areas. These areas also tend to feel cold to the touch because the flow of blood is constricted and the lymph system, which is responsible for eliminating toxins, can't work properly. This can worsen the problem and make the cellulite feel puffy and spongy.

HAVE I GOT CELLULITE?

Try squeezing the skin of your upper thigh between your thumb and index finger. If the flesh feels lumpy and looks bumpy, you have cellulite. Further clues may be that these areas look whiter, and feel colder than elsewhere on your legs.

Common causes

Cellulite can be caused and/or aggravated by the following:
● A poor diet is full of toxins and puts the body under great strain to get rid of vast quantities of waste. Also, an unhealthy low-fibre, high-fat diet means that the body's digestive system can't work effectively to expel toxins from the body.
● Stress and lack of exercise make your body sluggish and can slow down blood circulation and the lymphatic system.
● Hereditary factors – if your mother has cellulite, it's a fair bet you will have, too.
● Hormones, such as the contraceptive pill or hormone replacement therapy, may be contributory.

TAKING THE SENSIBLE APPROACH

There are dozens of products around designed to deal with cellulite but to really tackle the problem you should follow a three-pronged approach, combining:
• Circulation boosting tactics
• Diet
• Exercise.

Boost your circulation

Here are several ways to boost your circulation and your lymphatic system. Whichever one you choose, aim to follow it for at least 5 minutes a day.
● Use a soft body brush on damp or dry skin, brushing in long sweeping movements over the afflicted area, and working in the direction of the heart.
● Use a massage glove or rough sisal mitt in the same way as above.
● Use a cellulite cream. These usually contain natural ingredients such as horse chestnut, ivy and caffeine to pep up your circulation. However, you can make them doubly effective by massaging them in thoroughly with your fingertips. Or, some cellulite creams come with their own plastic or rubber hand-held mitts to help boost the circulation.

MAKE YOUR OWN CELLULITE CREAM

Some women swear by aromatherapy to treat their cellulite. There are many ready blended oils on the market, but you can make your own. Just add two drops each of rosemary and fennel essential oils to three teaspoons of carrier oil, such as almond oil. Massage this mixture daily thoroughly into the affected areas.

Follow a detox diet

To detoxify your body you need to follow a healthy low-fat, high fibre diet – one that contains plenty of fresh fruit and vegetables. The great news is, if you have any excess weight to lose it will naturally fall away by following these rules.
● Eat at least 5 servings of fresh fruit and vegetables every day.
● Cut down on the amount of fat you eat. For instance, grill rather than fry foods, and cut off visible fat from meat. For many foods you buy, look out for a low-fat alternative.
● Water cleanses your system and flushes toxins from body cells, so drink at least 2 litres (quarts) of pure water every day.
● Change from caffeine-laden tea and coffee to herbal teas and decaffeinated coffee. Sip pure fruit juices rather than fizzy drinks.
● Steer clear of alcohol as much as possible as it adversely affects your liver – your body's main de-toxifier.
● Drink a glass of hot water containing the juice of a fresh lemon when you get up in the morning – it's a wonderful way to detoxify your body.
● Avoid sugary snacks between meals – eat a piece of fruit, raw vegetables or rice cakes instead.

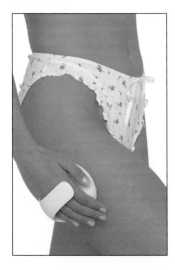

Right: Pep up your circulation and lymphatic system to help beat that cellulite.

Step up your exercise

Exercise will boost your sluggish circulation and lymphatic system, and encourage your body to get rid of the toxins causing your cellulite. Do a regular aerobic workout, exercising for 20-40 minutes, 3-5 times a week, and choose from these: brisk walking, jogging, swimming, cycling, tennis, badminton, aerobic classes or running. (It is always wise to consult your doctor before embarking on a new form of exercise.)

Tone it up!

On a more specific level, you can also try these exercises to firm up your legs and give them a better shape. Carried out daily, they will help you win the cellulite battle.

Bottom toner

Lie on your front with your hands on top of one another, resting your chin on them if you wish. Raise one leg about 13 cm (5 in) off the floor, and hold for a count of 10. Bring your leg back to the floor, and repeat 15-20 times with each leg.

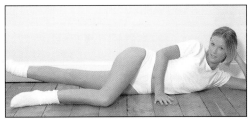

Inner thigh toner

Lie on your side on the floor, supporting your head with your arm. With your top leg resting on the floor in front, raise the lower leg off the floor as far as you can without straining, then gently lower it again. Repeat 10 times, then turn over and work the other leg.

Hip toner

Stand sideways with your hand resting on a chair. Your knees should be slightly bent and your shoulders relaxed. Slowly raise your right leg, keeping your body and raised foot facing forward. Carefully and slowly lower your leg, and then repeat this movement 10 times. Turn round and repeat with the other leg.

Outer thigh toner

Lie on your side, supporting your head with your hand. Bend your lower leg behind you and tilt your hips slightly forward. Place your other hand on the floor in front of you for balance. Slowly lift your upper leg, then bring it down to touch the lower one, and repeat this action 6 times. Repeat on the other side.

BROWNIE POINTS IN THE SUN

There's nothing that lifts your spirits like spending time in the sunshine. However, you need to take special care of your skin against the potential dangers of suntanning. The secret is to give your skin the protection it needs, whilst you gradually develop a light attractive colour.

THE RIGHT PRODUCT

There are so many sun creams and lotions on the market, but it's essential to use the right one because going for the burn can age your skin and increase your chances of skin cancer. So, play safe by following our two-step plan.

STEP 1: KNOW YOUR SPFS

The initials SPF stand for Sun Protection Factor. The higher the number of the SPF, the more protection the product will give you from the burning ultraviolet B (UVB) rays. For instance, an SPF 2 will let you stay out in the sun for twice as long as you usually would without burning, whereas an SPF 8 will let you stay out eight times as long.

STEP 2: GO BY SKIN-TYPE

To decide which SPF suits you, you need to know how vulnerable your skin is to the sun's UVB rays. Dermatologists divide skins into six types, each needing a different level of protection. By knowing your skin-type you can ensure it is always well protected, wherever you travel.

Skin-type 1

Always burns, never tans. Fair-skinned, usually with freckles. Red or blonde hair. Typical Irish or Anglo-Saxon skin-type.
UK/North Europe: Total sunblock, or keep out of the sun.
USA/Tropics/Africa: Total sunblock.
Mediterranean : Total sunblock.

Skin-type 2

Burns easily and tans with difficulty. Fair hair and pale skin. Typical North European skin-type.
UK/North Europe: Start with SPF 20 and use sunblock on delicate areas. Progress gradually to SPF 15.
USA/Tropics/Africa: Start with sunblock and progress gradually to SPF 20.
Mediterranean: Start with SPF 20, use sunblock on delicate areas, and progress gradually to SPF 15.

Skin-type 3

Sometimes burns but tans well. Light brown hair and medium skin tone. Again, a typical North European skin-type.
UK/North Europe: Start with SPF 10 and progress to SPF 8.
USA/Tropics/Africa: Start with SPF 20, moving to SPF 15, then SPF 10.
Mediterranean: Start with SPF 15, moving to SPF 10.

Skin-type 4

Occasionally burns but tans easily. Usually with brown hair and eyes, and olive skin. The typical Mediterranean skin-type.
UK/North Europe: Start with SPF 8, moving to SPF 6.
USA/Tropics/Africa: Start with SPF 15, moving to SPF 8.
Mediterranean: Start with SPF 10, moving to SPF 6.

Skin-type 5

Hardly ever burns and tans very easily. Dark eyes, dark hair and olive skin. A typical Middle Eastern or Asian skin-type.
UK/North Europe: Use SPF 6 throughout.
USA/Tropics/Africa: Start with SPF 8 and move to SPF 6.
Mediterranean: Start with SPF 8 and move to SPF 6.

Skin-type 6

Almost never burns. Has dark hair, eyes and skin. Typical African or Afro-Caribbean skin-type.
UK/North Europe: No sunscreen needed.
USA/Tropics/Africa: Start with SPF 8, moving to SPF 6.
Mediterranean: Use SPF 6 throughout.

A TIP FOR STAR QUALITY!

Many companies producing suntan products have recently introduced a star rating system. This indicates how well the product will protect you against the UVA rays of the sun – the ones that are responsible for the signs of ageing, such as lines and wrinkles. It is worth catching onto if you seriously want to keep your skin young-looking. The more stars your suntan product has, the better.

★

1 star gives moderate UVA protection.

★★

2 stars give good UVA protection.

★★★

3 stars give superior UVA protection.

★★★★

4 stars give maximum UVA protection.

If a product doesn't have this star rating, then doublecheck on the packaging that it does offer good UVA protection.

YOUR SAFE TAN PLAN

● Apply suntan lotion (block) before you go into the sun, and before you dress, to ensure that you don't miss any areas.
● Gradually build up the time you spend in the sun. Never be tempted to burn – it's a sign of skin damage.
● Stay out of the sun between 12 noon and 3 o'clock when the sun is at its hottest. Move into the shade or cover up with a t-shirt and broad-brimmed hat.
● If you're playing a lot of sport or swimming, choose a special sports formula or waterproof formulation.
● Lips need a good lip screen to protect them from burning and chapping.
● Like skin-care ranges, there are hypoallergenic products around, so ask at your pharmacist.

Opposite page, right: Protect and survive. Guard against ageing and the burning rays of the sun with an effective sun cream.
Opposite page far right: Go for the glow with a light golden tan.
Photographs courtesy of Nivea.

JOIN THE BROWNIES –
WITH A FAKE TAN!

The safest tan of all is one that comes out of a bottle! There are three main ways to fake a tan.

Bronzing powders

For use on your face, these act in the same way as a blusher. Make sure that the one you use is not too pearlized, or you'll really shimmer in the sunshine.

Wash-off tanners

These are the simplest way to create an instant tan on your face and body. You simply smooth on the cream, then wash it away at the end of the day.

Self-tanners

If you haven't tried these formulations for years because you remember the awful smell, orange colour and streaky results, then you'll be pleasantly surprised at the dramatic improvements that have been made. In fact, choose carefully, and you'll create an acceptable alternative to the real thing. These products contain an active ingredient called dihydroxyacetone (DHA), which is absorbed by surface skin cells, and turns brown in the presence of oxygen – which creates the "tan". This process usually takes 3-4 hours, and the effects last until these skin cells are naturally shed – which can be from a few days right up to a week.

SELF-TANNING TIPS

● Use a body scrub first to rub away the dead flaky skin that can soak up colour and create a patchy finish.

● Massage in plenty of body lotion over the area to be treated. This will combat any remaining dry areas, and give a smooth surface on which to apply the tanning lotion.

● If there's a shade choice, go with the lighter one, because you can always apply more to get a darker colour.

● Use only a small amount of the product at a time – you can always apply a second layer later on.

● Work the product firmly into the skin until it feels completely dry. Any excess left on the surface is likely to go patchy.

● If you've applied self-tan to your body, wipe areas that don't normally tan with damp cottonwool (cotton) – armpits, nipples, soles of feet and fingers. On the face, work the cottonwool (cotton) around eyebrows, hairline and jawline.

● While there are self-tanning products which offer some protection from the sun until your wash your skin, it's best to use them in conjunction with the best sunscreen for your skin-type.

MAKE-UP FOR EVERY WOMAN

Being considered beautiful today no longer means conforming to one accepted ideal. The contemporary approach to beauty places the emphasis firmly on the individual, and her own particular needs, aspirations and lifestyle. For although every woman is concerned to some extent about how she looks, everyone is very different. For instance, the make-up needs of a blue-eyed blonde are not the same as a dark-eyed woman with an Oriental skin-tone.

The great news is that make-up can be used to enhance everyone's features. Applied with a light touch it should create a subtle emphasis, rather than a mask disguising the features.

PRODUCT KNOW-HOW

No two women are alike. When we're buying a pair of jeans, we don't just pick the same size, colour and pair as our sister, because we have different requirements. Make-up is the same. We need to choose carefully from the vast array of products and formulations around to create a look that's made-to-measure for our own complexions and features. Simply buying the most expensive product on the shelves is no guarantee of success, as it may not be the most suitable for your colouring or skin-type.

These pages will take you through the myriad of bottles, compacts and colours around, and guide you on how to find the ones that work the best for you, and how to apply them.

Tailor-made make-up

The perfect make-up for you will be effortless once you choose the correct shades for your skin-tone and hair colour. It'll also work wonderfully, because you'll still look like you, only better! Checking your hair colour is easy – whether or not it's natural or comes out of a bottle. Deciding whether your skin is "warm" or "cool" can be slightly more difficult – however, there is an easy way to check. Simply look in a mirror and hold a piece of gold and a piece of silver in front of

your face. These can just as easily be pieces of foil or costume jewellery as the real thing. The right metal will bring a healthy glow to your skin, whereas the wrong one will make it look grey. If gold suits your skin, then it's "warm" toned. If silver suits it, it's "cool" toned. A further clue is how well you tan in the sun – cool skin-tones tend to colour less easily.

Inspirational ideas

Sometimes make-up should be used just for the sheer fun of it. Try out a different look for a special occasion, bringing out the make-up artist in you. Whether you want to create an impact in the office, or turn heads at a party, there are lots of ideas to help you put on the perfect face.

Above: Every woman can use make-up to emphasize her best features.
Right: We're all different. What works for one woman may not work for another. Understanding this helps you to bring out the best in yourself.

Problem solvers

Don't just read about them but actually put new ideas into practice! Brush up on tips and tricks to help you maximize your looks, and deal with your own particular beauty needs. Perhaps you need a new look on a budget, speedy ideas or some expert help. Spend a little time to make the most of yourself.

FOUNDATION THAT FITS

Many women avoid foundation, because they're scared of an unnatural, mask-like effect. In fact, finding the right product for you is simpler than you might think. There are two keys to success, the first is to pick the right formulation, and the second is to choose the perfect shade for your skin.

FIND YOUR FORMULATION

Long gone are the days when you could only buy heavy pancake foundation. Now you can choose from many formulations, so you can get the best coverage for your particular skin-type. Here's what's on offer, and who they're best for.

Tinted moisturizers

These are a cross between a moisturizer and a foundation, as they'll soothe your skin while giving a little coverage. They're ideal for young or clear skins. They're also great in the summer, when you want a sheer effect or to even out a fading tan. Unlike other foundations, you can blend tinted moisturizers on with your fingertips.

Liquid foundations

These are the most popular and versatile of all foundation types, because they smooth on easily and offer a natural-looking coverage. They suit all but the driest skins. If you have oily skin or suffer from breakouts, look for an oil-free liquid foundation, to cover affected areas without aggravating them.

Cream foundations

These are thick, rich and moisturizing, making them ideal for dry or mature skins. As they have a fairly heavy texture, make sure you blend them well into your skin with a damp cosmetic sponge.

Mousse foundations

Again these are quite moisturizing, and ideal for drier skins. The best way is to dab a little of the product onto the back of your hand, then dot onto your skin with a sponge.

Above: Spend time finding the right foundation colour for you.

Compact foundations

These are all-in-one formulations, which already contain powder. They come in a compact, usually with their own sponge for application. However, they actually give a lighter finish than you'd expect. They're great on all but dry skin-types.

Stick foundations

These are the original foundation, dating back to the days of Hollywood. They have a heavy texture, and so are best confined for use on badly blemished or scarred skin. Dot a little foundation directly onto the affected area, then blend gently with a damp sponge.

SHADE SELECTION

Once you've chosen the ideal formulation for you, you're ready to choose the perfect matching shade to your skin. At last cosmetic companies have woken up to the fact that not everyone has an "American tan" complexion! Now, there is a good selection of foundation shades from a pink-toned English rose to a yellow-hued, olive skin, as well as from the palest skin to the darkest one. Here's how to select the perfect one for you.

● Ensure you're in natural daylight when trying out foundation colours, so you can see exactly how your skin will look once you leave the shop or counter.
● Select a couple of shades to try, which look as though they'll match your skin.
● Don't try foundation on your hand or on your wrist – they're a different colour to your face.
● Stroke a little colour onto your jawline to ensure you get a tone that will blend with your neck as well as your face. The shade that seems to "disappear" into your skin is the right one for you.

Above: Liquid foundations are popular.

APPLICATION KNOW-HOW

● Apply foundation to freshly moisturized skin to ensure you have a perfect base on which to work.
● Use a cosmetic sponge to apply most types of foundation – using your fingertips can result in an uneven, greasy finish.
● Apply foundation in dots, then blend each one with your sponge.
● Dampen the sponge first of all, then squeeze out the excess moisture – this will prevent the sponge from soaking up too much costly foundation.

● Check for tell-tale "tidemarks" on your jawline, nose, forehead and chin.

HIGH PERFORMANCE FOUNDATION

Companies these days have made wonderful improvements to their foundations. Here are some benefits to look out for.

● Many companies have added sunscreens to their foundations, so they'll protect you from the ageing effects of the sun while you wear them. Look out for the the words UV Protection and Sun Protection Factor (SPF) numbers on the tube or bottle.

● Look for the new "light-diffusing" foundations, which are great for older skins. They contain hundreds of tiny light-reflective particles that bounce light away from your skin – making fine lines, wrinkles and blemishes less noticeable.

COLOUR CORRECT

Colour corrective foundations can be worn under your normal foundation to alter the skin-tone. They can seem quite strange at first glance, but are, in fact, highly effective at toning down a high colour or boosting the colour of your complexion. Use them sparingly at first

until you feel confident that you have achieved an effective, but subtle, result.

● Green foundation cools down rosiness and is great for those who blush easily. Princess Diana wore it under her normal foundation on her wedding day.

● Lavender foundation will brighten up a sallow complexion, and is great for when you're feeling tired.

● Apricot foundation will give a subtle glow to dull skin, and is a great beauty booster in the winter.

● White foundation gives a wonderful glow to all complexions, and is perfect for a special night out.

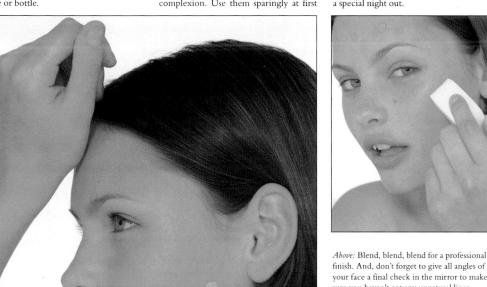

Above: Blend, blend, blend for a professional finish. And, don't forget to give all angles of your face a final check in the mirror to make sure you haven't got any unnatural lines where your foundation finishes.
Left: Before buying, check different foundation colours on your jawline for the perfect match.

CLEVER CONCEALER

Concealers are a fast and effective way to disguise blemishes, shadows, scars and red veins, so your skin looks perfect.

FIND YOUR FORMULATION

Concealers are the ideal way to cover a multitude of sins. They're a concentrated form of foundation with a very high pigment content, so they offer complete coverage to problem areas. Make-up artists argue as to whether concealer should be applied before or after foundation. I think applying it after foundation is best, as it's only applied to specific areas, and these would be disturbed when the foundation was being applied.

If you're after a light make-up effect, apply concealer directly onto clean skin, then apply powder or all-in-one foundation/powder over the top.

Stick concealers

These are easy to apply as you can simply stroke them straight onto the skin. They're the most readily available type on the market. Some have quite a heavy and thick consistency, so it's worth trying the samples in the shop before buying.

Cream concealers

These usually come in a tube, with a sponge-tipped applicator. The coverage isn't as thick as the stick type, but the finished effect is very natural.

Liquid concealers

Again, these come in a tube. Just squeeze a tiny amount of product onto your finger and smooth over the affected area. Look for the cream-to-powder formulations, which slick on like a cream and dry to a velvety powder finish.

> ### CONCEALER TIP
> When choosing a concealer look for the colour nearest to your own skin-tone rather than a lighter one. Covering a problem area with a paler shade will simply accentuate it.

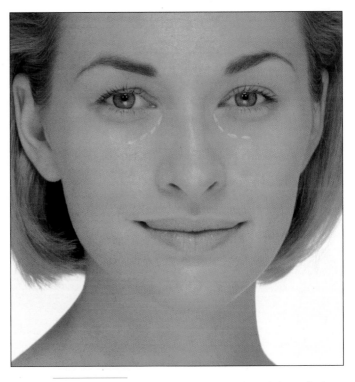

Above: Hide undereye shadows with a few dots of concealer.

TAKING COVER

Here's how to conceal all your beauty problems effectively.

Spots and blemishes

The ideal solution is to use a medicated stick concealer as this contains ingredients to deal with the pimple or blemish as well as cover it. Only apply the concealer exactly on the pimple or blemish, as it can be quite drying, and then smooth away the edges with a clean cotton bud (swab). Applying concealer all around the area will make the spot more noticeable and create a "halo" effect.

Under-eye shadows

Opt for a creamy stick concealer or a liquid one, as dry formulations will emphasize fine lines around your eyes. If you're blending with your fingertips, use your ring finger, as this is the weakest finger on your hand and less likely to drag at the delicate skin around your eyes.

Scars

Scars, including old acne or chickenpox marks, can be effectively covered by concealer but it can be time-consuming to get a perfect result. You need to build the indentation up to skin level by dotting on layers of concealer with a fine brush. Take your time, to allow each layer to settle into the skin properly.

Red veins

Stick or liquid concealer is ideal for this problem. Apply concealer over the area with a fine eyeliner brush or clean cotton bud (swab), then feather out the edges to stop them from being noticeable.

POW! WOW! POWDER!

Face powder is the make-up artist's best friend, as it can make your skin look really wonderful and is very versatile in its uses.

THE POWER OF POWDER

Here are four good reasons for putting on that powder!
● Powder gives a super-smooth sheen to your skin – with or without foundation.
● It "sets" your foundation, so it stays put and looks good for longer.
● Powder absorbs oils from your skin, and helps prevent shiny patches appearing.
● It helps conceal open pores.

CHOOSE YOUR POWDER

You'll need two types of powder – a loose form, and a powder compact for your handbag.

Loose powder

This gives the best and longest-lasting finish and is the choice of professional make-up artists and models. The best way to apply loose powder is to dust it lightly onto your skin using a large, soft powder brush. Then lightly brush over your face again to dust off the excess.

Pressed powder

Compacts containing pressed powder are ideal for carrying in your make-up bag as they're very quick to use and lightweight. Most come with their own application sponges, but you'll find you get a better result if you apply them with a brush. Look for brushes with retractable heads to carry in your make-up bag.

If you do use the sponge, use a light touch, and wash it regularly, or you'll transfer the oils in your skin onto the powder and get a build-up.

Shade away

Don't make the mistake of thinking that one shade of powder suits all. Instead, choose one that closely matches your skin-tone for a natural effect. Do this by dusting a little on your jawline, in the same way as you would with foundation.

Above: Powder gives a perfect featherlight finish to your skin.
Right: Choose the shade that best suits your skin colouring.

POWDER TIP

When dusting excess powder away from your skin, use your brush in light, downward strokes to help prevent the powder from getting caught in the fine hairs on your skin. Pay particular attention to the sides of the face and jawline which aren't so easy for you to see.

BEAUTIFUL BLUSHER

Give your complexion a bloom of colour with this indispensable beauty aid.

BLUSH BABY

Blusher is an instant way to give your looks a lift. It's old fashioned to use blusher to sculpt your face, as it looks so unnatural. Instead, it should be applied in the way it was first intended to be used – to recreate a youthful flush.

Powder blusher

This should be applied over the top of your foundation and face powder. To apply powder blusher, dust over the compact with a large soft brush. If you've taken too much onto your brush, tap the handle on the back of your hand to remove the excess. It's better to waste a little blusher than apply too much! A good guide is to use half as much blusher, and twice as much blending as you first think you need.

Start the colour on the fullest parts of your cheeks, directly below the centre of your eyes. Then smile and dust the blusher over your cheekbones, and up towards your temples. Blend the colour well towards the hairline, so you avoid harsh edges. This will place colour where you would naturally blush.

Right: Brush your cheeks with colour.
Below: Be a blushing beauty with a light touch of powder blusher.

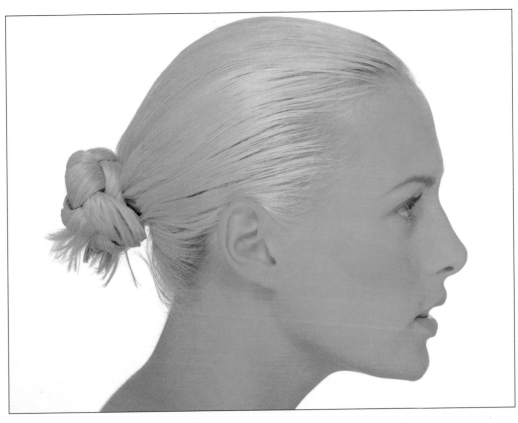

Cream blusher

Cream blusher breaks all the traditional beauty rules, as it's applied with your fingertips. It's put on after foundation, and before face powder. It's been out of fashion for some years, but has recently made a comeback. This is for good reason, as it can give a lovely fresh glow to every skin-type.

To apply, dab a few dots of cream blusher over your cheeks, from the plump part up towards your cheekbone. Using your fingertips, blend well. Build up the effect gradually, adding more blusher to create just the look you want. Or, if you prefer, you can use a foundation wedge to blend in cream blusher.

Colour choice

There's always a kaleidoscope of blusher shades to choose from. However, as a general rule, it's best to opt for a shade that tones well with your skin colouring, and co-ordinates with the rest of your make-up. You can opt for lighter or darker shades, depending on the season.

COLOUR GUIDE

Colouring	Choose
Blonde hair, cool skin	Baby pink
Blonde hair, warm skin	Tawny pink
Dark hair, cool skin	Cool rose
Dark hair, warm skin	Rosy brown
Red hair, cool skin	Soft peach
Red hair, warm skin	Warm peach
Dark hair, olive skin	Warm brown
Black hair, dark skin	Terracotta

Right: Powder blusher is a quick and easy option.
Below: Get a glow with cream blusher.

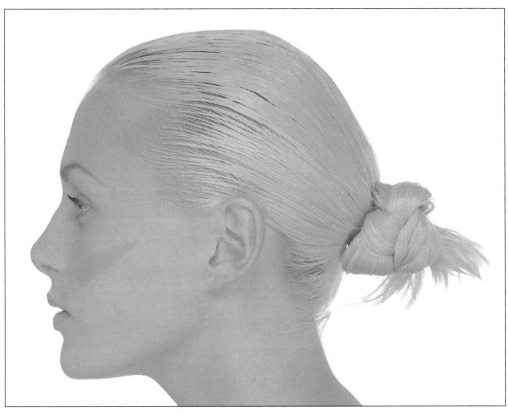

EYE-CATCHING MAKE-UP

Eye make-up is the most popular type of cosmetic, and for good reason. Just the simplest touch of mascara can open up your eyes, while a splash of colour can transform them instantly. Whatever your eye shape and colour, you can ensure they always look beautiful.

MASTERING THE BASICS

Many women hesitate to experiment with eye make-up, because it seems too time-consuming and complicated. The sheer quantity of products on the shelves and make-up counters can make it even more confusing. However, you can create a huge variety of looks – from the simplest to the most extreme – by opening your eyes to the basic techniques.

EYEBROW KNOW-HOW

Many women overlook their eyebrows, or sometimes even worse, overpluck them. When it comes to eye make-up, the eyebrows make an important impression. They can provide a balanced look to your face so it's well worth making the effort to get them looking right.

Natural brows

For perfectly groomed brows in an instant, try combing through them with a

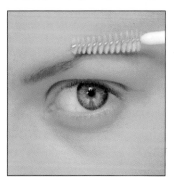

brush to flick away any powder or foundation. Comb the hairs upwards and outwards. This will also help give you a wide-eyed look. Then lightly slick them with clear gel to hold the shape in place.

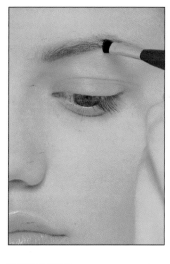

Eyebrow colour

To define your brows you can use eyebrow powder or pencil. Apply powder, with an eyebrow brush, dusting it through your brows and taking care not to sweep it onto the surrounding skin.

This gives a natural effect, and requires little blending. Alternatively, use a well-sharpened pencil to draw on tiny strokes, taking care not to press too hard or the finished effect will be unnatural. Then

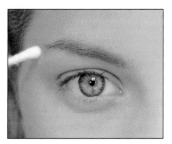

soften your the lines you've made with the eye pencil by lightly stroking a clean cotton bud (swab) through your brows.

LINING UP LINER

The different methods of eyelining change as often as fashions change. However, the basic idea of using eyeliner is a good one. Eyeliner is a great way to flatter all eye shapes and sizes. If you've never applied liner before and feel a bit nervous, try this technique.

Sit down at a table in a good light with a mirror. Take your eyeliner in your hand and rest your elbow on the table to keep your arm and hand steady. You can also give yourself extra support by resting your little finger on your cheek. Eyeliner should be applied after eyeshadow and before your mascara.

Liquid liners

These have a fluid consistency, and usually come with a brush attached to the cap. However, these aren't as easy to apply as the "ink-well" sponge-tipped variety. If you find the brush is too thick, you can pluck away hairs from it using tweezers, as this will allow you to create a thinner line. To apply the liner, look down into your mirror to prevent the liquid smudging. You should stay like this for a few seconds after applying the liner to give it time to dry thoroughly.

Pencil liners

This is the easiest way to add extra emphasis to your eyes. A pencil should be used to draw a line close to your upper and lower lashes. It's a good idea to sharpen the pencil between uses, not only to ensure you have a fine tip with which to work, but also to keep it bacteria-free.

Draw a soft line close to your lashes. If you find this quite difficult, try dotting it on along your lashes, then joining up the dots afterwards! Run over the pencil line with a brush. Alternatively, look for pencils that come with a smudger built in at the other end.

Eyeshadow as eyeliner

Make-up artists often use eyeshadow to outline the eyes, and it's a trick worth stealing! It looks great because it gives a very soft smoky effect. Use a small brush to apply shadow under your lower lashes

and to make an impact over the top of the eyelid, taking care to keep the shadow close to the eyelashes.

To create a softer, more modern effect simply sweep over the eyeshadow liner with a cotton bud (swab).

MASCARA MAGIC

If there's one item of make-up most women would take to a desert island, it's mascara. It's an invaluable way to create a fluttering fringe to your eyes – particularly if your lashes are fair. Most mascaras are applied with a spiral wand, as this makes them quick and easy to use. Some contain fibres to add extra length and thickness to your lashes. Opt for the waterproof variety to withstand tears, showers and swimming – but remember you'll need a suitable eye make-up remover to take it off as it clings more fiercely to your lashes than the other type.

The original block mascara is still quite popular with those who want to build up the thickness and length of their lashes gradually. Simply wet the brush with water before running the bristles over the mascara block and applying.

Applying mascara

Here are a few simple steps to perfect lashes. Start by applying mascara to your upper lashes first. Brush them downwards to start with, then brush your lashes upwards from underneath. Use a tiny zig-zag movement to prevent mascara from clogging on your lashes.

Next, use the tip of the mascara wand to brush your lower lashes, using a gentle side-to-side technique. Take care to keep your hand steady whilst you are applying the mascara, and not to blink whilst the mascara is still wet.

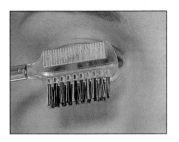

Comb through your lashes with an eyelash comb to remove any excess the wand has left behind, and to prevent your lashes from clumping together. For a more defined effect, repeat the two previous steps once or twice more, allowing each layer of mascara to dry for a few minutes before applying the next.

FALSE EYELASHES

These are great to try for party looks, although they can be tricky to apply. The strip lashes can look obvious unless you apply them perfectly. It's a better idea to use the individual lashes on the outer corners of your eyes. Dot the roots with a little glue, then use a pair of tweezers to place them exactly where you want them.

EYEING UP EYESHADOWS

Choose neutral colours to subtly enhance your looks, or play with a kaleidoscope of different shades.

Powder eyeshadows

The most popular type, these come in pressed cakes of powder either with a small brush or a sponge applicator. You can build up their density from barely-there to dramatic. Apply using a damp brush or sponge if you want a deep colour for an evening look.

Cream shadows

These are oil-based and come in little pots or compacts. They're applied either with a brush or your fingertips. They're a good choice for dry or older skins that need extra moisturizing.

Stick shadows

Wax-based, you smooth these onto your eyelids from the stick. Ensure they have a creamy texture before you buy them, so they won't drag at your skin.

Liquid shadows

Usually these come in a slim bottle with a sponge applicator. Look for the cream-to-powder ones that smooth on as a liquid and blend to a velvety powder finish.

Left: Beautiful eyes – naturally.
Below: Experiment with different coloured powder shadows.

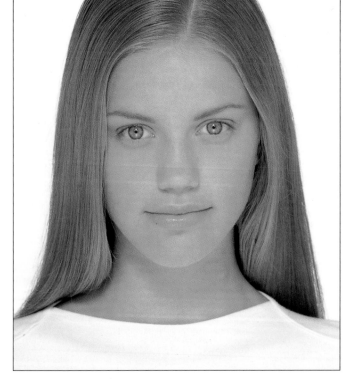

BRUSH UP YOUR MAKE-UP

Even the most expensive make-up in the world won't look particularly great if it's applied carelessly and using your fingertips.

BASIC TOOLS

For a professional finish you need the right tools. This means investing in a set of good brushes and applicators. Here's your basic tool kit.

Make-up sponge

Have a wedge-shaped one, so you can use the finer edges to help blend in foundation round your nose and jawline, while the flatter edges are great for the cheeks, forehead and chin. However, if you prefer not to use a synthetic sponge try the small, natural ones instead.

Powder brush

Get used to using a powder brush each time you put make-up on. To prevent a caked or clogged finish to your face powder, use a large, soft brush to dust away any excess.

Blusher brush

Use to add a pretty glow to your skin with a light dusting of powder blusher. A blusher brush is slightly smaller than a powder brush to make it easier to control.

Eyeshadow brush

Smooth on any shade of eyeshadow with this brush.

Eyeshadow sponge

An sponge applicator is great for applying a sweep of pale eyeshadow that doesn't need much blending or applying highlighter to your brow bones.

All-in-one eyelash brush/comb

Great for combing through your lashes between coats of mascara for a clump-free finish. Flip the comb over and use the brush side to sweep your eyebrows into shape, or soften pencilled-in brows.

Lipbrush

Use to create a perfect outline for your lips and then use to fill in the shape with your lipstick.

Eyebrow tweezers

It is essential to have a good pair of tweezers for regularly tidying up the eyebrows.

Eyelash curlers

Once used, they'll soon become a beauty essential! Curlier eyelashes make a huge difference to the way your lashes look and help open up the eyes.

Below: Bring out the make-up artist in you with a good set of brushes.

EYE MAKE-UP MASTERCLASS

Now that you know where to start, you can experiment with more sophisticated eye make-up methods to create a variety of stunning looks. Here's a look you can try, using a wide range of techniques to create the ultimate in glamorous eye make-up.

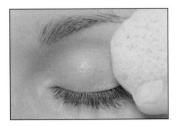

1 Smooth over your eyelids with foundation to create an even base on which to work, and to give your eye make-up something to cling to.

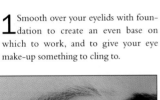

2 Sweep over your eyelids with a brush loaded with translucent face powder.

3 Dust a little translucent powder under your eyes to catch any flecks of fallen eyeshadow.

4 Use a sponge applicator to sweep a neutral ivory shade over your eyelids. Work it right up towards your eyebrows for a balanced overall effect.

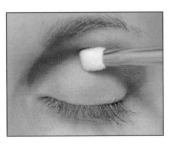

5 Smudge a brown eyeshadow into the socket line of your eyes, using a sponge applicator. If you find blending difficult, try using a slightly shimmery powder as these are easier to work in.

6 Use a brush to sweep over the top of the brown shadow as this will remove any harsh edges.

7 To create a perfectly blended finish, sweep some more ivory shadow over the edges of the brown eyeshadow using a sponge applicator.

8 Now that you've completed your eyeshadow, flick away the powder from under your eyes.

9 Looking down into a mirror and keeping your hand steady, apply liquid eyeliner along your upper lashes.

10 Use a clean cotton bud (swab) to work some brown eyeshadow under your lower lashes to add some subtle definition.

11 Squeeze your lashes with eyelash curlers to make them bend, before applying mascara. This will "open up" the eye area.

Above: For our main look here, we used a palette of ivory and blue eyeshadow, combined with black eyeliner and mascara. Take time to experiment with different colours to find a look that suits you and your colouring.

12 Apply mascara onto your upper lashes and use the tip of the mascara wand to coat your lower lashes.

13 Stroke your eyebrows with pencil to shape them and fill in any patches.

14 Smooth over the top with a cotton bud (swab) to soften the eyebrow pencil line.

LIP SERVICE

Lipstick has been around for about 5,000 years, and women have always loved it. Indeed, during the cosmetic shortages of the Second World War, British women said that lipstick was the item of make-up they missed the most. It's the easiest and quickest way to give your face a focus and give it an instant splash of colour.

A LICK OF COLOUR

Lipsticks in a bullet form are the most popular way to use lip colour. The more pigment a lipstick has, the longer it'll last on your lips. The best way to apply lipstick is with a lipbrush.

Above: A slick of colour will make you love your lips.
Right: A selection of lipstick colours is the key to creating different looks.

Another way of applying colour is with a lip gloss. These can be used alone to give your lips an attractive sheen, or over the top of lipstick to catch the light.

Lip liners are used to provide an outline to your lips before applying lipstick. You can also use them over your entire lip for a dark, matte effect. However, you may need to add a touch of lipsalve (balm) over the top to prevent drying out this delicate area of skin.

STEP-BY-STEP TO PERFECT LIPS

SPECIAL INGREDIENTS

Today's lipsticks offer more than just a pigment to give your lips colour. In just the same way as technology has been used in skin-care products, lipsticks often contain other ingredients to care for the delicate skin on your lips. Here are some that may be included in your lipstick.

● Vegetable wax to make your lipstick smooth on easily, and give a lovely sheen.
● Liposomes containing active moisturizing ingredients, to keep your lips soft.
● Chamomile to soothe and heal the skin on your lips.
● Shea butter to deep-moisturize your lips, especially in extremes of weather and

the wind, which can have drastic effects.
● Silica to help give your lipstick a slightly matte effect.
● UV filters to protect your lips against the ageing effects of the sun's rays.
● Vitamin E to heal any cuts, and to protect your lips against the fine lines associated with ageing.

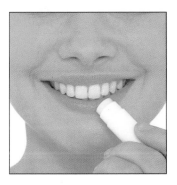

1 Ensure your lips are soft and supple by smoothing over some lipsalve (balm) before you start.

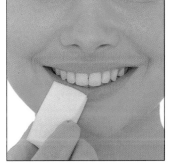

2 Prime your lips by smoothing them with foundation, using a make-up sponge so you reach every tiny crevice on the surface.

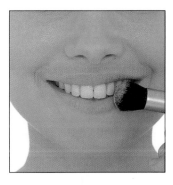

3 Dust over the top of the foundation with a light dusting of your usual face powder, to ensure your lipstick will stay put for longer.

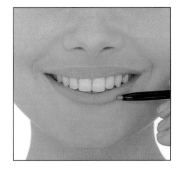

4 Rest your elbow on a firm surface and carefully draw an outline using a lip pencil. So it doesn't drag your skin, it may help to warm it slightly in your palm. Start by defining the Cupid's bow on the upper lip, then draw a neat outline on your lower lip. Finish by completing the edges of the outline to your upper lip.

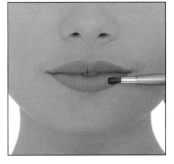

5 Use a lipbrush to fill in the outline with lipstick, ensuring you reach into every tiny crevice on the surface. Open your mouth to brush the colour into the corners of your lips.

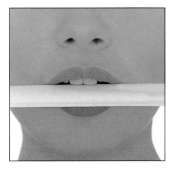

6 You'll make your lipstick last longer if you blot over the surface with a tissue. It'll also give an attractive, semi-matte finish to your lips.

COOL SKIN, BLONDE HAIR

With your porcelain complexion and pale hair, you should opt for baby pastel tones with sheer formulations and a hint of shimmer. This way you'll flatter your colouring with a light, fresh make-up look, without over-powering it.

THIS LOOK SUITS YOU IF...

- You have pale blonde to mousey or mid-blonde hair. It also suits women with white hair or steel-grey hair.
- Your eyes are blue, grey, hazel or green.
- You have pale skin, including whiter-than-white, ivory or a pinky "English rose" complexion.

TIPS
- If you're over 35, or unsure about wearing blue eyeshadow, swap it for a cool grey shade. This will create the same soft effect, but it's slightly more subtle.
- Shimmery eyeshadow can highlight crepey eyelids, so you may prefer to switch to a matte ivory shadow instead.

1 Your delicate skin doesn't need heavy coverage, so use a light tinted moisturizer. Dot it lightly onto your nose, cheeks, forehead and chin, then blend it in with your fingertips.

2 Cool pink, cream blusher will give a soft glow to your skin. Dot onto your cheeks, then blend in with your fingertips. You can either skip powder to leave your skin with a dewy glow, or dust a little over your face. However, use a gentle touch, as you want to let your natural skin-tone shine through.

3 Take a baby blue eyeshadow onto an eyeshadow brush and sweep it evenly over your entire eyelid. Stroke the brush gently over your eyelid a few times until you've swept away any obvious edges to the eyeshadow. Also work a little colour under your lower lashes.

4 Sweep a shimmery ivory shadow from the crease of your eyelid up towards the brow bone. Finish with two coats of brown/black mascara.

5 Stroke your eyebrows into shape with an eyebrow brush. This will also flick away any powder that's got caught in the hairs.

6 Cool pink lipstick should be applied with a lipbrush. If you like, you can slick a little lipgloss or lip balm on top for a sexy shimmer.

WARM SKIN, BLONDE HAIR

Although you have a warm skin-tone, your overall look is quite delicate. This means you should opt for tawny, neutral shades of make-up, and apply them with a light touch so you enhance your basic colouring.

THIS LOOK SUITS YOU IF...
- You have golden, warm blonde or dark blonde hair. This look also suits women with greying hair that has warm or yellow undertones.
- Your eyes are brown, blue, hazel or green – it will work equally well.

- You have a warm skin-tone which can develop a light, golden tan.
- Your skin tone and blonde hair mean your overall look is quite delicate. If so, you need to choose make-up shades that are not too intense, like those here.

1 After applying a light, tinted moisturizer, stroke concealer onto problem areas. Blondes tend to have fine skin, often prone to surface thread veins. Cover these effectively with concealer, applied with a clean cotton bud (swab).

2 Dip a powder puff into loose powder and lightly press over the areas of your face that are prone to oiliness. This will absorb excess oil throughout the day, and leave your skin beautifully matte. Dust off any excess powder with a clean powder brush.

3 Sweep peach eyeshadow over your entire eyelid. It will blend with your natural skin-tone, but give a clean, wide-eyed look to your make-up.

4 Use an eyeshadow brush to work a tiny amount of soft brown eyeshadow into the crease of your eyelid to create depth and definition to your eyes. Sweep it out towards the outer corner of your eyes as well.

5 Still using the same brown eyeshadow, work a little underneath your lower lashes. This gives a softer effect than traditional kohl pencil or eyeliner, and is particularly suitable for those with pale or blonde hair who often can't carry off very strong eye make-up. Finish with two coats of brown/black mascara.

6 Apply a barely-there shade of nude lipstick with a lipbrush. Then apply your tawny blusher, sweeping it a little at a time over your cheeks, forehead, and chin. You can even dust a little over the tip of your nose! The advantage of applying blusher after you've completed your make-up is that you can assess exactly how much you need.

COOL SKIN, DARK HAIR

Pale-skinned brunettes look fabulous with strong, cool shades of cosmetics. The density of colour provides a striking contrast to ivory skin-tones, while their coolness tones in beautifully with your natural beauty.

THIS LOOK SUITS YOU IF...

● You have medium brown to dark brown hair.
● Your eyes are brown, blue, hazel, grey or green.
● You have a cool, China doll skin-tone, that tans slowly in the sun.

Tips
● To stop your mascara from clogging wiggle the mascara wand from side to side as you pull it through your lashes.
● If you find cream blusher hard to apply you can opt for the powder variety, applying it after face powder.

1 Apply foundation or tinted moisturizer. If using foundation, it's likely you'll need the palest of shades. Blend in a few dots of tawny cream blusher. Finish with a dusting of loose powder.

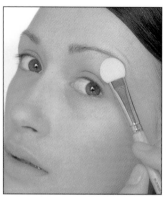

2 Smudge a cool ivory shadow over your eyelids, right up to your eyebrows. Stroke over it with a cotton bud (swab) to blend it if you find it gathers in creases close to your upper eyelashes.

3 Add extra definition with a touch of taupe or khaki eyeshadow on your eyelids. This shade works beautifully on your cool colouring, and emphasizes the colour of your eyes really well.

4 Now move onto your eyelashes. You need to apply two thin coats of black mascara to create a wonderful frame to your eyes.

5 Slick your eyebrows into place with an eyebrow brush. If they tend to look untidy, hold them in place by spritzing the brush with a little hairspray first.

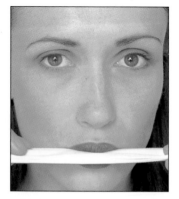

6 Choose a clear shade of berry lipstick to give your look a polished finish. Blot after one coat with a tissue, then re-apply for a longer-lasting finish.

WARM SKIN, DARK HAIR

Your skin-tone can carry off burnished browns, warm reds and earthy shades beautifully. They'll complement your complexion and emphasize your features.

THIS LOOK SUITS YOU IF...
● You have mid to dark brown hair.
● Your eyes are brown, dark blue, grey, hazel or green.
● You have a warm skin-tone that usually tans quite well. Even if it is pale in winter, your skin still has a yellow undertone.

Tip
Carry a powder compact with you during the day to blot break-through shine on nose, forehead and chin.

1 Dot liquid foundation onto your skin and blend in with a damp cosmetic sponge. Blend the colour into your neckline for a natural effect. Then apply concealer to any blemishes that need them.

2 Pat your face with translucent loose powder, then fluff off the excess with a large, soft brush.

3 Use a sponge-tipped eyeshadow applicator to sweep a red-brown shadow over your entire eyelid. The advantage of the sponge over a brush is that it doesn't tend to flick colour around. Complete your eyes with two thin coats of mascara.

4 Your eyebrows need subtle emphasis for this look. Either pencil them in with soft strokes of brown eyebrow pencil, or use a brown eyeshadow for a softer effect. Whichever method you use, brush them with an eyebrow brush to blend the strokes and slick the hairs in place.

5 Opt for a warm, tawny brown shade of powder blusher, dusted over your cheeks and up towards your temples. As this colour is quite strong, you may need to tone it down a little afterwards by dusting lightly over the top with translucent loose powder.

6 A fiery red lipstick balances the overall look. Use a lipbrush to ensure you fill in every tiny crease and crevice on the lip surface – this will help your lipstick colour stay put for longer as well as create a perfect finish.

COOL SKIN, RED HAIR

Redheads with cool skin-tones often stick to wishy-washy colours, but you can experiment with brighter colours to contrast with your wonderful colouring. Greens give an exciting dimension to your eyes, and strong earthy shades supercharge your lips.

THIS LOOK SUITS YOU IF...
● You have strawberry-blonde or pale red hair, even if the colour has faded.
● Your eyes are blue, grey, hazel or green.
● You have pale skin, ranging from ivory to a pink-toned complexion.

Tip
If you've got freckles, don't fall into the trap of trying to cover them with a dark-toned foundation. Instead, match your foundation to your skin-tone to avoid a mask-like effect.

1 Apply foundation and concealer, then dot a peachy shade of cream blusher onto your cheekbones. Unlike powder blusher, you can blend the cream variety with your fingertips – as the warmth from your skin will help smooth it in evenly. Apply a little cream blusher at a time. Finish with a dusting of translucent powder.

2 A neutral, peach-toned eyeshadow swept over your eyelids will emphasize your eye colour without fighting with it. Ensure you take care to work it close to your eyelashes, to create a balanced effect.

3 Redheads usually have fair eyebrows, so don't forget to emphasize them to create a frame to your eyes. Otherwise the rest of your make-up will look unbalanced as the focus will be placed on your forehead. Opt for a very pale eyebrow pencil, in a subtle grey-brown tone. Stroke it through your eyebrows, taking care to fill any bald spots. Then soften the lines by brushing through with an eyebrow comb.

4 Brush a hint of gold, shimmery eyeshadow into the arch under your eyebrows to give your eyes an extra dimension and bring them subtly into focus. This is a particularly good way to bring out gold flecks or warmth in the iris of your eyes.

5 Green eyeliner looks wonderful on your eyes and colouring! Don't fall into the trap of just smudging it under your lower lashes as this will drag your features downwards. Instead, work it along your upper lashes and into the corners of your eyes as well. Once you've applied it, smudge over the top with a clean cotton bud (swab) to give a softer finish. It's also a good idea to brush a little translucent powder over the top to ensure it stays put. Complete your eyes with two good coats of brown mascara.

6 Burnished orange lipstick complements this look. Begin by outlining your lips with a toning lip liner to prevent the colour from bleeding. Then use a lipbrush to fill in with the lipstick.

WARM SKIN, RED HAIR

Your vibrant Pre-Raphaelite colouring is suited to bold shades of wine, purple and brown. These deep, blue-toned colours look fabulous with your warm skin and hair tones, and can make you look truly stunning.

THIS LOOK SUITS YOU IF...

● You have medium to dark red hair. This look may also suit brunettes who have a lot of red tones to their hair.
● Your eyes are blue, grey, hazel, brown or green.

● You have a medium to warm skin-tone.
● Your skin takes on a golden colour in the summer, although you're unlikely to get a deep tan. It's quite likely that you have freckles.

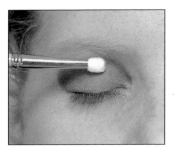

1 After applying foundation, concealer and powder, smooth a wine shade of shadow over your entire eyelid. Using a sponge-tipped eyeshadow applicator will give you more control when applying this colour. You may find it easier to blend in if you sweep some translucent powder over your eyelids first, to create a smooth base on which to work.

2 Use a pale mauve eyeshadow over your brow bone to balance your eye make-up. Blend it into the crease, to soften any harsh edges of the wine-toned eyeshadow. Take the time at this stage, for a professional-looking finish.

3 Smudge a little of the wine-toned eyeshadow under your lower lashes as well. This will give a modern look to your eye make-up, and give a softer effect than kohl pencil. Ensure you also work it into the outer corners of your eyes, sweeping it slightly upwards to give your eyes a lift. Then finish with two coats of brown mascara. Take care to take the mascara right to the roots of your lashes, especially if they're pale.

4 Use a soft brown eyeshadow on your eyebrows to give them subtle emphasis, using either a small brush, or a cotton bud (swab). Brush the eyebrows through afterwards with an eyebrow comb for a soft finish.

5 Choose a brown-toned blusher or bronzing powder to give your skin lots of warmth. Dust it on with a large blusher brush, blending it out towards your hairline for a natural glow. The key is to use a little at a time, increasing the intensity of colour as you go. It's best to avoid shimmery blushers, as these can sometimes give your skin a rather unnatural looking sheen.

6 You can carry off a deep plum shade of lipstick, outlined with a toning lip pencil. This strong colour needs perfect application to look good, so apply two coats, blotting in between with a tissue. This will also ensure your lipstick stays put for ages, and avoids the need for constant retouching.

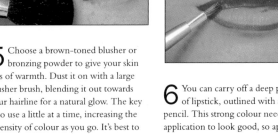

OLIVE SKIN, DARK HAIR

Your skin-tones are easy to complement with rich browns, oranges and a hint of gold or bronze. These rich shades define your features and work well on your wonderful skin-tones.

THIS LOOK SUITS YOU IF...
- You have dark brown to black hair.
- Your eyes are brown, hazel or green.
- Your olive skin tans beautifully, or you have Asian or Indian colouring.

TIP
To create a perfect lip line, stretch your mouth into an "O" shape and fill in the corners with your lip pencil.

1 Even out minor skin blemishes with a tinted moisturizer, blending it in with fingertips. If you need more coverage, opt for a liquid or cream foundation. Now apply a concealer and a light dusting of face powder.

2 After sweeping a golden shade of shadow across your entire eyelid, apply a darker bronze shade into the crease and then apply some under the lower lashes. This gives a wonderfully sultry look to your eyes.

3 Take a warm brown eyeliner, and work it along your upper and lower lashes for a strong look that you can carry off beautifully. If you find the effect too harsh, smudge with a clean cotton bud (swab). Apply two coats of black mascara.

4 A peach-brown powder blusher adds a sunkissed warmth to your cheeks. Apply just a little at a time, increasing the effect as you go.

5 Outline your lips with an orange-brown lip pencil. Start at the Cupid's bow on the upper lip, and move outwards. Then complete the other side, and finish with the lower lip.

6 To complete the look fill in with a sunny orange shade of lipstick. If you like a glamorous, glossy finish, don't blot your lips with a tissue You can even add a dab of lip balm for extra shine if you wish. But if you like a semi-matte look, blot after one coat with a tissue, then re-apply your lipstick for a longer-lasting finish.

OLIVE SKIN, ORIENTAL COLOURING

Your black hair, and pale – but yellow-toned – skin are best complemented by soft, warm colours. These will define your looks and counteract any sallowness in your complexion.

THIS LOOK SUITS YOU IF...

● You have very dark brown to blue-black hair. It also works if you have grey flecks in your hair.
● Your eyes are hazel or brown.
● You have a pale to medium skin-tone. It does tan, although it has a tendency to look quite yellow.

TIP
Oriental eyelashes are often poker-straight and so you can really benefit from the use of eyelash curlers.

1 After applying foundation, concealer and powder, sweep some lilac eyeshadow over your eyelid. This pale colour is a better option than using darker eyeshadows near the eyes as they have a tendency to make them look deep-set, particularly as your eyelids tend to be quite small.

2 Lightly fill in your eyebrows with a dark brown eyeshadow or eyebrow pencil to provide a strong frame to your eyes. This will help balance the eyeliner which is going to be applied next.

3 A lick of blue-black eyeliner will emphasize your beautifully-shaped eyes, and help correct any droopiness. Slick it along the lower lashes and into the outer corners of your eyes to create balance. To prevent the overall look from seeming too harsh, use a cotton bud (swab) to soften the eyeliner slightly.

4 Place your eyelashes between the edges of a curler, and gently squeeze for a few seconds. Then apply two coats of black mascara.

5 A warm pink blusher gives a wonderful boost to your complexion, and brings out its natural glow. Dust it over the plumpest part of your cheeks.

6 A baby pink lipliner and lipstick bring your lips fashionably into focus. The cool blue-tone to this shade works wonderfully on your colouring.

BLACK HAIR, PALE BLACK SKIN

Try emphasizing your looks with earthy shades. Your gold or red-toned skin works wonderfully with beige, brown and copper colours.

THIS LOOK SUITS YOU IF...

- You have black hair with golden or reddish highlights. It also works if you have grey flecks in your hair.
- You have hazel or brown eyes.
- You have a black skin.

1 After applying foundation, dust on a translucent face powder, ensuring it perfectly matches your skin-tone to avoid a chalky looking complexion. Dust off the excess with a large powder brush, using downward strokes.

2 Use an eyeshadow brush to dust an ivory-toned eyeshadow over your entire eyelid, to create a contrast with your warm skin-tone.

3 Smudge a deep-toned brown eyeshadow into the crease of your eyelid, blending it thoroughly. Also work a little of this colour into the outer corners, and underneath your lower lashes to make your eyes look really striking.

4 Black liquid eyeliner swept along your upper lashes will give a super-model look to your eyes. A sponge-tipped applicator is easier to use than a brush. Apply the eyeliner whilst looking down into a mirror, as this stretches any creases out of your eyelid. Rest your elbow on a firm surface. Complete your eyes with two coats of black mascara.

5 Use a brown lipliner pencil to outline your lips. You can use an ordinary brown eyeliner pencil if this is the only thing you have to hand. Blend the line lightly into your lips, using a cotton bud (swab) for a softer effect.

6 A neutral pink-brown lipstick gives a natural looking sheen to your lips, and instantly updates your looks. Apply it with a lipbrush for an even finish.

BLACK HAIR, DEEP BLACK SKIN

You can experiment with endless colour possibilities as your dark eyes, hair and skin provide the perfect canvas on which to work. The key to success is to choose bold, deep colours as your skin demands these to achieve a wonderful glow.

THIS LOOK SUITS YOU IF...

● You have deep black hair, even if it has flecks of grey.
● You have dark hazel or brown eyes.
● You have a dark black skin.

TIP
While dramatic colours suit your skin-tone and colouring perfectly, be sure to apply them with a light touch to get a fresh, up-to-date look.

1 Take care to find a foundation that matches your skin-tone exactly. Apply it with a sponge so it blends in perfectly. Dampen the sponge with water first to give it extra "slip", and to prevent the sponge from absorbing too much pricey foundation. Blend in thoroughly along your jaw and hairline to avoid tide-marks. Finally, set with a light dusting of translucent loose powder.

2 Next, sweep a dark blackcurrant eyeshadow over your eyelids. Dust a little loose powder under your eyes first to catch any falling specks of this dark shade, and prevent it from ruining your completed foundation.

3 Apply a dark charcoal eyeshadow into the crease of your eyelid, using an eyeshadow brush. Only take a little colour at a time onto the brush to prevent it from spilling onto your eyelid. If necessary, tap the brush on the back of your hand first to shake away any excess.

4 Use an eyeliner brush to work some of this charcoal shade under your lower lashes – as this is the ideal colour to outline your eyes with. Hold the mirror slightly above your eyeliner so you can achieve an accurate liner effect. Finish with two coats of black mascara.

5 A tawny brown shade of blusher complements your skin beautifully. With a large round brush, dust it over the apple of your cheeks, working it lightly out towards your hairline.

6 After outlining your lips with a toning lip pencil, fill in with a dark plum shade of lipstick, using a lipbrush.

TAKE FIVE FOR NIGHT-TIME GLAMOUR

When you haven't got time to spare, but want to look presentable, try this quick routine for evening sophistication. This isn't the time to experiment with new ideas, so the key is to choose simple looks, applied with minimum of fuss when you're racing the clock... in other words, simple steps to a sexy look!

Five minutes to go...

The all-in-one foundation/powder formulations give your skin the medium coverage it needs for this look in half the normal time. Also, take it over your lips and eyelids as this will make the rest of your make-up easier to apply and ensure it lasts the whole evening.

Four minutes to go...

Cream eyeshadow applied straight from the stick is quick and easy to apply. Opt for a brown shade as it'll bring out the colour of your eyes, and give them a sexy, sultry finish. Slick it over your entire eyelid, right up to the crease of the eye socket.

Three and a half minutes to go...

A swift way to blend in your eyeshadow is to brush over the top with translucent loose powder. This will tone down the colour and blend away any harsh edges.

Two and a half minutes to go...

Apply a coat of mascara to your lashes, taking care to colour your lower lashes as well as your upper ones. Use the tip of the mascara wand to coat the lower lashes, as this will prevent it from clogging on the hairs – and prevent you from spending valuable time having to use an eyelash comb.

One and a half minutes to go...

A warm berry red blusher will give your skin a fabulous flush. Apply it with a blusher brush, sweeping it from your cheeks up towards your eyes to give your face a lift.

Thirty seconds to go...

Choose a berry shade of lip gloss to add instant bold colour to your lips, sweeping it straight on with the sponge-tipped applicator. Cover your lower lip first, then press your lips together to transfer some of the colour onto your upper lip. Touch up any areas you've missed with the applicator, and you're ready to go!

Right: Six quick steps to a sexy look.

MAKE-UP TO LOOK YOUNGER!

If you haven't changed your make-up in years, it's a fair bet you're not making the most of your looks. Wearing out-of-fashion make-up is a sure way to add years to your appearance. Our simple make-up rules will help you break out of a beauty rut.

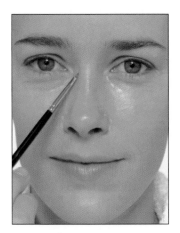

Simple steps to perfect skin

A dull, lifeless skin-tone can make you look, and feel, drab. The great news is, there are now foundations and concealers on the market specially designed to deal with this problem. Basically, the formulations contain hundreds of light-reflective particles and these bounce light away from your skin. This gives your skin the illusion of added vitality, and helps disguise problem areas such as fine lines and under-eye shadows.

And, the great news is that these light-reflective foundations and concealers are not just limited to expensive prestige beauty counters – these days, the price-conscious companies offer them too.

Apply your foundation with a damp sponge, blending away any harsh edges to avoid tell-tale tidemarks. This is the stage to apply concealer, dotting it onto under-eye shadows, blemishes and thread veins with a brush. Apply a tiny amount at a time, and blend thoroughly.

BEFORE YOU START

Avoid extremes of fashion and bright colours when you're over 40. While younger skins can just about get away with garish make-up, it'll simply emphasize fine lines and wrinkles on most women. Concentrate instead on flatter-ing your looks with subtle colours. So, throw away those traffic-stopping blue eyeshadows and neon lipsticks!

Add a youthful glow with blusher

Forget about adding colour to your skin with foundation – you'll be left with a mask effect, and "tidemarks" on your jawline. Instead, recreate a youthful bloom with a light touch of blusher. Remember though, to use half as much blusher and twice as much blending as you originally think! The cream variety of blusher is a good one to try, because it will give your skin a soft glow. Dot the blusher onto your skin, and blend with your fingertips.

Lightly set your foundation and blusher with translucent powder. A common mistake among many women is to be heavy-handed with face powder. Applying too much can make it settle into fine lines and wrinkles on your face, and emphasize them. Aim for a light touch, which will just blot out shine and set your make-up.

The best way to apply powder is only to blot the areas that need it, then brush away the excess with a large powder brush, stroking the brush downwards to prevent tiny particles catching in the fine hairs on your face.

If you haven't got a clue where to start, make an appointment for a free make-over at a local beauty counter. This way you'll be able to see which shades suit you, before you launch out and buy.

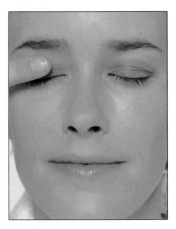

Be subtle with eyeshadow

Lots of women never perfect the technique of applying eyeshadow properly. Thankfully, now there's a new type of eyeshadow formulation that is a cinch to apply - cream-to-powder eyeshadow. It applies as a smooth cream, and dries quickly to a super-soft powder finish. Opt for a subtle shade, such as mid-brown, grey or taupe.

A good tip if your eyes look rather droopy is to blend eyeshadow upwards and outwards at the outer corners. Remember to blend it in well.

Give eyeliners a miss

Harsh lines of colour close to your eyes can be hard and unflattering. You'll emphasize your eyes much better if you smudge a little neutral-toned powder eyeshadow under your lower lashes with a clean cotton bud (swab).

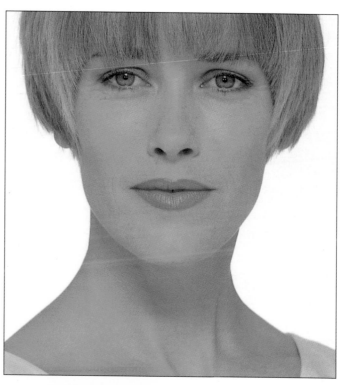

Above: Follow these six simple ideas to help you break out of a beauty rut.

Check your mascara colour

Most women's colouring fades slightly over the years. This means that the black mascara you're used to wearing can now look too obvious and harsh. So, try switching to a lighter shade for a more flattering effect. Apply two thin coats, allowing time for the first to dry thoroughly before you apply the second one.

Recreate your lip line

If your lip line has started to fade, and your lipstick tends to "bleed" into the lines around your mouth, try using a toning lipliner before you apply lipstick. Check it's firm enough to give a precise line, yet soft enough not to drag your skin. Apply by outlining your top lip first, working from the Cupid's bow outwards to each corner. Then outline your lower lip. Next dust your lips with loose powder to set the lipliner.

Finally, fill in your outline with a moisturizing lipstick. This will also help give a glossy shine to your lips which makes them look fuller. Apply with a lip-brush, blot with a tissue, then reapply for a longer-lasting finish.

CLASSIC CHIC

Whatever your age or colouring, this simple but highly effective classic look will always make a pleasing impact!

3 Sweep some pale ivory eyeshadow across your entire eyelid using a blender brush. Then complete your eyes with two thin coats of brown-black or black mascara.

4 Well-groomed eyebrows are essential. Brush them against the growth to remove any stray flecks of powder or foundation. Then lightly fill in any gaps with a toning eyeshadow. This gives a softer, more natural effect than pencil.

1 Apply a sheer all-in-one foundation-powder. This will give your skin the perfect coverage it needs to carry off strong lips, without clogging up your skin. Thick foundation is very much out of fashion these days. Natural-looking skin is much more attractive.

2 The eye make-up for this look is very understated. So, use an eyelash curler to open up your eyes and give them a fresh look.

COLOUR CODING

Believe it or not, everyone can wear red lipstick. The key to success is to choose just the right shade for your colouring.

Colouring	Choose
Blonde hair, cool skin	If you're daring enough your can wear any bright red shade, such as crimson or fire engine red. Any bold shade will look really effective and striking on you.
Blonde hair, warm skin	Lovely pink-reds look wonderful with your colouring. They're delicate enough not to look too harsh, while the pinky undertones complement the warmth of your skin.
Dark hair, cool skin	Rich blue reds, such as wine, burgundy and blood-red look wonderful on your China doll features. The contrast of dark hair, pale skin and red lips is really stunning!
Dark hair, warm skin	Rich brick reds and ruby jewel-like shades. Their warmth is very flattering to your complexion, while the intensity of colour looks great against your hair.
Red hair, cool skin	Choose a delicate orange-red, a paler version of the one mentioned above. This will add a wonderful splash of colour without overpowering you.
Red hair, warm skin	Warm, fiery reds with brown undertones, to complement your rich hair colour and rosy skin.
Dark hair, olive skin	Rich red, with orange undertones will flatter your skin. Go for a bold colour, as you can carry it off.
Black hair, brown skin	Berry reds and burgundy reds look wonderful on your skin.

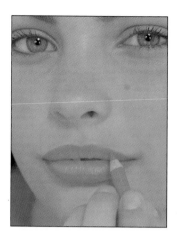

5 Your lips are the focus of this chic look. To ensure that you create a perfect outline, use a toning red lip pencil. Rest your elbow on a hard surface when using the pencil to prevent your hand from wobbling.

6 Use a lipbrush to fill in with a bold shade of red lipstick. Apply one coat, blot with a tissue, then reapply for a long-lasting finish.

Right: Make-up trends come and go, but red lipstick is always in fashion!

COUNTRY GIRL MAKE-UP

If you want a fresh, outdoor look, try this summery make-up – complete with fake freckles!

1 You need to avoid heavy foundations when you're outside, so tinted moisturizer is the perfect solution. It'll both nourish your skin and lightly cover any minor blemishes. Apply with your fingertips for ease.

2 If you already have freckles, don't try to hide them – they're perfect for a fresh-air look. If you don't have them, then fake them! Use an eyebrow pencil rather than an eyeliner pencil as it has a harder consistency and is less likely to melt on the skin. Use a mid-brown shade, and dot on the freckles, concentrating them on the nose and cheeks. Be extra creative, and apply different sizes of freckles for a realistic look.

3 To make your faux freckles look real, soften the edges with a clean cotton bud (swab). Then dust your skin with loose powder to set them in place.

4 A bronzing powder rather than a blusher will give your skin a sunkissed outdoor look. Choose one with minimum pearl or shimmer. Apply it to the plumpest part of your cheeks, where the sun would naturally catch your face. Dust the bronzing powder over your temples, too.

5 Swap to an eyeshadow blending brush to sweep some of the bronzing powder over your eyelids. Natural

colours like brown work best for this look. Remove any harsh edges with a clean cotton bud (swab).

6 Keep mascara to a minimum. Choose a natural-looking brown or brown/black shade, and apply just one coat. The waterproof type is great for hot days and sudden downpours but remember you'll need a waterproof eye make-up remover, too.

7 Don't overpower the look with bold lipstick. Opt for a muted brown-pink shade that's close to your natural lipcolour or use a tinted lipgloss for a natural sheen.

Right: A light, fresh, outdoor look.

CITY CHIC MAKE-UP

This super-successful look is great for work and in the city. Simple, perfectly applied colours can help you put together a polished working image. This stylish, balanced look will make you feel really confident and will leave you to ready to get on with the more important things in your day!

your eyes into focus. Take care not to leave flecks of powder in your eyebrow hairs – if necessary, flick them away with an eyebrow brush. Finish with two coats of mascara – blondes should use brown or brown-black mascara, while other colourings can opt for black.

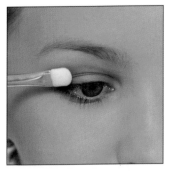

1 After applying a light foundation, and dusting your skin with powder to blot out shine, sweep your eyelids with a mid-grey eyeshadow. Use a matte powder formulation as this doesn't tend to crease as much during the day. Use a sponge-tipped applicator to make the eyeshadow easier to apply.

3 Brush your eyebrows with brown eyeshadow to fill in any gaps. This helps to create a strong frame to your make-up look.

5 Try soft blackcurrant shades as these can work beautifully on your lips, and make a welcome alternative to red lips. Start by using a lipliner to outline, ensuring you take it well into the outer corners. If you create any wobbly edges, whisk over the top with a clean cotton bud (swab) dipped in a little cleansing lotion. Then re-powder and try again!

2 Use a beige highlighting eyeshadow over your brow bone to soften the edges of the grey shadow and to bring

4 A soft pink shade of blusher will give your skin a rosy glow, and co-ordinate the rest of your make-up. And, it will give pale work-a-day faces an immediate lift!

6 Fill in your lips with a matching shade of blackcurrant lipstick. Blot your lips with a tissue afterwards for a semi-matte finish that's perfect for a day at the office.

WORKING WOMAN BASICS

You need to bear some simple pointers in mind to ensure you look good right through from 9 'til 5 – and beyond! Here are some tips to bear in mind.

● Choose a clear, plastic make-up bag so you can find what you're looking for in an instant – it saves rummaging around!

● Buy a make-up mirror in its own case, so it's always dust and make-up free. Powder compacts tend to become covered by the make-up inside, and are usually too small to be particularly effective.

● Look out for retractable powder and lipbrushes, so you can simply twist them up and they're ready to use. It's unhygienic to use a brush which has bristles that are gathering dust and grime in the bottom of your make-up bag.

● Also carry a nail file for emergency tears or splits, and a small hairbrush and travel-size hairspray to keep your hair looking preened and polished, too.

Below: Clever make-up moves for a smart 9 'til 5 look.

GO FOR GLAMOUR!

If there's one time you want to make a special effort with your make-up and pull out all the stops, it's a big night out! We'll show you how to create this stunning look, which combines a mixture of dark and light tones.

and provide a smooth base on which to apply your eyeliner at the next stage. The emphasis is on glamour and impact!

1 This is a sophisticated look, with the focus very much on the eyes. Once you've applied foundation, concealer and powder, you're ready to start work on your eye make-up. Sweep a smoky dark brown eyeshadow over your entire eyelid and blend it carefully into the crease. A simple sponge applicator is less likely to flick colour away than a brush, but still take the precaution of sweeping a line of loose powder under your eyes to catch any falling specks of dark shadow.

3 Whereas black eyeliner is usually too severe for harsh daylight, it's perfect for this look, which is designed to be seen in softer, sexier light! Using a pencil, carefully draw a fine line above and below your eyelashes. If you find it hard to create a steady line, try drawing a series of tiny dots, then blend them together with a clean cotton bud (swab).

5 Tawny blusher or a bronzing powder is ideal for this look, as this natural colour won't compete with the rest of your make-up. Sweep it over your cheekbones, blending away the edges into your hairline.

2 Apply a little of the same eyeshadow under your lower lashes to accentuate the shape of your eyes. This will give a balanced look to your eye make-up,

4 To contrast the dark, smoky look on your eyelids, sweep a pearlized ivory shadow over your brow bones for a wide-eyed look. Apply a little at a time, building up the effect gradually. Complete the look with two coats of black mascara.

6 Keeping the lips neutral gives this look its real impact, and updates it. Opt for a pinkish-beige shade of lip pencil and smudge it over your entire mouth for a matte, understated effect.

Right: Smoky eyes and neutral lips make for a sexy, sultry look!

20 PROBLEM SOLVERS

Whether you've made a beauty mistake, have run out of a vital product or are stuck for inspiration on how to make the most of your looks, the following problem solvers are just what you need!

Problem 1

Polish remover has run out

If you want to re-paint your nails, but have run out of remover, try coating one nail at a time with a clear base coat. Leave to dry for a few seconds, then press a tissue over the nail and remove it at once – the base coat and coloured polish will come off in one quick move. Your nail is now ready for a fresh coat of colour.

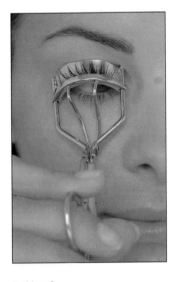

Problem 2

Poker-straight lashes

Do invest in a set of eyelash curlers, as they really make a difference to the way your eyes look. You'll never know how effective they are until you try them for the first time. Gently squeeze your lashes between their cushioned pad

Problem 3

Patchy powder

Provided you apply your powder with a light touch to freshly moisturized skin or on top of foundation that's applied with a clean sponge, it should look perfect. Check you're not making the common mistake of using the wrong colour powder for your skin. It needs to be matched closely to your natural skin-tone, as closely as your foundation. So, try dusting a sample of powder onto your skin in natural daylight before buying it, to make sure you've bought the perfect match for you.

Problem 4

Yellow nails

Yellow nails are usually caused by wearing dark-coloured nail polish without using a protective clear base coat, so wear one in future to prevent this from happening. You can also try switching to paler coloured polishes, as these contain lower levels of pigment that are less likely to stain your nails.

To cure yellow nails, rub them with lemon juice to remove the stains, then massage your hands and nails with hand cream to replenish the moisture levels. Try going polish free one day a week. If your problem recurs, consult your doctor to check that there's no underlying cause.

Problem 5

Flaky mascara

This usually means the mascara is too old and the oils that give it a creamy consistency have dried out. This can be made worse by pumping air into the dispenser when replacing the cap – so go gently. Replace your mascara every few months.

You can try to revive an old mascara by dropping it into a glass of warm water for a few minutes before applying it. If mascara flakes on your lashes, the only solution is to remove it thoroughly and to make a clean start.

Problem 6

A blemish appears

The immediate solution is to transform the blemish into a beauty mark! Start by calming down the blemish by dabbing it with a gentle astringent on a clean cotton bud (swab). This will help dry out excess oils from the skin and make the beauty mark stay in place for longer. To create your beauty mark dot over the top

with an eyebrow pencil – this is better than using an eyeliner pencil as it has a drier texture and so is less likely to melt and smudge. Finally, set your beauty mark in place with a light dusting of loose powder.

Problem 8

Smudged eyeliner

Tidy up the under-eye area by dipping a cotton bud (swab) into some eye make-up remover. Whisk it over the problem area to remove smudges, then re-powder. In future, remember to run a little loose powder over eyeliner to combat the smudging that occurs when the wax in the pencil melts.

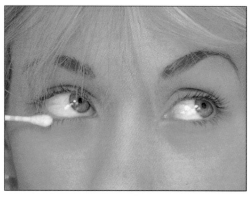

Problem 7

Melting lipstick

If you're out and about, and your lipstick is starting to move in the heat, then dust over the top with a little loose powder. This will give it a slightly drier texture, to help it stay put for longer. A little loose powder will also create a lovely matte finish.

Problem 9

Red-toned skin or embarrassing blushes

A red skin colour can be toned down by smoothing your skin with a specialized green-tinted foundation. Apply with a light touch, just to the areas that really need it. The green pigment in the cream has the effect of cancelling out the red in your skin.

However, to avoid a ghostly glow, you'll need to apply a light coating of your ordinary foundation on top, and then set with a dusting of loose powder. This tip is also good for covering the occasional angry spot or blemish.

Problem 10

Foundation has turned orange

This tip sounds strange, but really works! Mix a spoonful of bicarbonate of soda into your loose face powder, then dust the powder mixture lightly over your skin before applying your foundation. The bicarbonate of soda will give your skin a slightly acid pH-balance to prevent it from turning orange.

Problem 11

Bleeding lipstick

Use lipliner to prevent your lipstick from bleeding into the fine lines around your mouth. Trace the lip outline, then apply lip colour with a brush. Choose a drier textured matte lipstick as they're less prone to bleed than moisturizing variety. Also, lightly powder over and around your lips before you start.

Problem 12

Disappearing foundation

If your foundation seems to sink into your skin on hot or damp days, then rethink how you apply it in the first place. The trick to help foundation last longer is to apply it to cool skin. Do this by holding a cold, damp facecloth onto your skin for a few moments, then apply your foundation.

You can also store your foundation in the refrigerator to ensure it's cool when it goes on. Apply the foundation with a damp sponge, not your fingers, as the natural oils from them will leave a streaky finish on your skin. Finally, set with a light dusting of loose powder.

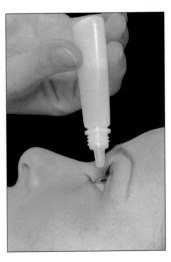

Problem 13

Bloodshot eyes

Red eyes are caused by the swelling of the tiny blood vessels on the eye surface, which can be caused by lack of sleep, excessive time in front of a computer, a smoky atmosphere or an infection. If it's a continual problem, consult your doctor, or ask your optician for an eyesight examination to ensure there's nothing to worry about.

Also, take care to avoid the source of the problem in future. On a temporary basis, you can use eye drops to bring the sparkle back to your eyes. These contain ingredients to reduce the swelling in the blood vessels that will decrease redness and cut down on dryness and itching.

Problem 14

Tidemarks of foundation

If you find obvious edges to your foundation on your chin, jawline or hairline, blend them away with a damp cosmetic sponge. Do this in natural daylight so you can check the finished effect. Powder as usual afterwards.

Problem 17

Droopy eyes

To help lift the appearance of droopy eyes, sweep a light-toned eyeshadow all over your eyelid. Then apply a little eye-shadow with a clean cotton bud (swab) under your eyes, sweeping it slightly upwards. Apply extra coats of mascara on the lashes just above the iris of the eye to draw attention to the centre of your eye rather than the outer corners.

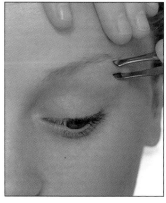

Problem 15

Unhealthy looking nails

Sometimes, however strong your nails are, their overall effect can be spoilt by clear or yellowing tips. However, you can immediately improve them by running a white manicure pencil underneath the free edges of nail to give them a cleaner appearance. Combine with a coat of clear polish for a fresh, natural nail look.

Problem 16

Yellow Teeth

First of all, consult your dentist or dental hygienist for regular check-ups and thorough cleaning to ensure your teeth are as white as possible. Take heart that yellow teeth tend to be stronger than their whiter counterparts! To make them look whiter, avoid coral or brown-based lipsticks as the warm colours will emphasize the yellow ones in your teeth. Clear pink or red shades will make them look much whiter in comparison.

Problem 18

Straggly eyebrows

It's a fair bet you won't even notice your eyebrows until they look messy! Try tidying them with regular tweezing sessions. The ideal time is after a bath, when your pores will be open from the heat, so the hairs will be easier to remove. Before bedtime is also a great idea, so you don't have to face the day with reddened skin!

Quickly brush your brows into place, so you can see the natural shape. Then pluck one hair at a time, in the direction of growth. First remove the hairs between your brows, and then weed out the undereye area. Tweeze any stray hairs at the outer sides. As a general rule, don't pluck above the eyebrow area or you'll risk distorting the shape of your brows. The only exception is if there are hairs growing well above the natural browline.

Problem 19

Over-applied blusher

If you've forgotten the golden rule about building up your blusher slowly and gradually, you may need to tone down an over-enthusiastic application of colour. The quickest and easiest way is to dust a little loose powder over the top of the problem area, until you've reached a depth of blusher shade that you're happy with.

Problem 20

Sore ears from cheap earrings

If you can't bear to throw away cheap earrings that make your ears react, try coating the posts and back of the earrings with some hypo-allergenic clear nail polish. This will make them less likely to react with your sensitive skin. However, always give the skin on your ears time to heal up before wearing troublesome earrings again.

HANDS UP TO BEAUTIFUL NAILS

A little manual labour is all it takes to have hands to be proud of – rather than ones you want to hide!

LAYING THE FOUNDATIONS FOR HEALTHY NAILS

There's no point in slicking your nails with colour if they're not in good condition to start with. Following this advice will ensure they're ultra-tough.

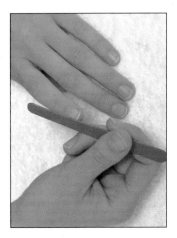

Filing know how

Keep your nails slightly square or oval – not pointed – to prevent them from breaking. Filing low into the corners and sides can weaken nails. File gently in one long stroke, from the side to the centre of the nail. The classic length that suits most hands is just over the fingertip.

Condition-plus

Smooth your nails every evening with a nourishing oil or conditioning cream. This helps seal moisture into your nails to prevent flaking and splitting. A tiny drop of olive oil is a great cheap alternative.

Cuticle care

Go carefully with tough or overgrown cuticles. Most manicurists are against cutting them with scissors, as this can lead to infection of the nail bed. Instead, soak your nails in warm soapy water to soften

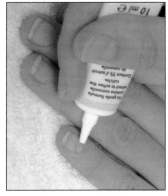

the cuticles. Then smooth them with a little cuticle softening cream or gel, before gently pushing them back with a manicure hoof stick or clean cotton bud (swab). You can then gently scrub away the flakes of dead skin that are still clinging to the nail bed.

Above: Give your nails a splash of colour for instant glamour.

POLISH UP YOUR FRENCH!

When it comes to nail trends, there's one look that never goes out of fashion, and that's the French manicure. It leaves your nails looking clean, fresh and healthy – and matches any make-up you happen to be wearing.

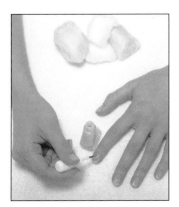

1 The basis of the French manicure is two coats of pale pink polish. Copy the professionals and do it in three strokes – one down the middle and one on each side. This prevents the polish from going lumpy and clogging, as you don't continuously have to work over the same area of nail. Apply two coats, giving each one plenty of time to dry. To turn a French manicure into an "American manicure", switch the pink polish for a beige one.

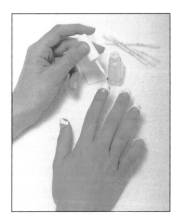

2 Now it's time to paint the tips of your nails with a white polish. If you find it difficult to paint them freehand, try using the stick-on nail guards that come with many French manicure sets. Simply press them onto the nail bed,

leaving the free edges of nail clear. Then apply the white polish, being careful not to overload the brush or the varnish will flow down it too quickly for you to control. Rest your hand on a firm surface to keep your hands steady and create a professional-looking finish.

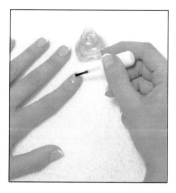

3 Once the white tips of your nails are dry, paint on a clear top coat of polish to seal in the colour and create a chip-free finish.

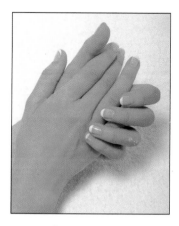

Above: French polish your nails to make them look clean and fresh.

COLOUR CODING

● If you have long, elegant fingers, you can carry off any shade of polish, including the dramatic deep reds, russets and burgundies.

● Short nails look their best with pale or beige-toned polish.

● Pale colours also suit broad nails. However, you can make them look slightly narrower by leaving a little space on the sides of each nail unpainted.

● If you love nude, barely-there shades for the daytime, but prefer something more exotic at night, try a pale pearlized polish – the shimmer will be caught by the evening light.

● If you find strong colours too bold on

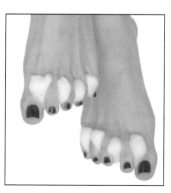

your hands, try painting your toenails instead. A glimpse of wonderful colour in open-toed shoes or on bare feet can look very sophisticated. You can create our model look by mixing a little dark red and black nail polish together before applying.

● Coral polish and pearlized formulations work wonderfully against a tanned skin.

TOP 10 NAIL TIPS

1 Avoid using acetone nail polish removers, as these can strip your nails of essential moisture. Choose the conditioning variety, instead.

2 Apply hand cream every time you wash your hands. The oils in the cream will seal moisture into your nails.

3 The most common cause of soft nails is exposure to water, so wear rubber gloves when doing the dishes!

4 If you have very weak nails, try painting your base coat and nail polish under the tip of your nails to give them extra strength.

5 Dry wet nails in an instant by plunging them into ice cold water.

6 To repair a split nail, tear a little paper from a teabag or coffee filter paper and glue it over the tear with nail glue. Once it's dry, buff until smooth, and then apply your polish.

7 If you're planning to do some gardening or messy work, drag your nails over a bar of soap. The undersides of your nails will fill up with soap, which means dirt won't be able to get in.

8 Clean ink and stains from your fingertips, by using a toothbrush and toothpaste on the affected areas.

9 Never file your nails immediately after a bath, as this is when they're at their weakest and likely to split.

10 Use a cotton bud (swab) with a pointed end to clean under your nails – it's gentler than scrubbing with a nail brush.

50 FAST, EFFECTIVE BEAUTY TIPS

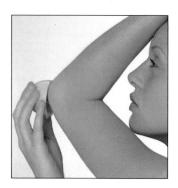

1 Brighten grey elbows by rubbing them with half a fresh lemon – it has a natural bleaching effect. Moisturize the skin afterwards to counteract the drying effects of the juice.

2 Turn foundation into a tinted moisturizer by mixing a few drops of it with a little moisturizer on the back of your hand before applying. It's the perfect blend for summer.

3 Carry a spray of mineral water in your handbag to freshen up your foundation while you're out and about.

4 Sleeping on your back helps stop wrinkles, according to recent research. It's certainly worth a try!

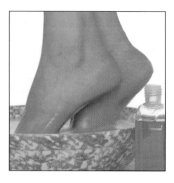

5 Dunk feet into a bowl containing warm water and 4 tablespoons of Epsom salts to help ease swollen ankles.

6 If you have very soft nails, file them while the polish is still on to prevent them from cracking.

7 If you find eyebrow tweezing painful, hold an ice cube over the area first to numb the area before you start.

8 Warm up your looks by dusting a little blusher over your temples, chin and the tip of your nose as well as your cheeks.

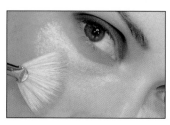

9 Sweep a little loose powder under your eyes when applying dark shades of eyeshadow to catch any falling specks and prevent them from staining your skin.

10 Make your lips look larger by wearing a bright, light lipstick. Make them appear smaller by wearing dark or more muted colours.

11 Soak nails in a bowl of olive oil once a week to strengthen them.

12 Keep your smile looking its best by changing your toothbrush as soon as the bristles begin to splay. This means at least every three months. You should brush for at least two minutes, both morning and evening.

13 If you don't have a specialized contouring product for your cheeks, simply use an ordinary face powder a couple of shades darker than your usual one to slim round cheeks.

14 Add a drop of witch hazel – available from all good pharmacists – to turn ordinary foundation into a medicated one – it'll work wonders on oily or blemish-prone skins.

15 Mascara your lashes before applying false ones to help them stick properly.

16 If you look tired, blend a little concealer just away from the outer corner of your eye – it makes you look as though you had a good night's sleep!

17 Go lightly with powder on wrinkles around the eyes – too much will settle into them and emphasize them.

18 If you haven't got time for a full make-up, but want to look great, paint on a bright red lipstick – it's a happy, glamorous colour which immediately brightens your face.

19 When plucking your eyebrows, coat the hairs you want to remove with concealer – it'll help you visualize exactly the shape of brow you're after.

20 Never apply your make-up before blow-drying your hair – the heat from the dryer can make you perspire and cause your make-up to smudge.

21 The colour of powder eyeshadow can be made to look more intense by dipping your eyeshadow brush in water first.

22 Keep lashes smooth and supple by brushing them with petroleum jelly before going to bed at night. It's also a good way to emphasize natural-looking lashes in the daytime.

23 Apply cream blusher in light downward movements, to prevent it from creasing and specks of colour from catching in the fine hairs on your face.

24 If mascara tends to clog on your lower lashes, try using a small thin brush to paint colour onto individual lashes.

25 Make sure you give moisturizer time to sink in before you start applying your make-up – it'll help your make-up go on more easily.

26 For eyes that really sparkle, try outlining them just inside your lower eyelashes with a soft white cosmetic pencil.

27 Lip gloss can look sophisticated if you apply just a dot in the centre of your lower lip.

28 Hide cracked or chipped nails under stick-on false ones.

29 If your eyeliner is too hard and drags your skin, hold it next to a light bulb for a few seconds before applying.

30 If you find your lashes clog with mascara, try rolling the brush in a tissue first to blot off the excess, leaving a light, manageable film on the bristles.

31 If you're unsure where to apply blusher, gently pinch your cheeks. If you like the effect, apply blusher in the same area – it'll look wonderfully natural.

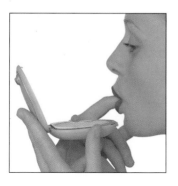

32 To prevent lipstick from getting on your teeth, try this tip: after putting it on, put your finger in your mouth, purse your lips and pull it out.

33 Women who wear glasses need to take special advice on make-up. If you're near-sighted, your glasses will make your eyes look smaller. So, opt for brighter, bolder shadows and lots of mascara to ensure they don't disappear. If you're far-sighted, your lenses will make your eyes look bigger and your eye make-up more prominent. So, opt for more muted colours that won't seem so obvious.

34 For a long-lasting blush on sunny days or hot nights, apply both cream and powder blusher. Apply the cream formulation

first, set with translucent powder then dust with a little powder blush.

35 Let your nails breathe by leaving a tiny gap at the base of the nail where the cuticle meets the nail – this is where the new nail cells are growing.

36 A little foundation lightly rubbed through your eyebrows and brushed through with an old toothbrush will instantly lighten them.

37 Coloured mascara can look super-effective if applied with a light hand. Start by coating your lashes with two coats of black mascara. Once the lashes are dry, slick a little coloured mascara – try blue, violet or green – onto the underside of your upper lashes. Each time you blink your eyelashes will reveal a dash of unexpected colour.

38 If you use hypo-allergenic make-up for your sensitive skin, remember to use hypo-allergenic nail polish, too – you constantly touch your face with your hands and can easily trigger a reaction.

39 Make over-prominent eyes appear smaller by applying a wide coat of liquid liner. The thicker the line, the smaller your eyes will look.

40 Calm down an angry red blemish by holding an ice cube over it for a few seconds and then apply your usual medicated concealer.

41 If you've run out of loose powder, use a light dusting of unperfumed talcum powder instead.

42 Use a little green eyeshadow on red eyelids to mask the ruddiness.

43 If you've run out of liquid eyeliner, dip a thin brush into your mascara and apply in the same way. It works perfectly.

44 You can dry nail polish quickly by blasting nails with a cold jet of air from your hairdryer.

45 Use a toothpick or dental floss regularly to clean between your teeth.

46 Apply powder-foundation with a damp sponge for a thicker, more opaque coverage. Applied with a dry sponge, the effect will be sheerer.

47 Run your freshly sharpened eyeliner pencil across a tissue before use. This will round off any sharp edges and remove small particles of wood.

48 If you have hard-to-cover under-eye shadows, cover them with a light coat of blue cream eyeshadow before using your ordinary concealer. It really works.

49 Get together with a friend and make each other up – it's amazing how other people picture you – and it's a great way to find yourself a new look.

50 Remove excess mascara by placing a folded tissue between your upper and lower lashes and then blinking two or three times.

50 BEST BUDGET BEAUTY TIPS

12 Dust blusher over your eyelids as an instant subtle eyeshadow. It's quick to apply, and will give a balanced look to your make-up.

13 Rub a dab of petroleum jelly around the neck of a new nail polish bottle, and it should be easy to open for the entire life of the product.

14 A cheap way to boost the shine of dark hair is to rinse it with diluted vinegar. Blonde hair benefits from lemon juice. Both act by sealing down the outer cuticles of the hair, helping your hair reflect the light more effectively.

15 De-fuzz using a razor with replaceable blades – it works out much cheaper in the end than buying disposable razors.

16 Swap commercial face scrubs for a handful of oatmeal massaged directly onto your skin – it works really well.

17 Don't use too much toothpaste – it's the brushing action that gets teeth really clean. A pea-sized blob is enough.

18 Pick the largest sized products you can afford – it's much cheaper that way.

19 Don't just shop for beauty goodies in glitzy department stores and fancy pharmacies. These days, your local supermarket can offer a surprisingly good range.

20 If you're happy to forgo a fancy label, look out for great value own-label product ranges at leading drug store chains.

21 Sometimes you're just as well off with cheap alternatives. Opt for those when you can, and indulge yourself with the

1 Cottonwool (cotton) balls soak up liquids like toner, so dampen them with water first. Squeeze out the excess, then use as usual.

2 A drop of remover added to a bottle of dried-up nail polish will revive it in a few seconds. Shake well to encourage it to mix in thoroughly.

3 Stand a dried-up mascara in a glass of warm water to bring it back to life.

4 Keep new soaps from getting too soft by putting them in a warm cupboard until you need them. This helps dry the moisture out, which makes them harder and longer-lasting.

5 To get the last drop out of almost-empty bottles store them upside-down overnight. You'll reap the rewards the next morning.

6 Don't rip the cellophane cover off translucent powder – prick a few holes in it instead – it'll stop you spilling and wasting it.

7 Keep perfume strips from magazines in your bag for an instant freshen-up.

8 Sachets in magazines make ideal travel packs for weekends away.

9 If you've run out of blusher, dot a little pink lipstick on your cheeks and blend well with your fingertips.

10 Look out for "2 for the price of 1" special offers on your favourite products. Perhaps split the savings with a friend.

11 Turn ordinary mascara into the lash-lengthening variety by dusting eyelashes with a little translucent powder first.

products that are really worth it! For instance, buy cheap and cheerful lip liners, then show off with a fancy lipstick. As well as looking good, expensive lipsticks tend to contain more pigment than cheaper ones – which means they look better and last longer.

22 Buy cheap but effective body moisturizers instead of expensive fragranced ones. Then save your money to splash out on your favourite perfume.

23 It used to be that only the pricier ranges offered hi-tech products. However, these days more companies are offering state-of-the-art products – at budget prices. This means you'll get all the benefits without spending a fortune. For instance, there are now affordable skin creams that contain the anti-ageing alpha-hydroxy ingredients at a third or quarter of the price of prestige brands.

24 Many of the more expensive prestige make-up, skin-care and fragrance companies offer sample products at their counters. It's generally at the discretion of the consultant. However, it's always worth asking, especially if you're already buying something from them.

25 There's a great trend at the moment for 2-in-1 products. They're worth trying, because they can save you money – as you only buy one product instead of two. They include shower gels with added moisturizers, shower gels that also act as body scrubs and hair shampoos with built in conditioners.

26 If you want to indulge in some new make-up, then ask for a makeover at a cosmetic counter. It's the best way to see how the colours and formulations look on your skin before you buy anything – and can also mean you'll look great for an evening out!

27 Store your make-up and fragrance in a cool dark place to extend their life span.

28 One length hair with no layers is the easiest and cheapest hairstyle to maintain as it doesn't require as many visits to the hairdresser to keep it looking good.

29 Don't throw away an item of make-up just because the colour's not in fashion at the moment – you might like it again in a few months.

30 Make cheap nail polish last longer by sealing it with a clear top coat.

31 Pure glycerine is an extremely cheap and effective moisturizer when you don't have much to spend.

32 Turn lipstick into lip gloss with a coat of lip balm after applying colour.

33 Double up your lip liner to fill in your lips as well as outline them.

34 Prise eyeshadows out of their cases, and stick into an old paint-box or lid to create a make-up artist's colour palette. It's a sure way to ensure you use the products you've got because you can see them all at a glance.

35 Add a few drops of your favourite eau de toilette to some olive oil, and use as a scented bath oil as a cheap treat.

36 Neutral make-up colours are a better investment than brighter ones because they look great at any time, any place.

37 Eyeshadow doubles up as eyeliner, if applied with a cotton bud (swab). Dampen the end of the bud (swab) first for a more dramatic effect.

38 If you're choosing a new fragrance, buy the weaker and cheaper eau de toilette first before splashing out on the stronger and more expensive perfume strength.

39 Check out the model nights at your local hairdressers when trainee hairdressers will style your hair for a fraction of the normal price.

40 Mix different colour lipsticks on the back of your hand with a brush – to create new shades for free!

41 A drop of olive oil rubbed nightly into your nails will help them grow long and strong, and is cheaper than shop-bought manicure oils.

42 When you're out of toothpaste, brush with plain baking soda – it'll make them extra white, too.

43 Put your lip and eye pencils in the refrigerator before sharpening, as this means they're less likely to break – and you won't waste so much.

44 Make powder eyeshadows last longer and stay crease-free by dusting eyelids with translucent powder first. It'll absorb the oils from your skin, and keep your make-up looking fresh.

45 Sharpen dull eyebrow tweezers by rubbing sandpaper along the tips.

46 Add a drop of water to the last remains of a foundation to ensure you use every last dot.

47 Keep the plastic seals or paper discs that come with products and replace after each use. It helps prevent air from distributing in the product and bacteria breeding – which means your product stays fresh until the very end.

48 Spritz your hair lightly with water and re-blow dry to revive products already in the hair, and make your style look as good as new.

49 Add half a cup of baking soda to your bath water as a cheap and cheerful water softener in hard water areas.

50 Use an old clean toothbrush to slick unruly eyebrows into shape.

YOUR TOP 10 MAKE-UP QUESTIONS

1 Blush baby

Q *"Can I reshape my face using blusher?"*

A The best way to apply blusher is to smile, find the apples of your cheeks, and blend the colour upwards. For special occasions, try using your normal blusher – combined with a barely-there highlighter colour and a colour that is slightly darker than your usual blusher – to reshape your face. Check your face shape and try the following:

● **Slim a round face...** by blending your usual blusher upwards from your cheeks into your hairline. Then, highlight along

● **Balance a heart-shaped face...** by dusting your blusher slightly lower than your cheekbones into the actual hollows of your cheeks. Dust some highlighter onto the tip of your chin, and apply shader to your temples, blending it well into your hairline.

2 24-hour lipstick

Q *"Is there any way to make my lipstick stay put all day?"*

A Unfortunately there's no such thing as a 24-hour lipstick, no matter what some cosmetic manufacturers claim! The

3 Over-plucked brows

Q *"I plucked my eyebrows very thin last year. Now I'd like to grow them back. How can I do it successfully?"*

A Choose a natural-looking brown eyeshadow. Then apply it lightly and evenly with a firm-bristled eyebrow brush, using short sharp strokes across the brow. As the hairs that grow back are often unruly, a light coat of clear mascara can be applied to help keep them in place.

Try to ignore the periodic fashions for highly plucked eyebrows. The fashions don't last for long – but eyebrows can take ages to grow back! It's better to stick with the eyebrow shape you were born with, concentrating on just removing stray hairs from underneath the arch and between the brows.

4 Covering birthmarks

Q *"Can you recommend something that will cover my birthmark, even when I go swimming?"*

A You need a specialized foundation that will give ultimate coverage, look opaque and be waterproof. Look for a specialized range of camouflage creams tailor-made to cover skin imperfections, such as scars and port wine stains, as well as birthmarks. Their formulation means that they're applied differently to ordinary foundations. They're applied with the fingertips using a "dab, pat" motion. They're available from specialized make-up suppliers, and some dermatologists.

5 Spider Veins

Q *" What can I do about the spider veins on my face?"*

A Spider or thread veins, known by their medical name as "telangiectases", are a very common beauty problem. An electrolysist qualified in diathermy or a dermatologist can treat them for you, by inserting a very fine needle into the vein. The heat from the needle coagulates the blood inside the vein, rendering it inac-

your cheekbones, and use the shader in the hollows of your cheeks.

● **Soften a square-shaped face...** by concentrating your blusher in a circle on the rounded parts of your cheeks. Apply shader into the hollows of your cheeks, and also lightly on the square edges of your chin. Lightly dust highlighter onto the bridge of your nose and the tip of your chin.

longest lasting lipsticks are those with the thickest, driest textures, although this can mean they leave your lips feeling quite dry, especially if you use them day in, day out. However, you can look for lipstick sealers, which are clear gels that you paint over your lips after you've applied your lipstick. Once they're dry, these lipstick sealers help your lipstick stay put at least past your first cup of coffee of the day.

tive. The number of treatments varies depending on the size of the area to be treated, and the number of spider veins you have. In the meantime, you can cover the veins with a light covering of concealer, applied with a fine brush and set with a dusting of loose powder.

6 Mascara matters

Q *"My mascara always seems to run onto my skin, and leave me with 'panda eyes'. What can I do?"*

A Obviously you should opt for the waterproof variety of mascara if you're prone to this problem, or you can "seal" your normal mascara with a coat of clear mascara. You should also try holding a piece of tissue just underneath your lower lashes while you're applying your mascara to prevent it from getting as far as your skin in the first place.

Alternatively, dip a cotton bud (swab) in eye make-up remover for fast touch-ups before the mascara has a moment to dry on your skin. Another, more long-term, solution is to regularly have your eyelashes permanently dyed at a reputable beauty salon.

7 Colour coding

Q *"Are there colours which some people can never wear?"*

A As a general rule, everyone can wear every colour. However, if you want to wear a particular colour, you should

choose the particular shade of it very carefully. For instance, everyone can wear red lipstick, but in different shades. A pale-skinned blonde will suit a soft pink-red, whereas a warm-toned redhead will be able to carry off an orange-based fiery shade of the colour.

In the same way, a blue-eyed, cool-skinned blonde can carry off a pale pastel, baby blue eyeshadow, whereas her brunette colleague will look much better wearing a darker version to complement her skin-tone.

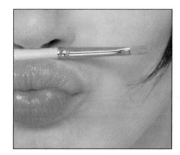

8 Smoother lips

Q *"Lipstick always looks awful on my mouth because my lips are so flaky, and it's impossible to create a smooth finish. Is there a solution to this problem?"*

A Slick your lips with petroleum jelly, and leave for 10 minutes to give it time to soften hard flakes of skin. Then cover your index finger with a damp flannel and gently massage your lips. This will remove the petroleum jelly and the flakes of dead skin at the same time.

9 Problem polish

Q *"I always seem to be left with lots of bottles of nail varnish which I can't use, because they're either dried up, or full of bubbles which means they don't go on smoothly. What can I do?"*

A There are some simple solutions to your problem. Dried-up polish can be revived by stirring in a few drops of polish remover before using. You can help prevent it from thickening in the first place by storing it in the refrigerator, as the cold temperature will stem evaporation and thereby stop it changing in texture.

Bubbles of air in the polish will ruin its finish, as it won't create an even surface. You can prevent this by rolling the bottle between the palms of your hands to mix it up before using, rather than shaking it vigorously – as it's this which creates the bubbles in the first place.

10 The changing face of foundation

Q *"I have difficulty keeping up with the changing colour of my skin in the summer, as I gradually get a tan. It's so expensive constantly buying new foundations!"*

A Stick with the the colour that suits you when you're at your palest in the middle of winter. Then, also buy a small tube of dark foundation designed for black skins. Blend just a drop or two into your ordinary foundation on the back of your hand before applying to darken it to match your tan. This means you can change your foundation daily, without having to spend a fortune on different shades.

HAIRCARE
AND
STYLING

BEAUTIFUL, SHINING HAIR IS A VALUABLE ASSET.
IT CAN ALSO BE A VERSATILE FASHION ACCESSORY, TO
BE COLOURED, CURLED, DRESSED UP OR SMOOTHED
DOWN — ALL IN A MATTER OF MINUTES. HOWEVER, TOO
MUCH ATTENTION COMBINED WITH THE EFFECTS OF A
POOR DIET, POLLUTION, AIR-CONDITIONING, AND
CENTRAL HEATING CAN MEAN THAT YOUR HAIR
BECOMES THE BANE OF YOUR LIFE RATHER THAN YOUR
CROWNING GLORY. A DAILY HAIRCARE ROUTINE AND
PROMPT TREATMENT WHEN PROBLEMS DO ARISE ARE
THEREFORE OF VITAL IMPORTANCE IN MAINTAINING THE
NATURAL BEAUTY OF HEALTHY HAIR.

THE STRUCTURE OF HAIR

A human hair consists mainly of a protein called keratin. It also contains some moisture and the trace metals and minerals found in the rest of the body. The visible part of the hair, called the shaft, is composed of dead tissue: the only living part of the hair is its root, the dermal papilla, which lies snugly below the surface of the scalp in a tube-like depression known as the follicle. The dermal papilla is made up of cells that are fed by the bloodstream.

Each hair consists of three layers. The outer layer, or cuticle, is the hair's protective shield and has tiny overlapping scales, rather like tiles on a roof. When the cuticle scales lie flat and neatly overlap, the hair feels silky-soft and looks glossy. If, however, the cuticle scales have been physically or chemically damaged or broken the hair will be dull and brittle and will tangle easily.

Under the cuticle lies the cortex, which is made up of fibre-like cells that give hair its strength and elasticity. The cortex also contains the pigment called melanin, which gives hair its natural colour. At the centre of each hair is the medulla, consisting of very soft keratin cells interspersed with spaces. The actual function of the medulla is not known, but some authorities believe that it carries nutrients and other substances to the cortex and cuticle. This could explain why hair is affected so rapidly by changes in health.

Hair's natural shine is supplied by its own conditioner, sebum, an oil composed of waxes and fats and also containing a natural antiseptic that helps fight infection. Sebum is produced by the sebaceous glands present in the dermis. The glands are linked to the hair follicles and release sebum into them. As a lubricant sebum gives an excellent protective coating to the entire hair shaft, smoothing the cuticle scales and helping hair retain its natural moisture and elasticity. The smoother the surface of the cuticle, the more light will be reflected from the hair, and therefore the higher

HAIR STRUCTURE

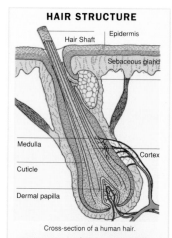

Cross-section of a human hair.

Centre and above: Pictures of a human hair magnified 200 times. A strand of hair in good condition is smooth, but if it has been damaged the outer layer is frayed and broken. Photographs courtesy of Redken Laboratories.

will be the gloss. This is why it is more difficult to obtain a sheen on curly hair than on straight hair.

Under some circumstances, for example excessive hormonal activity, the sebaceous glands produce too much sebum, and the result is greasy hair. Conversely, if too little sebum is produced the hair will be dry.

THE GROWTH CYCLE

The only living part of hair is underneath the scalp – when the hair has grown through the scalp it is dead tissue. Hair goes through three stages of growth: the anagen phase when it actively grows; the catagen, or transitional phase when the hair stops growing but cellular activity continues in the papilla; and the telogen, or resting phase, when growth stops completely. During the telogen phase there is no further growth or activity at the papilla; eventually the old hair is pushed out by the new growth and the cycle begins again. The anagen phase continues for a period of two to four years, the catagen phase for only about 15-20 days, and the telogen phase for 90-120 days. At any given time, about 93 per cent of an individual's hair is in the anagen phase, 1 per cent is in the catagen phase, and 6 per cent is in the telogen phase. Scalp

FACT FILE

○ Hair grows about 12 mm/ ½ in per month.
○ A single strand lives for up to seven years.
○ If a person never had their hair cut it would grow to a length of about 107 cm/42 in before falling out.
○ Women have more hair than men.
○ Hair grows faster in the summer and during sleep.
○ Hair grows fastest between the ages of 16 and 24.
○ Between the ages of 40 and 50 women tend to lose about 20 per cent of their hair.
○ Hair becomes drier with age.

hair, which reacts to hormonal stimuli just like the hair on the rest of the body, is genetically programmed to repeat its growth cycle 24-25 times during the average person's lifetime.

THE IMPORTANCE OF DIET

What you eat is soon reflected in the health of your hair. Like the rest of the body, healthy, shining hair depends on a good diet to ensure it is supplied with all the necessary nutrients for sustained growth and health. Regular exercise is also important as it promotes good blood circulation, which in turn ensures that vital oxygen and nutrients are transported to the hair root via the blood. Poor eating habits and lack of exercise are soon reflected in the state of the hair; even a minor case of ill-health will usually make the hair look limp and lack-lustre.

An adequate supply of protein in the diet is essential. Good sources include lean meat, poultry, fish, cheese, and eggs as well as nuts, seeds, and pulses. Fish, seaweed, almonds, brazil nuts, yogurt, and cottage cheese all help to give hair strength and a natural shine.

Whole grain foods and those with natural oils are highly recommended for the formation of keratin, the major component of hair. Seeds are a rich source of vitamins and minerals as well as protein. Try to eat at least three pieces of fruit a day – it is packed with fibre, vitamins, and minerals. Avoid saturated fat, which is found in red meat, fried foods, and dairy products. Choose skimmed or semi-skimmed milk rather than the full-fat varieties, and low-fat cheese and yogurt instead of full-fat cheese and cream. Substitute vegetable oils such as sunflower, safflower, and olive oil for animal fats. These foods all provide nutrients that are essential for luxuriant hair.

If you eat a balanced diet with plenty of fresh ingredients you shouldn't need to take any supplementary vitamins to promote healthy hair growth.

PROMOTING HEALTHY HAIR

○ Cut down on tea and coffee – they are powerful stimulants that act on the nervous, respiratory, and cardiovascular systems, increasing the excretion of water and important nutrients. They also hamper the absorption of minerals crucial for hair health. Drink mineral water (between six and eight glasses a day), herbal teas, and unsweetened fruit juice.
○ Alcohol dilates blood vessels and so helps increase blood flow to the tissues. However, it is antagonistic to several minerals and vitamins that are vital for healthy hair. Limit yourself to an occasional drink.
○ Regular exercise stimulates the circulatory system, encouraging a healthy blood supply to all cells and nourishing and helping to regenerate and repair.
○ Some contraceptive pills deplete the B-complex vitamins and zinc. If you notice a change in your hair after starting to take the Pill, or changing brands, ask your family doctor or nutritionist for advice.

COLOUR

Hair colour is closely related to skin colour, which is governed by the same type of pigment, melanin. The number of melanin granules in the cortex of the hair, and the shape of the granules, determines a person's natural hair colour. In the majority of cases the melanin granules are elongated in shape. People who have a large number of elongated melanin granules in the cortex have black hair, those with slightly fewer elongated granules have brown hair, and people with even less will be blonde. In other people the melanin granules are spherical or oval in shape rather than elongated, and this makes the hair appear red.

Spherical or oval granules sometimes appear in combination with a moderate amount of the elongated ones, and then the person will have rich, reddish brown tinges. If, however, spherical granules occur in combination with a large number of elongated granules then the blackness of the hair will almost mask the redness, although it will still be present to give a subtle tinge to the hair and differentiate it from pure black.

Hair colour darkens with age, but at some stage in the middle years of life the pigment formation slows down and silvery-grey hairs begin to appear. Gradually, the production of melanin ceases, and all the hair becomes colourless – or what is generally termed grey.

When melanin granules are completely lacking from birth, as in albinos, the hair is pure white.

Hair colour is determined by the amount of pigment in the hair and the shape of the pigment granules. People with dark hair have a larger amount of pigment than people with blonde hair. In both brunettes and blondes the pigment granules are elongated in shape: red hair results from the presence of oval-shaped granules. Photograph courtesy of Silvikrin.

Right: Red hair looks attractive whether it is worn smooth or curly. To create movement in longer hair, mist with styling lotion and set on shapers. If each strand of hair is twisted before winding, you will achieve a more fulsome curl. Thick, straight hair can be left to dry naturally and just finished with a shine serum. By Patrick Cameron at Alan Paul, Wirral, England.

Below left: Brunettes look good with precision bobs that are cut to increase volume in the hair. By Yosh Toya, San Francisco, Photography Gen.

Below right: This naturally curly blonde hair has been quickly styled by scrunch-drying to achieve maximum volume. By Nicky Clarke, London, Photography Paul Cox.

STRANGE BELIEFS

The Ancient Greeks regarded blonde as the hair colour of gods and heroes, but they viewed people with red hair with suspicion, and believed that strangers, rogues, and redheads should be treated with contempt. The idea that redheads were untrustworthy, deceitful, and quick-tempered was widespread in many cultures. In the Christian tradition Judas, who betrayed Christ, was said to have red hair, and artists of the early Christian period and beyond portrayed him as a redhead.

TEXTURE AND TYPE

Hair with a very curly texture needs intensive moisturizing treatments to keep the spring in the curl. On this type of hair always use a wide-toothed comb, never a brush, which will make the hair frizz. Leave-in conditioners are good for curly hair as they help to give curl separation. To revitalize curls mist with water and scrunch with the hands.

ETHNIC DIFFERENCES

Scandinavians normally have thin, straight, baby-fine hair, and mid-Europeans hair that is neither too fine nor too coarse. People native to the Indian subcontinent have coarse textured tresses while Middle Eastern populations have strong hair. In general the further east you travel the coarser hair becomes.
The hair of Chinese and Japanese people is very straight; that of Latin-speaking and North African peoples can be very frizzy and thick.

The texture of your hair is determined by the size and shape of the hair follicle, which is a genetic trait controlled by hormones and related to age and racial characteristics.

Whether hair is curly, wavy, or straight depends on two things: its shape as it grows out of the follicle and the distribution of keratin-producing cells at the roots. When viewed in cross section, straight hair tends to be round, wavy hair tends to be oval, and curly hair kidney-shaped. Straight hair is formed by roots that produce the same number of keratin cells all around the follicle. In curly hair however the production of keratin cells is uneven, so that at any given time there are more cells on one side of the oval-shaped follicle than on the other. Furthermore, the production of excess cells alternates between the sides. This causes the developing hair to grow first in one direction and then in the other. The result is curly hair.

The natural colour of the hair also affects the texture. Natural blondes have finer hair than brunettes while redheads have the thickest hair.

Generally speaking, hair can be divided into three categories: fine, medium, and coarse and thick. Fine hair can be strong or weak; however, because of its texture, all fine hair has the same characteristic – it lacks volume. As the name suggests, medium hair is neither too thick nor too thin, and is strong and elastic. Thick and coarse hair is abundant and heavy, with a tendency to grow outwards from the scalp as well as downwards. It often lacks elasticity and is frizzy.

A single head of hair may consist of several different textures. For example, fine hair is often found on the temples, and the hairline at the front and on the nape of the head, while the texture over the rest of the head may be medium or even coarse.

NORMAL, DRY, OR OILY?

Hair type is determined by the hair's natural condition – that is, by the amount of sebum the body produces. Treatment programmes such as perming, colouring, and heat styling will also have an effect on hair type. Natural hair types and those produced by applying various treatments are described below, together with advice on haircare where appropriate.

Dry hair looks dull, feels dry, tangles easily, and is difficult to comb or brush, particularly when it is wet. It is often

Thick straight hair can be made sleeker if you remember to always blow-dry downwards, which encourages the cuticles to lie flat and reflect the light. Photography courtesy of Braun.

Fine hair needs expert cutting to maximize the volume. Here gel spray was used to give lift at the roots and the hair was then blow-dried. By Taylor Ferguson, Glasgow, Scotland.

Normal hair responds well to regular brushing, smoothing, and polishing. By Antoinette Beenders at Trevor Sorbie, London, for Denman, Photography Simon Bottomley.

quite thick at the roots but thinner, and sometimes split, at the ends.

Causes Excessive shampooing, over-use of heat-styling equipment, misuse of colour or perms, damage from the sun, or harsh weather conditions. Each of these factors depletes the moisture content of hair, so that it loses its elasticity, bounce, and suppleness. Dryness can also be the result of a sebum deficiency on the hair's surface, caused by a decrease in or absence of sebaceous gland secretions.

Solutions Use a nourishing shampoo and an intensive conditioner (see page 18). Allow hair to dry naturally whenever possible.

Normal hair is neither greasy nor dry, has not been permed or coloured, holds its style, and looks good most of the time. Normal hair is ideally suited to the daily use of two-in-one conditioning shampoos. These are formulated to provide a two-stage process in one application. When the product is lathered into wet hair the shampoo removes dirt, grease, and styling products. At this stage

the conditioner remains in the lather. As the hair is rinsed with more water, the grease and dirt are washed away. At the same time, the micro-fine conditioning droplets are released on to the hair leaving it shiny and easy to comb.

Greasy hair looks lank and oily and needs frequent washing.

Causes Overproduction of sebum as a result of hormone disturbances, stress, hot, humid atmosphere, excessive brushing, or constantly running hands through the hair, perspiration, or a diet rich in saturated fat. The hair becomes oily, sticky, and unmanageable in just a few days, or sometimes within hours.

Solutions Use a gentle, non-aggressive shampoo that also gives the hair volume. A light perm will lift the hair at the roots and limit the dispersal of sebum. Rethink your diet: reduce dairy fats and greasy foods. Try to eat plenty of fresh food, and drink six to eight glasses of water every day.

Combination hair is greasy at the roots but dry and sometimes split at the ends.

Causes Chemical treatments, using detergent-based shampoos too frequently, overexposure to sunlight, and overuse of heat-styling equipment. Such repeated abuse often provokes a reaction in sebum secretion at the roots and a partial alteration in the scales, which can no longer fulfil their protective role. The hair ends therefore become dry.

Solutions Use products that have only a gentle action on the hair. Excessive use of formulations for oily hair and those for dry hair may contribute to the problem. Ideally, use a product specially designed for combination hair. If this is not possible try using a shampoo for oily hair and finish by applying a conditioner only from the middle lengths to the ends of the hair.

Coloured or permed hair is very often more porous than untreated hair, so it needs gentle cleansers and good conditioners. Colour-care products help prevent fading by protecting the hair from damaging rays of sunlight. Specialist products for permed hair help maintain elasticity, giving longer-lasting results.

THE CUT

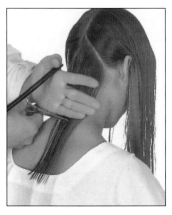

Before she had her hair cut, our model's long hair had natural movement but the weight was pulling the hair down and spoiling the shape. For her new style she wanted a shorter, more sophisticated look, and one that would be easy to maintain.

First the model's hair was shampooed, conditioned, and then combed through to remove any tangles. The stylist was then ready to start cutting. He began by sectioning off the front hair so that the hair at the back could be cut to the required length.

Next the front hair was combed forward and cut straight across at an angle. This ensured that when the model's hair was dry it would fall easily into shape.

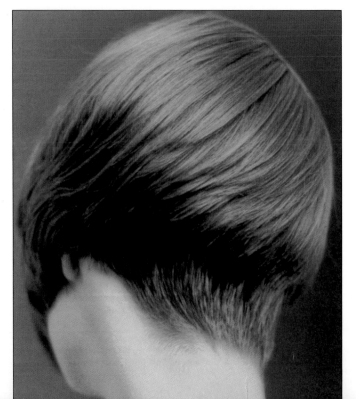

Hair growth varies over different parts of the head. This is why your cut can appear to be out of shape very quickly. As a general rule, a short precision cut needs trimming every four weeks, a longer style every six to eight weeks. Even if you want to grow your hair long it is essential to have it trimmed regularly – at least every three months – to prevent splitting and keep the ends even.

Hairdressers use a variety of techniques and tools to make hair appear thicker, fuller, straighter, or curlier, whatever the desired effect. The techniques and tools they use are explained below.

Blunt cutting, in which the ends are cut straight across, is often used for hair of one length. The weight and fullness of the hair is distributed around the perimeter of the shape.

Clippers are used for close-cut styles and sometimes to finish off a cut. Shaved clipper cuts are popular with teenagers.

This heavily layered, graduated bob was cut close into the nape, and then the shape of the hair was emphasized by using a vegetable colour to give tone and shine. The hair was styled by blow-drying. By Trevor Sorbie, London.

The top hair was graduated to help build volume and lift into the style. This type of cut makes it possible for the hair to be styled either towards the face or towards the back.

To finish, the stylist scrunched the hair, using a blow-dryer and some mousse to encourage the formation of curls. On this type of style a diffuser fitted to the dryer will spread the airflow and give added movement to the hair. By Carlos Galico, Madrid.

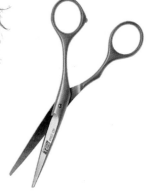

Graduated hair is cut at an angle to give fullness on top and blend the top hair into shorter lengths at the nape.

Layering the hair evenly distributes the weight and fullness, giving a round appearance to the style.

Slide cutting (also called slithering or feathering) thins the hair. Scissors are used in a sliding action, backwards and forwards along the hair length. This technique is often done when the hair is dry.

Razor cutting creates softness, tapering, and internal movement so that the hair moves more freely. It can also be used to shorten hair.

Thinning, either with thinning scissors or a razor, removes bulk and weight without affecting the overall length of the hair.

CLEVER CUTS

Fine, thin, flyaway hair can be given volume, bounce, and movement by blunt cutting. Mid-length hair can benefit from being lightly layered to give extra volume, while short, thin hair can be blunt cut and the edges graduated to give movement.

Some hairdressers razor cut fine hair to give a thicker and more voluminous

effect. It is best not to let fine hair grow too long. As soon as it reaches the shoulders it tends to look wispy.

Thick and coarse hair can be controlled by reducing the weight to give more style and direction. Avoid very short styles because the hair will tend to stick out. Try a layered cut with movement.

Layering also helps achieve height and eliminate weight. On shorter styles the weight can be reduced with thinning scissors expertly used on the ends only.

Sometimes hair grows in different directions, which may cause styling problems. For example, a cow lick is normally found on the front hairline and occurs when the hair grows in a swirl, backwards and then forwards. Clever cutting can redistribute the weight and go some way to solving this problem. A double crown occurs when there are two pivots for natural hair at the top of the head, rather than the usual one. Styles with height at the crown are most suitable here.

To maximize the effect of a widow's peak the hair should be taken in the reverse direction to the growth. This gives the impression of a natural wave.

Scissors can be used to reduce the bulk in thick hair. Scissors by Wella Tondeo.

For this style the model's straight hair was cut so that it would swing back into shape with every movement of the head. The shine was improved by using a longer-lasting semi-permanent colour. By L'Oréal.

SHAMPOOING

Shampoos are designed to cleanse the hair and scalp, removing dirt and grime without stripping away too much of the natural sebum. They contain cleansing agents, perfume, preservatives, and conditioning agents that can coat the hair shaft to make the hair appear thicker. The conditioning agents smooth the cuticle scales so the hair doesn't tangle, and help eliminate static electricity from the hair when it dries.

THE pH FACTOR

The letters pH refer to the acid/alkaline level of a substance. It is calculated on a scale of 1 to 14. Numbers below 7 denote acidity, those over 7 alkalinity. Most shampoos range between a pH factor of 5 and 7; medicated varieties have a pH of about 7.3, which is near neutral.

Sebum has a pH factor of between 4.5 and 5.5, which is mildly acidic. Bacteria cannot survive in this pH, so it is important to maintain this protective layer in order to keep the skin, scalp, and hair in optimum condition.

Many shampoos are labelled "pH balanced", and this means they have the

Shampoos are available in different formulas to suit all hair types and conditions. Make sure you choose one that is right for your hair and use it as often as necessary to keep your hair clean. Rinse out the shampoo thoroughly. Photograph courtesy of Silvikrin.

SHAMPOO TIPS

○ Use the correct shampoo (and not too much) for your hair type. If in doubt use the mildest shampoo you can buy.
○ Don't wash your hair in washing-up liquid, soap, or other detergents; they are highly alkaline and will upset your hair's natural pH balance by stripping out the natural oils.
○ Read the instructions first. Some shampoos need to be left on the scalp for a few minutes before rinsing.
○ If you can, buy small sachets of shampoo to test which brand is most suitable for your hair.

○ Never wash your hair in the bath; dirty bath water is not conducive to clean hair, and it is difficult to rinse properly without a shower attachment or separate jug.

○ Always wash your brush and comb when you shampoo your hair.
○ Change your shampoo every now and then; hair seems to develop a resistance to certain ingredients after a period of time.
○ Don't throw away a shampoo that doesn't lather. The amount of suds are determined by the active level of detergent. Some shampoos have less suds than others but this has no effect on their cleansing ability. In fact, quite often, the more effective the product, the fewer the bubbles.

same acidity level as hair. Individuals with fragile, permed, or coloured hair should use a shampoo of this type. However, for strong hair in good condition a pH balanced shampoo is unnecessary, provided shampooing is followed by conditioning.

SHAMPOO SUCCESS

Always use a product formulated for your hair type – dry, normal, greasy, or chemically treated – and before shampooing brush your hair to free any tangles and loosen dirt and dead skin cells. Use lukewarm water, as hot water can be uncomfortable.

Wet the hair, then apply a small amount of shampoo and gently massage into the roots, using the pads of your fingertips; never use your nails. Pay special attention to the hairline area, places where make-up and dirt become trapped. Allow the lather to work its way to the ends of the hair. Don't rub vigorously or you will stretch the hair.

When you have finished shampooing rinse thoroughly until the water runs clean and clear. Repeat the process only if you think your hair needs it, again using only a small amount of shampoo. Finally, blot the hair with a towel to remove excess water before applying conditioner.

MASSAGING THE SCALP

Massage helps maintain a healthy scalp. It brings extra blood to the tissues, which enhances the delivery of nutrients and oxygen to the hair follicle. It also reduces scalp tension – which can contribute to hair loss – loosens dead skin cells, and helps redress the overproduction of sebum, which makes hair greasy.

You can give yourself a scalp massage at home. Use warm olive oil if the scalp is dry or tight. Try equal parts of witch hazel and mineral water if you have an oily scalp. For a normal scalp, use equal parts rose and mineral waters.

Begin the massage by gently rotating your scalp using the tips of your fin-

A head massage reduces scalp tension as well as promoting healthy hair growth. It is also a relaxing and pampering treatment that you can do yourself at home.

gers. Start at the forehead, move to the sides, and work over the crown to the nape of the neck. Then place your fingertips firmly on the scalp without exerting too much pressure. Push the fingers together then pull them apart through the hair in a kneading motion, without lifting or moving them. When you have massaged for about a minute, move to the next section. Continue until your entire scalp and upper neck have been treated.

ELABORATE HAIR STYLES

In the 17th and 18th centuries hair washing was a biennial event. Fashionable women contrived towering heads of hair adorned with vegetables, fruit, feathers, and even vases of flowers. Many ladies sat up all night dozing in chairs rather than spoil their head pieces by lying in bed.

GETTING INTO CONDITION

Long hair needs a regular conditioning regime to keep it healthy and shiny. By Daniel Galvin, London, for L'Oréal Coiffure, Photography Iain Philpott.

In an ideal world a regular shampoo would be sufficient to guarantee a glossy head of hair. Unfortunately very few people are able to wash their hair and let the matter rest at that; most need some sort of help just to overcome the effects of modern living, not to mention the occasional problem that needs treatment. Here is a guide to the vast array of products available to get the hair in excellent condition.

THE CONDITIONERS

Glossy hair has cuticle scales that lie flat and neatly overlap, thus reflecting the light. Perming and colouring, rough handling, and heat styling all conspire to lift the cuticles, allowing moisture to be lost from the cortex and making hair dry, lack lustre, and prone to tangle. Severely damaged cuticles break off completely, which means that the hair gets thinner and eventually breaks.

To put the shine back into hair and restore its natural lustre it may be necessary to use a specific conditioner that meets the hair's requirements. Conditioners, with the exception of hot oils, should be applied to freshly shampooed hair that has been blotted dry with a towel to remove excess moisture.

Today there is a large, and sometimes confusing, number of conditioners on the market. The following list describes those which are widely available.

Basic conditioners coat the hair with a fine film, temporarily smoothing down the cuticle and making hair glossier and easier to manage. Leave for a few minutes before rinsing thoroughly.

Conditioning sprays are used prior to styling and form a protective barrier against the harmful effects of heat. They are also good for reducing static electricity on flyaway hair.

Hot oils give an intensive, deep nourishing treatment. To use, place the unopened tube in a cup of hot tap water and leave to heat for one minute. Next, wet the hair and towel it dry before twisting off the tube top. Massage the hot oil evenly into the scalp and throughout the hair for one to three minutes. For a more intensive treatment cover the head with a shower cap. To finish, rinse the hair and shampoo.

Intensive conditioners help hair to retain its natural moisture balance, replenishing it where necessary. Use this type if the hair is split, dry, frizzy, or difficult to manage. Distribute the conditioner evenly through the hair and then allow it to penetrate for two to five minutes, or longer if required. Rinse very thoroughly with lots of fresh water, lifting your hair from the scalp to ensure any residue is washed away.

Leave-in conditioners are designed to help retain moisture, reduce static, and add shine. They are especially good for fine hair as they avoid conditioner overload, which can cause lankness. Convenient and easy-to-use, they also provide a protective barrier against the effects of heat styling. Apply after shampooing but don't rinse off. These products are ideal for daily use.

Restructurants penetrate the cortex, helping to repair and strengthen the inner part of damaged hair. They are helpful if the hair is lank and limp and has lost its natural elasticity as a result of chemical treatments or physical damage.

Split end treatments/serums condition damaged hair. The best course of action for split ends is to have the ends trimmed, but this does not always solve the whole problem because the hair tends to break off and split at different levels. As an intermediate solution, split ends can be temporarily sealed using these specialist conditioners. They should be worked into the ends of newly washed hair so that they surround the hair with a microscopic film that leaves the hair shaft smoother.

Colour/perm conditioners are designed for chemically treated hair. After-colour products add a protective film around porous areas of the hair, preventing colour loss. After-perm products help stabilize the hair, thus keeping the bounce in the curl.

PROBLEMS AND SOLUTIONS

Split ends, dandruff, and dry, itchy scalp are common problems that can detract from otherwise healthy hair. In most cases such problems can be overcome by giving the appropriate treatment.

Dandruff consists of scaly particles with an oily sheen that lie close to the hair root. This condition should not be confused with a flaky scalp (see below).
Causes Poor diet, sluggish metabolism, stress, a hormonal imbalance, and sometimes infection. These conditions produce increased cell renewal on the scalp, which is often associated with an increase in sebum. The scales will absorb the excess oil, but if the problem is untreated it will become worse.
Solutions Rethink your diet and lifestyle. Learn relaxation techniques if the problem appears to be caused by stress. Brush the hair before shampooing and scrupulously wash combs and brushes. Always choose a mild shampoo with an antidandruff action that gently loosens scales and helps prevent new ones. Follow with a treatment lotion, massaged into the scalp using the fingertips. The treatment must be used regularly if it is to be effective. Avoid excessive use of heat stylers. If the dandruff persists, consult your family doctor or trichologist.

Flaky/itchy scalp produces tiny white pieces of dead skin that flake off the scalp and are usually first noticed on the shoulders. This condition can often be confused with dandruff but the two are not related. Sometimes the scalp is red or itchy and feels tense. The hair has a dull appearance.
Causes Hereditary traits, stress, insufficient rinsing of shampoo, lack of sebum, using a harsh shampoo, vitamin imbalance, pollution, air conditioning and central heating.
Solutions Choose a moisturizing shampoo and a conditioner with herbal extracts to help soothe and remoisturize the scalp.

PROFESSIONAL TIPS

○ Blot hair to remove excess moisture before applying conditioner.
○ Gently massage conditioner into the hair, or use a wide-toothed comb to distribute it evenly.
○ Leave the conditioner on the hair for the time specified – check whether it is a "leave in" or "rinse out" variety.
○ If necessary, rinse thoroughly.
○ Treat wet hair with care; it is much more sensitive and vulnerable than when it is dry.
○ Avoid rubbing, pulling, or stretching wet hair.

Leave-in conditioners that come in mousse formulations can be applied straight on to the hair from the container.

Use a styling comb with widely spaced teeth to distribute the conditioner from the roots to the ends of the hair. Do not rinse out, simply style and dry the hair as desired.

Above and right: Limp, fine hair can be transformed easily using a volumizing spray or thickening mousse before setting on large rollers. Make sure the hair is completely dry before removing rollers and lightly brushing the hair through. Hold with hairspray. By Nicky Clarke, London, Photography Paul Cox.

Fine hair tends to be limp, looks flat, and is difficult to style because it does not hold a style.

Causes The texture is hereditary, but the problem is often made worse by using too heavy a conditioner, which weighs the hair down. Excessive use of styling products can have the same effect.

Solutions Wash hair frequently with a mild cleanser and use a light conditioner. Volumizing shampoos can help give body, and soft perms will make hair appear thicker.

Frizzy hair results from the merest hint of rain or other air moisture being absorbed into the hair. It looks dry, lacks lustre, and is difficult to control.

Causes Can be inherited or caused by rough treatment, such as too much harsh brushing or pulling the hair into rubber bands.

Solutions When washing the hair massage the shampoo into the roots and allow the lather to work its way to the ends. Apply a conditioner from the mid-lengths of the hair to the ends, or use a leave-in conditioner. The hair is often best styled with a gel, which should be applied when the hair is wet. Alternatively, allow the hair to dry naturally and then style it using a wax or pomade. Serums can also help. These are silicone-based products that work by surrounding the cuticle with a transparent microscopic film, which leaves the hair shaft smoother. Serums effectively prevent moisture loss and inhibit the absorption of dampness from the surrounding air.

Split ends occur when the cuticle is damaged and the fibres of the cortex unravel. The hair is dry, brittle, and prone to tangling, and can split at the end or anywhere along the shaft.

Causes Over-perming or colouring, insufficient conditioning, or too much brushing or backcombing, especially with poor quality combs or brushes. Careless use of spiky rollers and hair pins, excessive heat styling and not having the hair trimmed regularly can also cause the problem.

Solutions Split ends can't be mended; the only long-term cure is to have them

snipped off. What is lost in the length will be gained in quality. It may help if you reduce the frequency with which you shampoo, as this in itself is stressful to hair and causes split ends to extend up the hair shaft. Never use a dryer too near the hair, or set it on too high a temperature. Minimize the use of heated appliances. Try conditioners and serums that are designed to temporarily seal split ends and give resistance to further splitting.

Product build-up is the residue of styling products and two-in-one shampoo formulation left on the hair shaft.

Causes When these residues combine with mineral deposits in the water a build-up occurs, preventing thorough cleansing and conditioning. The result is hair that is dull and lacks lustre; it is often difficult to perm or colour successfully because there is a barrier preventing the chemicals from penetrating the hair shaft. The colour can be patchy and the perm result uneven.

Solutions Use one of the stripping, chelating or clarifying shampoos, which are specially designed to remove product build-up. This is particularly important prior to perming or colouring.

Top left and above: Frizzy hair can be controlled using a moisturizing shampoo and conditioner. Style using a mousse designed for curly hair, which will help to eliminate tangles and reduce static. Finish with a few drops of serum to add a final touch of gloss. By Nicky Clarke, London, Photography Paul Cox.

Above left: Split ends can't be mended, just temporarily sealed. The only permanent cure is to have your hair trimmed regularly.

Natural ingredients such as herbs and essential oils can help you achieve beautifully conditioned hair. Here a hot oil treatment was applied to the model's hair to enhance its shine and condition. Natural oils that are suitable for applying to the hair and scalp include vegetable oils, but rosemary, ylang ylang, and lavender essential oils are fragrant alternatives. Use according to the manufacturer's directions. By Daniel Galvin, London.

NATURAL SOLUTIONS

Since time immemorial herbs and plants have been used to heal, pamper, and beautify. Many of these age-old haircare recipes still apply today. The following are a few you might like to try at home. Remember to use them immediately after you have made them: they won't keep.

Dandruff solution

Mix a few drops of oil of rosemary with 30 ml/2 tbsp of olive oil and rub well into the scalp at bedtime. Shampoo and rinse thoroughly in the morning.

Egg shampoo

In a blender mix together two small eggs with 50 g/2 oz of still mineral water and 15 ml/1 tbsp of cider vinegar or lemon juice. Blend for 30 seconds at low speed. Massage well into the scalp and rinse very thoroughly using lukewarm water (if the water is any hotter the egg will begin to set).

Herbal shampoo

Crush a few dried bay leaves with a rolling pin and mix with a handful of dried camomile flowers and one of rosemary. Place in a large jug and pour over 1 litre/1¾ pints of boiling water. Strain after 2-3 minutes and mix in 5 ml/1 tsp of soft or liquid soap. Apply to the hair, massaging well. Rinse thoroughly.

Hot oil

Any vegetable oil is suitable for conditioning. Just heat the oil until slightly warm. Rub a little into your scalp and then through every part of your hair, massaging gently as you go. Cover your head with a plastic shower cap for 20 minutes; the heat from your head will help the oil penetrate the hair shaft. Shampoo and rinse thoroughly.

Intensive conditioning treatment

Warm 15 ml/1 tbsp each of wheat germ and olive oil and massage into the scalp. Wrap a warm towel around the head and leave for 10 minutes. Then rinse with a basin of water to which you have added the juice of a lemon.

Hair tonic

Beat 150 ml/ 5 fl oz of natural yogurt with an egg; add 5 ml/1 tsp of sea kelp powder and 5 ml/1 tsp of finely grated lemon rind. Mix thoroughly and work into the hair. Cover your hair with a plastic shower cap and leave in place for 40 minutes. Shampoo and rinse.

Using essential oils

Pure aromatherapy oils can be used for hair care. The following recipes come from world-famous aromatherapist Robert Tisserand. The number of drops of oil, as listed, should be diluted in 30 ml/2 tbsp of vegetable oil, which will act as a carrier oil.

Dry hair: rosewood 9, sandalwood 6.
Oily hair: bergamot 9, lavender 6.
Dandruff: eucalyptus 9, rosemary 6.
Mix the required treatment and apply to dry or wet hair. Massage the scalp using the fingertips. Leave for two to five minutes. Shampoo and rinse thoroughly.

You can grow your own herbs or find them and other ingredients such as essential oil and henna in many health food shops and pharmacies. They are also available through specialist shops selling natural remedies and beauty products. Many hair treatments can be made safely, economically, and easily at home.

HAIR RINSES

Lemon juice added to the rinsing water will brighten blonde hair, while 30 ml/2 tbsp of cider vinegar will add gloss and body to any colour hair.

Other rinses (to be used after shampooing) can be made up to treat a variety of hair problems. First you must make an infusion by placing 30 ml/2 tbsp of the fresh herb in a china or glass bowl. Fresh herbs are best, but if you are using dried herbs remember they are stronger so you will need to halve the amount required for fresh herbs. Add 600 ml/1 pint boiling water, cover and leave to steep for three hours. The longer the herbs steep the stronger the infusion. Strain before using. Make infusions with the following herbs for the specific uses as listed:

○ Southernwood to combat grease.
○ Nettle to stimulate hair growth.
○ Rosemary to prevent static.
○ Lavender to soothe a tight scalp.

Make a parsley hair tonic (see picture right) by blending a large handful of parsley sprigs and 30 ml/2 tbsp water in a food processor until well puréed. Apply to the scalp, cover with a shower cap, and leave for an hour before rinsing thoroughly.

TIMES OF CHANGE

Hair goes through many different stages during a lifetime. Each stage brings with it different requirements in haircare. The most significant stages are described below, together with recommendations for promoting hair health during each phase.

BEGINNINGS:
THE BABY AND CHILD

A baby's hair characteristics are determined from the very moment of conception. By the 16th week of pregnancy the foetus will be covered with lanugo, a downy body hair that is usually shed before birth. The first hair appears on the head at around 20 weeks gestation and it is at this time that the pigment melanin, which will determine the colour of the hair, is first produced.

A few weeks after birth the baby's original hair begins to fall out or is rubbed off. The new hair is quite different from the initial downy mass, so a baby born with blonde wispy curls might have dark straight hair by the age of six months.

Cradle cap, which appears as thick, yellow scales in patches over the scalp, causes many mothers concern. Cradle cap is the result of a natural build-up of skin cells. It is nothing to worry about and can be gently loosened by rubbing a little baby oil on to the scalp at night and washing it off in the morning. This may need to be repeated for several days until all the loose scales have been lifted and washed away.

Mothers often carefully trim their baby's hair as and when necessary, and it is not until the child is about two years of age that a visit to a hairdressing salon may be necessary. Children's hair is normally in beautiful condition and is best cut and styled simply.

At the onset of puberty young adults suddenly become much more interested in experimenting with their hair. This is when they may experience greasy hair and skin for the first time. A re-evaluation of the shampoos and conditioners currently in use is often necessary to keep hair looking good.

HAIRCARE DURING PREGNANCY

During pregnancy the hair often looks its best. However after the birth, or after breast-feeding ceases, about 50 per cent of new mothers experience what appears to be excessive hair loss. This is related to the three stages of hair growth (see page 8). During pregnancy and breast-feeding, hormones keep the hair at the growing stage for longer than usual, so it appears thicker and fuller. Some time after the birth – usually about 12 weeks later – this hair enters the resting stage, at the end of which all the hair that has been in the resting phase is shed. What appears to have been excessive hair loss is therefore simply a postponement of a natural occurrence, a condition that is known as post-partum alopecia.

A more significant problem that may occur during pregnancy is caused by a depletion in the protein content of the hair. As a result the hair becomes drier and more brittle. Combat this by frequent use of an intensive conditioning treatment.

GROWING UP

A baby's hair is soft and downy at first but it takes on its individual characteristics within six months of birth.

The toddler's hair requires a simple cut. At this stage the child is usually taken for her first visit to a salon.

Young boys need a hair cut that is easily combed into shape. By Regis, Europe.

Bobs suit most girls and are perfect for straight hair, but need regular trims. By Regis, Europe.

As women grow older the hair becomes thinner. A mid-length to short cut makes the hair less prone to droop. By Joseph and Jane Harling, Avon, England.

HAIR LOSS AND HRT

Medical opinion differs concerning the effect of Hormone Replacement Therapy (HRT) on the hair but it is generally accepted that in most cases it can be beneficial. However trichologists advise that if women have had permanent hair thinning prior to taking HRT the problem may be compounded. It is best to discuss this with your family doctor.

This is particularly true for those who live in a town or spend time in smoky atmospheres. Cigarette smoke and natural gas from cookers discolour white hair and make it look yellow. Mineral deposits from chlorinated water can give white hair a greenish tinge. Chelating, clarifying, or purifying shampoos will help to strip this build-up from the hair.

To counteract dryness associated with ageing, use richer shampoos and conditioning products. As well as regular conditioning, weekly intensive treatments are essential to counteract moisture loss.

Avoid perming during pregnancy because the hair is in an altered state and the result can be unpredictable. However, a new colour can give your hair and your spirits a lift.

GROWING OLDER

With ageing the whole body slows down, including the hair follicles, which become less efficient and produce hairs that are finer in diameter and shorter in length. Such shrinkage is gradual and the hair begins to feel slightly thinner, with less volume and density. At the same time the sebaceous glands start to produce less sebum and the hair begins to lose its colour as the production of melanin decreases.

Blonde hair fades, brunettes lose their natural highlights, and redheads tone down to brownish shades. When melanin production stops altogether the new hair that grows is white, not grey as is commonly perceived. The production of melanin is governed by genetic factors, and the best indication of when an individual's hair will become white is the age at which their parents' hair lost its colour. Pigment, apart from giving hair its colour, also helps to soften and make each strand more flexible. This is why white hair tends to become wirier and coarser in texture.

Because the texture changes, the hair is inclined to pick up dust and smoke from the atmosphere, so it soon appears to be discoloured and dirty.

AS THE YEARS GO BY

Medium-textured hair that needs a lift can be given height on the crown with a root perm. By Paul Falltricks, Essex, England, for Clynol.

The hair has been cut to create more movement and softness. It was then scrunch-dried and finished with wax. By Regis, Europe.

Long hair was softened by feathering the sides and cutting a full fringe. A semi-permanent colour added gloss. By Nicky Clarke, London.

Fine grey hair was highlighted and then toned using a rinse before blow-drying with a round brush. By Essanelle Salons, Britain.

HOLIDAY HAIRCARE

Permed hair needs extra protection from the drying effects of sun, salt, chlorine, and wind. Use plenty of conditioner and always rinse your hair after swimming. Curl revitalizers help by putting moisture back and keeping curls bouncy. Photograph courtesy of Bain de Terre Spa Therapy.

More damage can be done to the hair during a two-week holiday in the sun than the damage accrued during the rest of the year. The ultraviolet rays or radiation (UVRs) from sunlight that can cause damage to the skin can also have an adverse effect on the hair, depleting the natural oils and removing moisture. Strong winds whip unprotected hair into a tangle, causing breakage and split ends. Chlorinated and salt water cause colour fading and result in drooping perms.

Permed and coloured hair, weakened by chemicals, lose moisture at a faster rate than untreated hair. White hair is particularly susceptible to the effects of the sun because it has lost its natural pigmentation (melanin), which to some degree helps to filter out harmful UVRs.

OUT IN THE MID-DAY SUN

Protecting the hair from the sun's harmful rays makes as much sense as protecting the skin. Wear a hat or a scarf on the beach or use a sun protective spray to shield the hair from the sun's harmful rays. After a swim, rinse the salt or chlorinated water thoroughly from the hair using plenty of fresh, clean water. If fresh water is not available take some with you in an empty soft drinks bottle or use bottled water.

Sun screen gels are available for the hair and these offer a good deal of protection. Comb the gel through your hair and leave on all day. Remember to reapply the gel after swimming. Alternatively, use a leave-in conditioner, choosing one that protects the hair against UVRs.

On windy or blustery days keep long hair tied back to prevent tangles. Long hair can also be braided when it is wet and the braid left in all day. When evening comes and you undo the braids you will have a cascade of rippling, pre-Raphaelite curls.

If your hair does get tangled by the wind, untangle it gently by using a

Above. Slick short hair back with gel. Leave the gel in all day, then rinse out and style your hair in the evening. Photograph courtesy of Bain de Terre Spa Therapy.

BEFORE YOU GO

❍ Any hair colouring you are planning should be done at least one week prior to your holiday. This will allow the colour to "soften" and allow time for some intensive conditioning on any dry ends.

❍ If you want to have a perm before your holiday, book the appointment at least three weeks before departure to allow your hair to settle. You will also have the opportunity to learn how best to manage your new style and help overcome any dryness.

❍ Remember to pack all your holiday hair needs – your favourite shampoos, conditioners, and styling products. And pack a selection of scarves and hair accessories. You will have more time to experiment on holiday.

❍ If possible take a travel dryer with dual voltage, and remember to pack an adaptor.

❍ Gas-powered stylers are convenient for holidays but remember they must be carried in the hold of the aircraft, not in your hand luggage. Refill cylinders are not allowed on aeroplanes, so fit a new cartridge before you go.

❍ Soft, bendy rollers are a good alternative to heated ones – they are also kinder to the hair.

❍ Have a trim before you go, but not a new style, as you won't want to worry about coping with a new look. Whatever you do, don't be tempted to have your hair cut abroad. Wait until you are back home and can visit your regular stylist.

Above. When the sun sets apply mousse to straightened hair and sleek back behind the ears, flicking the ends up. Then leave to dry naturally. By Jon Pereira-Santos, Montage Hair Company, Windsor, England. Photography Suzy Corby.

Left. Breezy beach days whip the hair into a tangle. Take time to remove knots and snarls with a wide-toothed comb. Longer hair can be braided or knotted into a neat bun at the nape to keep it in place and prevent damage. Photograph courtesy of Silvikrin.

Top: After swimming rinse the hair in clean, clear water and comb through with a wide-toothed comb. Use a sun protective gel with a UVR filter for maximum care. By Daniel Galvin, London.

Above: To keep the hair in place, clasp it into a pretty slide. Colourful accessories are great for the beach; take a selection to mix and match with your swimwear. By Daniel Galvin, London.

Opposite: To get separation on long curls mix a little conditioner with water and use a spray to mist the solution on to the hair. Scrunch the hair with your hands to create a casual look. Photograph courtesy of Bain de Terre Spa Therapy.

Opposite below: Pin fresh flowers in your hair for an alluring, feminine after-sun style. By Joseph and Jane Harling, Avon, England.

wide-toothed comb and work from the ends of the hair up towards the roots.

Keep your head and hair protected even when you are away from the beach. Wear a sun hat when shopping or sightseeing, especially at mid-day. When the sun sets, shampoo and condition your hair and, if possible, let it dry naturally. Leave heat styling for those special nights out.

WINTER HAIRCARE

During the winter, and particularly on a winter break, your hair will be exposed to damaging conditions, such as harsh biting winds and the drying effects of low temperatures and central heating. Central heating draws moisture from the hair and scalp, which causes static. Extreme cold makes the hair brittle and dry, and wet weather spells disaster for a style, making curly hair frizz and straight hair limp.

Above left: Long hair that is lightly layered gives lift on the crown and movement in the ends. For this look, rough-dry the hair and mist with styling lotion before setting on large rollers. When the hair is completely dry, lightly brush through to create soft waves and curls. By Taylor Ferguson, Glasgow, Scotland.

Above: Short, naturally curly hair can be given a pretty style by drying it with a small round brush and working the hair upwards. By Andrew Collinge, Liverpool, and Harrods, London. Photography Iain Philpott.

These effects can be counteracted with a few simple measures. To reduce the drying effects of central heating, place large bowls of water near the radiators or use humidifiers. Use a more intensive conditioner on your hair in the winter to combat dryness caused by cold. In damp weather apply a mousse, gel, or hairspray; they are invaluable for keeping a style in place and giving some degree of protection.

ON THE PISTE

○ The sun's rays are intensified by reflection from the snow, so hair needs extra protection in the form of a hair sunscreen.
○ Wind, blasts of snow, and sunshine are a damaging combination for hair, so wear a hat whenever possible.
○ In freezing temperatures hair picks up static electricity, making it flyaway and unmanageable. Calm the static by spraying your brush with hairspray before brushing your hair.
○ With sudden temperature changes – from icy cold slopes to a warm hotel – and constantly changing headgear your hair may need daily shampooing. Use a mild shampoo and light conditioner.

COLOURING AND BLEACHING

Hair colorants have never been technically better; nowadays it is a simple matter to add a temporary tone and gloss to the hair or make a more permanent change. And there is a wide variety of home colouring products from which to choose.

THE CHOICE

Temporary colours are usually water-based and are applied to pre-shampooed, wet hair. They work by coating the outside, or cuticle layer, of the hair. The colour washes away in the next shampoo. Temporary colours are good

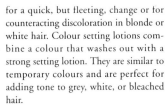

FACT FILE

○ Colouring swells the hair shaft, making fine hair appear thicker.
○ Because colour changes the porosity of the hair it can help combat greasiness.
○ Rich tones reflect more light and give hair a thicker appearance.
○ Highlights give fine hair extra texture and break up the heaviness of very thick hair.
○ Too light a hair colour can make the hair appear thinner.

for a quick, but fleeting, change or for counteracting discoloration in blonde or white hair. Colour setting lotions combine a colour that washes out with a strong setting lotion. They are similar to temporary colours and are perfect for adding tone to grey, white, or bleached hair.

Semi-permanent colours give a more noticeable effect that lasts for six to eight shampoos. They can only add, enrich, or darken hair colour, they cannot make it any lighter. Semi-permanent colours penetrate the cuticle and coat the outer edge of the cortex (the inner layer of the hair). The colour fades gradually and is ideal for those who want to experiment but don't want to commit themselves to a more permanent change.

Longer lasting semi-permanent colours remain in the hair for 12-20 shampoos and are perfect for blending in the first grey hairs. The colour penetrates even deeper into the cortex than in semi-permanent colours. This type is perfect for a more lasting change.

Permanent colours lighten or darken, and effectively cover white. The colour enters the cortex during the development time (around 30 minutes) after which oxygen in the developer swells the pigments in the colorant, and holds them in. The roots may need retouching every six weeks. When retouching it is important to colour only the new hair growth. If the new colour overlaps previously treated hair there will be a build-up of colour from the mid-lengths to the ends, which will make the hair more porous.

The model's fine hair was made to look thicker by working fine highlights of different tonal values throughout the hair. The feather cut was then styled forward and blow-dried into shape. A little wax was rubbed between the palms of the hands and applied to the hair with the fingertips to give further definition. By Nicky Clarke, London.

Below: Ash-blonde hair was tapered at the sides so that it feathered on to the face. Fine textured hair like this needs gentle styling to maintain it in good condition, especially after colouring, so regular conditioning treatments are essential. By Steven Carey, London.

Above: These copper tones were achieved by applying a permanent tint; the volume of hair was then increased by using a hot air brush to style the hair away from the face. You can get the same effect by working on one section of the hair at a time. Finish with firm-hold hairspray. Photograph courtesy of BaByliss.

Above: Here reddish hues were created with a longer-lasting semi-permanent colour that added deep tones and luminosity. The hair was blow-dried straight, pointing the nozzle of the dryer downwards in order to polish and encourage the shine. By Yosh Toya, San Francisco, Photography Gen.

Above: Russet tones were further emphasized by weaving a few lighter colours into the front hair. The hair was blow-dried with styling gel to get lift at the roots. By Daniel Galvin, London.

Left: The model's hair was lightened to achieve this soft shade of blonde. Remember, only lift your hair colour by one or two shades and don't forget that the roots will need retouching regularly. For this style the hair was graduated and blow-dried into shape. By Daniel Galvin, London.

NATURAL COLOURING – HENNA

Vegetable colorants such as henna and camomile have been used since ancient times to colour hair, and henna was particularly popular with the Ancient Egyptians. Although henna is the most widely used natural dye, others can be extracted from a wide variety of plants, including marigold petals, cloves, rhubarb stalks, and even tea leaves. Natural dyes work in much the same way as semi-permanent colorants by staining the outside of the hair. However, results are variable and a residue is often left behind, making further colouring with permanent tints or bleaches inadvisable.

Henna enhances natural highlights making colour appear richer. It is available today as a powder, which is mixed with water to form a paste. The colour fades gradually but frequent applications will give a stronger, longer-lasting effect. The result that is achieved when using henna depends on the natural colour of the hair. On brunette or black hair it produces a lovely reddish glow, while lighter hair becomes a beautiful titian. Henna will not lighten, and it is not suitable for use on blonde hair. On hair that is more than 20 per cent grey, white, tinted, bleached, or highlighted, the resultant colour will be orange.

The longer the henna is left on the hair, the more intense the result. Timings vary from one to two hours, but some Indian women leave henna on the hair for 24 hours, anointing their heads with oil to keep the paste supple.

The condition of the hair being treated is another factor that effects the intensity. The ends of long hair are always slightly lighter than the roots because they are more exposed to the sun, and henna will emphasize this effect. The resulting colour will be darker on the roots to the mid-lengths and more vibrant from the mid-lengths to the ends.

It is always wise to test the henna you intend to use on a few loose hairs (the ones in your hairbrush will do),

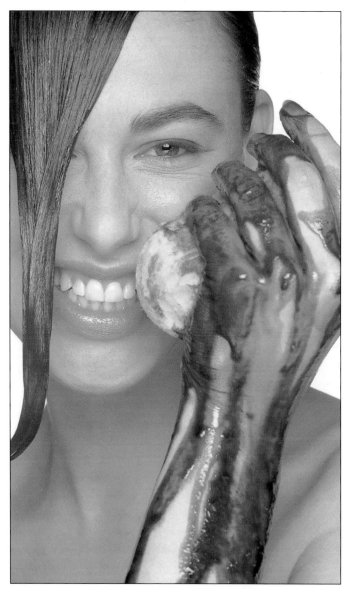

A variety of herbs and other plants have been used in the past to colour hair, and many of them have remained popular to this day. The natural dyes provide a semi-permanent colour, although the results that can be achieved will vary. They depend on the quality of the raw ingredients combined with the natural colour of the hair and how porous it is. Many top hairdressers mix their own vegetable dyes using a a wide range of ingredients, as well as using commercial colours. By Daniel Galvin, London.

noting the length of time it takes to produce the result you want.

Neutral henna can be used to add
gloss and lustre to the hair without
adding any colour. Mix the henna with
water to a stiff paste. Stir in an egg yolk
for extra conditioning, plus a little milk,
which will help to keep the paste pliable. Apply to the hair and leave for an
hour before rinsing thoroughly. Repeat
every two to three months.

CAMOMILE

Camomile has a gentle lightening effect
on hair and is good for sun-streaking
blonde and light brown hair. However,
it takes several applications and a good
deal of time to produce the desired
effect. The advantage of camomile over
chemical bleach is that it never gives a
brassy or yellow tone. Best for blonde
hair, it will also gently lighten red.

To make a camomile rinse to use
after each shampoo, place 30 ml/2 tbsp

Above: Brunettes are very suitable candidates
for having their hair coloured. Their hair can
be considerably enriched and enhanced with a
henna, which will produce brilliant depths and
tones. By Wella Living Colours.

Above right: These vibrant red tones were
achieved using a mixture of vegetable dyes and
by working highlights of different tones
through the hair. The hair was then styled by
blow-drying. By Daniel Galvin, London.

of dried camomile flowers in 600 ml/1
pint of boiling water. Simmer for 15
minutes, strain and cool before use.

To obtain more positive results add
125 g/1 cup of dried camomile flowers
to 300 ml/½ pint of boiling water and
leave to steep for 15 minutes. Cool, simmer, and strain. Add the juice of a fresh
lemon plus 30 ml/2 tbsp of a rich cream
conditioner. Comb through the hair and
leave to dry – in the sun, if possible.
Finally, shampoo and condition your
hair as usual.

DO'S AND DON'TS

○ Do rinse henna paste thoroughly,
or the hair and scalp will feel gritty.
○ Don't expose hennaed hair to
strong sunlight and always rinse salt
and chlorine from the hair
immediately after swimming.
○ Do use a henna shampoo
between colour applications to
enhance the tone.
○ Don't use shampoos and
conditioners containing henna on
blonde hair, grey hair, or hair that
has been chemically treated.
○ Do use the same henna product
each time you apply henna.
○ Don't use compound henna (one
that has had metallic salts added); it
can cause long-term hair colouring
problems.

CHOOSING A NEW COLOUR

When choosing a colour a basic rule is to keep to one or two shades at each side of your original tone. It is probably best to try a temporary colorant first; if you like the result you can choose a semi-permanent or permanent colorant next time. If you want to be a platinum blonde and you are a natural brunette, you should seek the advice of a professional hairdresser.

There are two important points to remember when considering a colour change. First, only have a colour change if your hair is in good condition; dry, porous hair absorbs colour too rapidly, leading to a patchy result. Second, your make-up may need changing to suit your new colour.

SPECIAL TECHNIQUES

Hairdressers have devised an array of colouring methods to create different effects. These include:

Flying colours, in which a combination of colours is applied with combs and brushes to the middle lengths and tips of the hair.

Highlights/lowlights, where fine strands of hair are tinted or bleached lighter or darker, or colour is added just to give varying tones throughout the hair. This technique is sometimes called frosting or shimmering, particularly when bleach is used to give an overall lighter effect.

Slices, a technique in which assorted colours are applied through the hair to emphasize a cut and show movement.

COVERING WHITE HAIR

If you just want to cover a few white hairs use a temporary or semi-permanent colour that will last for six to eight weeks. Choose one that is similar to your natural colour. If the hair is brown, applying a warm brown colour will pick out the white areas and give lighter chestnut highlights. Alternatively, henna will give a glossy finish, and at the same time produce stunning red highlights. For salt and pepper hair – hair with a

mixed amount of white with the natural colour – try a longer lasting semi-permanent colour. These last for up to 20 shampoos and also add shine.

When hair is completely white it can be covered with a permanent tint, but with this type of colorant it is necessary to update the colour every four to six weeks, a fact that should be taken into consideration before choosing this option. Those who prefer to stay with their natural shade of white can improve on the colour by using toning shampoos, conditioners, and styling products, which will remove any brassiness and add beautiful silvery tones.

CARING FOR COLOURED HAIR

Chlorinated and salt water, perspiration, and the weather all conspire to fade coloured hair, particularly red hair. However special products are available that will help counteract fading, such as those containing ultraviolet filters that protect coloured hair from the effects of the sun. Other protective measures include rinsing the hair after swimming and using a shampoo designed for coloured hair, followed by a separate conditioner. Gently blot the hair after shampooing – never rub it vigorously as this ruffles the cuticle and can result in colour "escaping". Finally, use an intensive conditioning treatment at least once a month.

BLEACHING

Strictly speaking, anything that lightens the hair bleaches it, but in the present context bleaching refers specifically to any treatment that removes colour from the hair – rather than adding colour, which is the purpose of permanent colorants. There are several different types of bleach on the market and they range from the mild brighteners that lift hair colour a couple of shades to the more powerful mixes that completely strip hair of its natural colour.

Bleaching is quite difficult to do and is best left to a professional hair-

Left: There is a wide range of natural tones to choose from when you are looking for a new hair colour.

Above: The alternative is to opt for more vibrant fashion shades. Colour swatches courtesy of L'Oréal Coiffure.

dresser. If misused it can be very harsh and drying on the hair. To get the best results make sure your hair is in optimum condition prior to bleaching. Once the hair has been bleached, regular intensive conditioning treatments are essential.

COLOUR CORRECTION

If you have been colouring your hair for some time and want to go back to your natural colour and tone consult a professional hairdresser. Hair that has been tinted darker than its normal shade will have to be colour-stripped with a bleach bath until the desired colour is achieved. Hair that has been bleached or highlighted will need to be re-pigmented and then tinted to match the original colour. For best results, all these processes must be carried out in a salon where the technicians have access to a variety of specialist products.

HELPFUL HINTS FOR HOME HAIR COLOURING

Always read the directions supplied with the product before you start, and follow them precisely. Make sure you do a strand and skin sensitivity test, as detailed in the directions.

If you are retouching the roots of tinted or bleached hair, apply new colour only to the regrowth area. Any overlap will result in uneven colour and porosity, which in turn will adversely affect the condition of your hair.

Don't colour your hair at home if the hair is split or visibly damaged, or if you have used bleach or any type of henna; you must allow previously treated hair to grow out before applying new colour. Avoid colouring your hair if you are taking prescribed drugs, as the chemical balance of your hair can alter. Check with your family doctor first.

If your hair has been permed consult a hairdresser before using a hair colorant. And if you are in any doubt about using a colour, always check with the manufacturer or consult a professional hair colourist.

FACT FILE

In the Middle Ages saffron and a mixture of sulphur, alum, and honey were used for bleaching and colouring hair. These concoctions were not always safe however, and in 1562 a certain Dr Marinello from Moderna, Italy, wrote a treatise warning of the possible and undesirable consequences of bleaching the hair. He warned: "The scalp could be seriously damaged and the hair be destroyed at the roots and fall out."

Top and above: Burnished Titian red tones give one of the most effective results when applied to natural brown hair. However reddish hues are particularly prone to fade so coloured hair should be protected from the sun. Specialist shampoos and conditioners should be used to help maintain colour. Photographs: top, Mark Hill for Wella; above, Zotos.

PERMANENT SOLUTIONS

Making straight hair curly is not a new idea. Women in Ancient Egypt coated their hair in mud, wound it around wooden rods and then used the heat from the sun to create the curls.

Waves that won't wash out are a more recent innovation. Modern perms were pioneered by A F Willat, who invented the "cold permanent wave" technique in 1934. Since then, improved formulations and ever more sophisticated techniques have made perms the most versatile styling option in hairdressing.

HOW THEY WORK

Perms work by breaking down inner structures (links) in your hair and re-forming them around a curler to give a new shape. Hair should be washed prior to perming as this causes the scales on the cuticles to rise gently, allowing the perming lotion to enter the hair shaft more quickly. The perming lotion alters the keratin and breaks down the sulphur bonds that link the fibre-like cells together in the inner layers of each hair. When these fibres have become loose, they can be formed into a new shape when the hair is stretched over a curler or a perming rod.

Once the curlers or rods are in place, more lotion is applied and the perm is left to develop to fix the new shape. The development time can vary according to the condition and texture of the hair. When the development is complete, the changed links in the hair are re-formed into their new shape by the application of a second chemical known as the neutralizer. The neutralizer contains an oxidizing agent that is effectively responsible for closing up the broken links and producing the wave or curl – permanently.

Specialist formulations enable your hairdresser to perm long hair while maintaining it in optimum condition. Here the hair was wound on to large rods to achieve a soft curl formation. Photograph courtesy of Clynol.

The type of curl that is produced depends on a number of factors. The size of the curler is perhaps the most important as this determines the size of the curl. Generally speaking the smaller the curler the smaller and therefore tighter the curl, whereas medium to large curlers tend to give a much looser effect. The strength of lotion used can also make a difference, as can the texture and type of hair. Hair in good condition takes a perm much better than hair in poor condition, and fine hair curls more easily than coarse hair.

After a perm it takes 48 hours for the keratin in the hair to harden naturally. During this time the hair is vulnerable to damage and must be treated with care. Resist shampooing, brushing, vigorous combing, blow-drying, or setting, any of which may cause the perm to drop.

Once hair has been permed it remains curly and shaped the way it has been formed, although new growth will be straight. As time goes by the curl can soften, and if the hair is long its weight may make the curl and the wave appear much looser.

HOME VERSUS SALON

Perming is such a delicate operation that many women prefer to leave it in the hands of experienced, professional hairdressers. The advantages of having hair permed in a salon are several. The hair is first analysed to see whether it is in fit condition to take a perm; coloured, out-of-condition, or over-processed hair may not be suitable. With a professional perm there is also a greater choice in the type of curl – different strengths of lotion and different winding techniques all give a range of curls that are not available in home perms.

Above. Spiral perming gives a ringlet effect on long hair. It is important with hair of this length to re-perm only at the roots when the hair grows, or you may cause damage to previously permed hair. By Terence Renati, London and Melbourne.

Right. The model's thick hair was given a volume perm in order to produce a stunning style with the fullest look possible. By Kevin Murphy International for Clynol, Photography Martin Evening.

POST PERM TIPS

○ Don't wash newly permed hair for 48 hours after processing as any stress can cause curls to relax.
○ Use shampoos and conditioners formulated for permed hair. They help retain the correct moisture balance and prolong the perm.
○ Always use a wide-toothed comb and work from the ends upwards. Never brush the hair.
○ Blot wet hair dry before styling to prevent stretching.
○ Avoid using too much heat on permed hair. If possible, wash, condition, and leave to dry naturally.
○ If your perm has lost its bounce, mist with water or try a curl reviver. These are designed to put instant volume and bounce into permed hair. They are also ideal for eliminating frizziness on naturally curly hair.
○ Expect your perm to last three to six months, depending on the technique and lotion used.

HOME RULES

If you do use a perm at home, it is essential that you read and follow the instructions supplied with the product. Remember to do a test curl to check whether your hair is suitable, and check to make certain you have enough curlers. You will probably want to enlist the help of a friend, as it's impossible to curl the back sections of your own hair properly, so you'll need a helping hand.

Timing is crucial – don't be tempted to remove the lotion before the time given or leave it on longer than directed.

Above. Short, straight hair was root permed and then blow-dried into place. By Paul Falltrick, Falltricks, for Clynol.

DON'T DO IT YOURSELF IF...

❍ Your hair is very dry or damaged.
❍ You have bleached or highlighted your hair: it may be too fragile. If in doubt, check with your hairdresser.
❍ The traces of an old perm still remain in your hair.
❍ You suffer from a scalp disorder such as eczema or have broken, irritated skin.

Above. A soft perm gives volume to short hair. Set the hair on rollers to achieve the maximum amount of lift. By Regis, Europe. *Above right*. Tinted hair can also be permed if the correct formulation is chosen. Your stylist will advise you. By Regis, Europe. *Right*. To achieve the best spiral perm the hair needs to be lightly graduated. By Patrick Cameron for Alan Paul, Wirral, England.

SALON PERMS – THE CHOICES

Professional hairdressers can offer a number of different types of perm that are not available for home use:

Acid perms produce highly conditioned, flexible curls. They are ideally suited to hair that is fine, sensitive, fragile, damaged, or tinted, as they have a mildly acidic action that minimizes the risk of hair damage.

Alkaline perms give strong, firm curl results on normal and resistant hair.

Exothermic perms give bouncy, resilient curls. "Exothermic" refers to the gentle heat that is produced by the chemical reaction that occurs when the lotion is mixed. The heat allows the lotion to penetrate the hair cuticle, conditioning and strengthening the hair from inside as the lotion moulds the hair into its new shape.

PERMING TECHNIQUES

Any of the above types of perm can be used with different techniques to produce a number of results.

Body perms are very soft, loose perms created by using large curlers, or sometimes rollers. The result is added volume with a hint of wave and movement rather than curls.

Root perms add lift and volume to the root area only. They give height and fullness, and are therefore ideal for short hair that tends to go flat.

Pin curl perms give soft, natural waves and curls, which are achieved by perming small sections of hair that have been pinned into pre-formed curls.

Stack perms give curl and volume to one-length hair cuts by means of different sized curlers. The hair on top of the head is left unpermed while the middle and ends have curl and movement.

Spiral perms create romantic spiral curls, an effect that is produced by winding the hair around special long curlers. The mass of curls makes long hair look much thicker.

Spot perms give support only on the area to which they are applied. For example, if the hair needs lift the perm is applied just on the crown. They can also be used on the fringe or side areas around the face.

Weave perms involve perming certain sections of hair and leaving the rest straight to give a mixture of texture and natural looking body and bounce, particularly on areas around the face such as the fringe.

REGROWTH PROBLEM

When a perm is growing out the areas of new growth can be permed if a barrier is created between old and new growth. The barrier can be a special cream or a plastic protector, both of which effectively prevent the perming lotion and neutralizer from touching previously permed areas.

There are also products that facilitate re-perming an entire length of hair without damaging the structure. These more complex solutions are only available from salons.

To keep a full perm looking its best, shampoo, apply mousse, then blow-dry using a diffuser or set the hair on rollers. By L'Oréal.

BLACK HAIR

Black hair is fragile yet difficult to control, therefore it needs specialist care and pampering if it is to look its best.

This type of hair is almost always curly, although the degree of wave varies enormously. As a general rule, black hair is brittle and has a tendency to split and break. This is because the sebaceous glands produce insufficient sebum to moisturize the hair. In addition, because the hair is tightly curled, the sebum is unable to travel downwards to condition it naturally. If the curl forms kinks, this makes the hair thinner, and therefore weaker, at each bend.

Other types of black hair can be very fine, making it difficult to style and hold a set.

To treat excessive dryness choose a specialist formulation that replaces the natural oils lacking in black hair. If the product is massaged in daily, or whenever necessary, the hair will become more manageable with improved condition and shine. It is also important to deep condition the hair regularly.

One of the most effective ways of styling very curly hair is to crop it close and short. With this type of cut you just need to shampoo, condition, and finish it with soft wax. By Macmillan, London.

Before: Long, thick natural hair can be totally transformed with the technique known as weaving. To do this the hair is corn-row braided and then weaves are sewn on to the braided base.

STRAIGHTENING THE HAIR

Straightening, or relaxing, is in fact perming in reverse. A hair straightener, also known as a chemical relaxer, is combed or worked through the hair to change the structure and to straighten it. The result is permanent, only disappearing as the hair grows. Chemical relaxers come in different strengths to suit different hair textures and styles.

PROFESSIONAL TIP

Hair needs to be strong and healthy to take any type of chemical treatment. To check hair strength and natural elasticity, pluck out a hair and hold it firmly between the fingers of both hands, then pull gently. If the hair breaks with hardly any stretching, it is weak and in poor condition, in which case all chemical treatments should be avoided.

Hair that has been straightened is blow-dried using a vent brush. Straightening irons could also be used to achieve a similarly smooth effect. By Richard M F Mendleson of David's Hair Designers, Maryland, USA.

After: Once the weave has been sewn into place, the new hair is cut and styled as desired. The result of all this work is a completely different look. By Eugene at Xtension Masters, London.

They are particularly effective on longer styles as the weight of the hair helps to maintain the straightened look. If you do this at home get advice first, and make sure you use high quality branded products and follow the instructions precisely to get the best results.

DEMI PERMING

Very curly hair can also be tamed by perming. This enables tight curls to be replaced by larger, looser ones. Demi-perms are good for short hair, giving a more controlled, manageable shape; on long hair they produce a softer, bouncier look. The more advanced perms involve softening the hair by weaving it on to rollers and then neutralizing it so that the curls are permanently set into their new shape.

To prevent frizziness and maintain the definition of curls, special lotions called curl activators and moisturizing sprays can be used to revive and preserve the formation of curls.

As with all chemical treatments, relaxing and perming can be potentially harmful to the hair, removing natural moisture and leaving hair in a weakened state. For this reason it is advisable to get skilled professional help and advice.

HOT COMBS

Before chemical relaxers became available the most popular hair straightening method was "hot pressing". This involved putting a pre-heated iron comb through the hair to loosen the curls. Up-to-date versions, called thermal texturizers, are electric pressing combs, which work in a similar way to loosen and soften very curly hair.

COLOUR OPTIONS

Because of its natural dryness and porosity, black hair should be coloured with caution, preferably by a professional hairdresser. If the hair has been straightened, relaxed, or permed it may be too weak to colour successfully.

Techniques such as highlighting, low-lighting, or tipping the ends are best for this type of hair.

SPECIAL PROBLEMS

Traction hair loss is caused by braiding or weaving hair too tightly. If the hair is pulled too forcibly too often, it will disrupt the hair follicles, cause scar tissue to form and, ultimately, hair loss. To help prevent this, avoid braiding or pulling the hair into tight braids. Similar problems can also result from misusing perming and relaxing chemicals.

After straightening or relaxing, black hair can be styled smooth using blow-drying techniques. *Left*: The hair has been smoothed into curls. *Centre*: Here it has been flicked up at the ends and the fringe curved. *Right*: For this style it was piled into soft curls and given a fuller fringe. By Richard M F Mendleson, David's Hair Designers, Maryland, USA.

KEEPING BLACK HAIR BEAUTIFUL

○ Use a wide-toothed afro comb for curly hair and a natural bristle brush for relaxed hair. Combing will help spread the natural oils through the hair, making it look shinier and healthier. Use intensive pre-shampoo treatments.

○ Massage the scalp regularly to encourage oil production.

○ Shampoo as often as you feel necessary but only lather once, using a small amount of shampoo. Rinse thoroughly. Towel-blot, don't rub hair.

○ Once a month try a hot oil treatment, which will lubricate dry scalp conditions as well as moisturize brittle hair.

○ If you have a delicate fringe or baby fine hair around the hairline (sometimes from breakage, sometimes an inherited trait), use a tiny round brush and a hairdryer to blend in this hair.

○ Gels are good for moulding black hair into shape; choose non-greasy formulas that give hair a healthy sheen.

○ If you use hot combs or curling tongs, make sure you shield the hair by using a protective product.

○ For extra hold and added shine use a finishing spray.

○ Braided hair needs a softening shampoo that maintains the moisture balance and helps eliminate a dry scalp.

CHOOSING A STYLE TO SUIT YOUR FACE

Make the most of your looks by choosing a style that maximizes your best features. The first feature you should consider is your face shape – is it round, oval, square, or long? If you are not sure what shape it is then the easiest way to find out is to scrape your hair back off your face. Stand squarely in front of a mirror and use a lipstick to trace the outline of your face on to the mirror. When you stand back you should be able to see into which of the following categories your face shape falls.

THE SQUARE FACE

The square face is angular with a broad forehead and a square jawline. To make the best of this shape, choose a hairstyle with long layers, preferably one with soft waves or curls, as these create a softness that detracts from the hard lines. The hair should be parted at the side of the head and any fringe combed away from the face.
Styles to avoid: Severe geometric cuts – they will only emphasize squareness; long bobs with heavy fringes; severe styles in which the hair is scraped off the face and parted down the centre.

THE ROUND FACE

On the round face the distance between the forehead and the chin is about equal to the distance between the cheeks. Choose a style with a short fringe, which lengthens the face, and a short cut, which makes the face look thinner.
Styles to avoid: Curly styles, because they emphasize the roundness; very full, long hair or styles that are scraped right back off the face.

THE OVAL FACE

The oval face has wide cheekbones that taper down into a small, often pointed, chin, and up to a fairly narrow forehead. This is regarded by many experts as the perfect face shape. If your face is oval in shape then you have the advantage of being able to wear any hairstyle you choose.

THE LONG FACE

The long face is characterized by a high forehead and long chin, and needs to be given the illusion of width. Soften the effect with short layers, or go for a bob with a fringe, which will create horizontal lines. Scrunch-dried or curly bobs balance a long face.
Styles to avoid: Styles without fringes, and long, straight, one-length cuts.

THE COMPLETE YOU

When choosing a new style you should also take into account your overall body shape. If you are a traditional pear-shape don't go for elfin styles; they will draw attention to the lower half of your body, making your hips look even wider. Petite women should avoid masses of very curly hair as this makes the head appear larger and out of proportion with the body.

IF YOU WEAR GLASSES . . .

Try to choose frames and a hairstyle that complement each other. Large spectacles could spoil a neat, feathery cut, and very fine frames could be overpowered by a large, voluminous style. Remember to take your glasses to the salon when having your hair restyled, so that your stylist can take their shape into consideration when deciding on the overall effect.

SPECIFIC PROBLEMS

○ Prominent nose: incorporate softness into your style.
○ Pointed chin: style hair with width at the jawline.
○ Low forehead: choose a style with a wispy fringe, rather than one with a full fringe.
○ High forehead: disguise with a fringe.
○ Receding chin: select a style that comes just below chin level, with waves or curls.
○ Uneven hairline: a fringe should conceal this problem.

Left: A wispy fringe stylishly disguises a low forehead. Hair by Sam Mcknight for Silvikrin. *Above*: A high forehead or uneven hairline can be hidden under a full fringe. Hair by Paul Falltrick, photography Iain Philpott. *Below*: Strong features benefit from a soft, full hairstyle. Hair by Jed Hamill of Graham Webb International for Clynol, Photography Ian Hooton.

STYLE GALLERY, SHORT HAIR

Short hair can be cut close,
cropped, or layered in a variety
of styles.

Fine, straight hair was lightly layered and
cut close into the nape. A root perm
provided extra volume at the crown of the
head. The hair was then finger-dried using
a styling mousse. By Yosh Toya, San
Francisco, Photography Gen.

Naturally wavy hair was lightly layered to
encourage movement. A wet-look gel was
applied and the hair was combed into soft
waves and side curls, then left to dry
naturally. By Regis, Europe, Photography
John Swannell.

Naturally wavy hair was cut into a one-
length bob and taken behind the ears,
using wet-look gel to give definition and
accentuate the waves. By Regis, Europe,
Photography John Swannell.

Far left: Thick hair was feather-cut into layers, with slightly longer lengths left at the nape. The hair was highlighted and then blow-dried into shape using a styling brush. *Left*: For a different look the hair was combed down over the ears. By Regis Europe, Photography John Swannell.

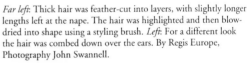

Left: Fine hair was softly layered and given an application of mousse, then the hair was ruffle-dried with the fingers to create just a little lift at the roots. *Right*: The same haircut was blow-dried forwards using a styling brush. By Regis, Europe, Photography John Swannell.

Medium-textured hair was cut into face-framing layers. Mousse was applied from the roots to the ends, then the hair was blow-dried forwards, using the fingers to rake through the hair from the back to the front. By Paul Falltrick, Falltricks, Essex, for Clynol, Photography Alistair Hughes.

A longer layered bob was blow-dried straight back from the face using a round brush to give height and a soft curl, then finished by smoothing with a few drops of serum, which gave added gloss. By Yosh Toya, San Francisco, Photography Gen.

Medium-textured hair was cut into layers of the same length, then blow-dried using a strong-hold mousse to get lift, and finished with a mist of firm-hold hairspray. By Daniel Galvin, London.

A short, urchin cut is good for all hair textures. Highlights give extra interest and add thickness to finer hair. By Nicky Clarke, London, Photography Paul Cox.

A short, feathery cut was set off with a straight, cropped fringe. For this style the hair can either be left to dry naturally, or blow-dried while ruffling with the fingers. By Anestis Kyprianou of Cobella, London, for Schwarzkopf, Photography Martin Evening.

Medium-textured hair was graduated to give this head-hugging cut. Mousse was applied from the roots to the ends, then the hair was blow-dried forwards from the crown. By Neville Daniel, London, for Lamaur.

Very curly, wiry hair was cropped close to the head, then dressed using just a little wax to give definition and separation. By Frank Hession, Dublin, Eire, for L'Oréal Coiffure.

This soft style is ideal for hair with more than a hint of natural wave; layering gives additional movement. After an application of a little mousse (styling gel would be equally suitable) the hair was left to dry naturally, occasionally running the fingers through to encourage curl. By Beverly Kyprianou of Cobella, London, for Schwarzkopf, Photography Martin Evening.

Thick hair was razor cut to give forward movement, then blow-dried for a few seconds with the dryer set on high heat, at the same time brushing in all directions to give extra movement. By John Frieda, London and New York.

A short cut was given extra interest by bleaching the hair honey-blonde. It was then blow-dried into shape and finished using wax to create separation. By Yosh Toya, San Francisco, Photography Gen.

One-length hair was parted at the side and slicked down with a wet-look gel to create this slick style. Pictures left to right by Joseph and Jane Harling, Avon, England, Photography Ruth Crafer.

Fine hair was softly layered and combed forwards. A little wax was rubbed between the palms and applied with the fingertips to strands of hair in order to achieve separation.

A thick, one-length bob was blow-dried very smooth from a side parting. The hair was misted with hairspray and smoothed with the hands to eliminate wisps.

Wispy, fine hair was given extra volume with a light perm, then blow-dried forwards. A semi-permanent colour gives this type of hair added depth.

Choppy layers give an uneven texture to this thick hair. The hair was blow-dried using mousse and a styling brush to create lift. By Alan Edwards for L'Oréal Coiffure.

A root perm helped to give lift at the crown on this short, layered look. Mousse was applied to give extra lift and the hair was blow-dried forwards from the crown. By Neville Daniel, London, Photography Will White.

Very straight hair was cut into a neat, face-framing shape, then blow-dried forwards. It was then finished with a mist of shine spray for added gloss. By Andrew Collinge, Liverpool, and Harrods, London, Photography Iain Philpott.

STYLE GALLERY, MID-LENGTH HAIR

Hair of medium length can be worn in a sleek bob or lightly layered to give versatility.

Layering gives this 70s inspired style a fresh look. The hair was misted with styling spray and rough-dried before finishing with a little gloss. By Trevor Sorbie, London, Photography Mark Havrilliak.

Above: Fine mid-length hair can be made to look thicker by blunt cutting just below ear level. This style can be roller-set and brushed through with a bristle brush to smooth, or simply blow-dried with a round brush. For L'Oréal.

Medium-textured hair was cut into a one-length bob. Styling spray was applied to partially dried hair, which was then wound on large rollers and heat set. After the rollers were removed the hair was brushed into shape. By Charles Worthington, Worthingtons, London, for L'Oréal Coiffure.

A longer, one-length, graduated bob is perfect for thick, straight hair. Add extra shine by using a longer-lasting semi-permanent colour. By Umberto Giannino, Kidderminster, England, for L'Oréal Coiffure.

A mid-length bleached bob was scrunch-dried with mousse to give a tousled look. Use a diffuser to encourage more volume. By Stuart Kirby of Eaton Hair Group, Portsmouth, for L'Oréal Coiffure.

A layered cut was permed to give lots of movement. The hair was scrunch-dried, with the head held forward to give maximum volume. By Anthony Mascolo, Toni & Guy, London, for L'Oréal Coiffure.

A bob was highlighted using a light, golden-blonde colour to give natural, warm lights, then styled and blow-dried using a soft sculpting spray. By Barbara Daley Hair Studio, Liverpool, England, for L'Oréal Coiffure.

A razor-cut bob gives graduation so the hair moves freely. The hair was coloured with a shade of mahogany to give more depth, and then blow-dried using mousse. For L'Oréal.

Left: Thick hair was cut into a bob, then sprayed with styling lotion before setting on large rollers. After drying, the hair was brushed through to give a smooth style that is full of volume. *Right*: The same cut was blow-dried smooth using a styling brush. By Mod Hair, France, for Schwarzkopf.

A smooth, graduated bob was cut long at the sides and shorter into the back. To add additional tone and shine use a longer-lasting semi-permanent colour, which also gives gloss. Blow-dry straight using a styling brush to smooth the ends under. For L'Oréal.

Left: Natural movement was encouraged by blunt cutting and leaving the hair to dry naturally. Alternatively, the hair could be dried using a flat diffuser attachment on the dryer. *Right*: The same style was sprayed with styling lotion and set on large rollers. When the rollers were removed the hair was ruffled through with the fingers, not brushed. By Regis, Europe, Photography John Swannell.

Thick, straight hair was heavily highlighted and cut into a blunt, short bob. Either blow-dry or leave to dry naturally. By Yosh Toya, San Francisco, Photography Gen.

Left: Wavy hair was cut in short layers. Layers encourage more curl and movement and give a soft, feminine style. The hair was dried using mousse and lifted with the fingers while drying to get height on the crown. By Cobella, London, for Schwarzkopf, Photography Martin Evening.

Left: A soft body perm gives volume to this one-length bob. The hair was gently dried using mousse for additional lift. By Yosh Toya, San Francisco, Photography Gen.

STYLE GALLERY, LONG HAIR

Long hair can be waved,
curled, or left to fall free.

Naturally wavy hair was roller-set and heat-dried before brushing through lightly. A similar look could be achieved with a soft perm. By Steven Carey, London.

After an application of styling spray the hair was set on large rollers. When dry the hair was combed to one side and allowed to fall into soft waves, with a tiny tendril pulled in front of one ear. By Neville Daniel, London, for Lamur.

Above: Long, straight hair was graduated at the sides to give interest. It was then shampooed and conditioned, and left to dry naturally. By Neville Daniel, London, for Lamaur.

A vegetable colour adds depth and makes hair appear even thicker. The hair was then simply styled by blow-drying. By Daniel Galvin, London.

Soft, undulating waves were achieved by tonging the hair, then lightly combing it through. Spray shine was applied to the finish. By Nicky Clarke, London.

Thick hair was cut with graduated sides and a heavy fringe to give this 60s look. The hair can be blow-dried smooth or left to dry naturally. By John Frieda, London and New York.

Setting lotion was applied to clean hair, which was set on large rollers and heat dried. When the hair was completely dry the rollers were removed and the hair gently back combed at the roots to give even more height and fullness. By Daniel Galvin, London.

Far left: The hair was shampooed and conditioned, then rough-dried before applying mousse and setting on heated rollers. The hair was then brushed through into soft waves. *Left*: This alternative style was achieved by tonging. It could also be set on shapers. For Silvikrin, London.

Left: A thick graduated cut was given maximum lift by spraying the roots with gel spray and backcombing lightly, then brushing over the top layers. By Daniel Galvin, London.

Naturally wavy hair was lightly layered, then set on large rollers. When the hair was dry it was brushed lightly to give broken up waves and curls. By Daniel Galvin, London.

The hair was sprayed with styling lotion and set on heated rollers. When it was dry a bristle brush was used to smooth it into waves. By Adam Lyons, Grays, Essex, England, for L'Oréal Coiffure.

Above: Coarse hair was rough-dried and then tonged all over before brushing through to give a soft movement. By Keith Harris for Braun.

Left: Long, straight hair was blunt-cut at the ends and simply styled from a centre parting. By Taylor Ferguson, Glasgow, Scotland.

Left: To give one-length hair extra body the head was tipped forwards and the hair misted with sculpting lotion. The roots were scrunched a little with the hands before straightening the head. By Paul Falltrick, Falltricks, Essex, England, for Clynol, Photography Alistair Hughes.

TAKE ONE GIRL

The following styles illustrate how one-length hair can be transformed using different styling techniques.

1 Soft waves were created with rollers.

2 The top hair was clipped up and the back hair tonged into tendrils.

3 High bunches were carefully secured and the hair crimped.

4 The top hair was secured on the crown. A band was wrapped with a small piece of hair and the length allowed to fall freely.

5 The hair was clipped back and two simple braids were worked at each side.

Hair by Taylor Ferguson, Glasgow, Scotland.

STYLE GALLERY, SPECIAL OCCASIONS

These styles will inspire you when you want to dress up long hair on those special occasions.

The hair was secured in a very high ponytail on the crown, then divided into sections and looped into curls. If your hair isn't long enough for this style, you could use a hairpiece. By Steven Carey, London, Photography Alistair Hughes.

The hair was softly scooped into large curls and pinned in place. One tendril was left to fall free to soften the style. By Zotos International.

Vibrant blond and copper lights add brilliance to the hair. The front hair was sectioned off and the back hair secured in a high ponytail. The hair was then divided and coiled into loops before pinning in place. The front hair was smoothed over and secured at the back. For Schwarzkopf.

The foundation for this style came from a roller-set. The back hair was then formed into a French pleat and the top hair looped, curled and pinned into place. The side tendrils were allowed to fall free. Hair by Regis, Europe, Photography Mark York.

Very curly hair was simply twisted up at the back and secured with pins. Curls were allowed to fall down on one side to give a feminine look. By Steven Carey, London, Photography Alistair Hughes.

Long hair was scooped up, but the essence of this style is to allow lots of strands to fall in soft curls around the face. By Partners, London.

A high ponytail forms the basis of this style. The hair was then looped into curls and pinned, and the fringe was combed to one side. Hair by Keith Harris for Braun.

THE SALON VISIT

London hairdresser Nicky Clarke always explains to his clients how to style their hair at home.

A professional cut is the basis of any style. Expert stylists evaluate your hair and lifestyle before they even pick up a pair of scissors. The best way to choose a salon is by personal recommendation. If a friend has a good haircut ask them for the name of their hairdresser. If this is not possible you will have to do some research.

See if there are any salons in your area that look promising. Remember that the exterior can be deceptive, so have a look at the interior as well. The salon should be clean and welcoming, with a style and ambience that appeals to you, and sales material that is new and fresh. The stylists should also reflect an image that you like.

THE FIRST VISIT

Once you have chosen a salon, make an appointment for a consultation. Wear clothes that reflect your lifestyle; for example, if you are a bank teller, don't wear a track-suit – you will give the stylist the wrong impression. Discuss your hair's idiosyncrasies and explain what you like and dislike about it. Spare a few minutes to discuss how you are going to manage the style between salon visits. If you want a wash-and-wear style that falls into place with the flick of a comb, say so. If you are prepared to spend 15 minutes a day scrunching a perm to perfection, then speak up.

Hairdressers are not mind readers: neither can they wave a magic wand. However they can, with technical expertise, make the most of any type of hair. Listen to what they offer, but never be coerced into something with which you don't feel happy. Good hairdressers translate fashion trends into what is right for you. Yet you must be realistic; if your hair is thick and curly it will never hang in a straight, shiny bob, no matter how good the cut.

TAKING NOTES

While you are having your hair done, watch how your stylist does your hair, how much mousse or gel they apply and how they dry your hair. A good haircut should need the minimum of styling products and drying to achieve the desired result. Ask for advice on how to achieve the same look at home.

As a general rule, you need to have your hair cut every six to eight weeks, and to have a tint or colour regrowth every four weeks; a highlight root application needs to be done at least every three months, and perms every four to six months.

TECHNICAL SKILL

With such a wide variety of perms and colours available in chemists' shops you may wonder why you should visit a salon to have your hair coloured or permed. Yet the fact is that what you are buying is expertise and artistry. At the salon the stylist will use techniques that can be varied to suit the individual's specific hair textures and solve specific problems. For example, colours can be blended and applied in various ways to achieve a wide range of effects; hair can be made to look thicker and glossier by colour shading; perms can be used to give body, not just curl; long hair can be spiral or corkscrew-permed for movement; and special products can be used to refresh colours and reactivate curls.

COMPLAINTS

If you are not satisfied with the service you have received, then complain. Ask to see the salon manager, explain the problem, and ask what they are prepared to do about it. You should expect an apology, but don't expect to be offered a refund. If your hair has been badly permed, don't accept any offer to have it re-permed. The remedy is to have a course of intensive conditioning treatments. Following this you should wait until the hair is in optimum condition before you have another perm or colour. If it is just a question of not liking the style, then that is a matter for discussion.

If you suffer serious damage, for example, an itchy burning scalp, blisters, cuts, hair breakage, or hair loss, then immediately seek advice from your family doctor or a trichologist. In the majority of cases remedial treatment should be prescribed and the damage minimized. If the practitioner feels that you have cause for complaint and compensation, then the practitioner should prepare a report giving full details and an analysis of the problem. However, remember that hair grows, blisters heal, and memories fade. So, act quickly and,

if necessary, make certain you have some photographs taken to reinforce your claim.

IMAGING

Imaging, which is available in some salons, is a means of previewing yourself on a video screen wearing a range of haircuts and colours. It is invaluable for experimenting with different looks before making a commitment to a particular style. Developed in France, the system is designed to take the stress out of choosing a style.

Watch how your stylist dries your hair. Here Trevor Sorbie, London, lifts the front hair to create lift and movement.

STYLING TOOLS

The right tools not only make hairstyling more fun, but also makes it much easier. Brushes, combs, and pins are the basic tools of styling. The following is a guide to help you choose what is most suitable from the wide range that is available.

BRUSHES

Brushes are made of bristles (sometimes termed quills or pins), which may be natural hog bristle, plastic, nylon, or wire. The bristles are embedded in a wooden, plastic, or moulded rubber base and set in tufts or rows. This allows loose or shed hair to collect in the grooves without interfering with the action of the bristles. The spacing of the tufts plays an important role – generally, the wider the spacing between the rows of bristles the easier the brush will flow through the hair.

The role of brushing

Brushes help to remove tangles and knots and generally smooth the hair. The action of brushing from the roots to the ends removes dead skin cells and dirt, and encourages the cuticles to lie flat, thus reflecting the light. Brushing also stimulates the blood supply to the hair follicles, promoting healthy growth.

Natural bristles

Natural bristles are made of natural keratin (the same material as hair) and therefore create less friction and wear on the hair. They are good for grooming and polishing, and help to combat static on flyaway hair. However, they will not penetrate wet or thick hair and you must use a softer bristle brush for fine or thinning hair. In addition, the sharp ends can scratch the scalp.

Plastic, nylon, or wire bristles

All of these bristles are easily cleaned and heat resistant, so they are good for blow-drying. They are available in a variety of shapes and styles. Cushioned brushes give good flexibility, as they glide through the hair, preventing tugging and helping to remove knots. They are also non-static.

A major disadvantage is that the ends can be harsh, so try to choose bristles with rounded or ball tips.

TYPES OF BRUSH

Circular or radial brushes come in a variety of sizes and are circular or semicircular in shape. These brushes have either mixed bristles for finishing, a rubber pad with nylon bristles, or metal pins for styling. They are used to tame and control naturally curly, permed, and wavy hair and are ideal for blow-drying. The diameter of the brush determines the resulting volume and movement, much the same way as rollers do.

Flat or half-round brushes are ideal for all aspects of wet or dry hairstyling and blow-drying. Normally they are made of nylon bristles in a rubber base. Some bases slide into position on to the plastic moulded handle. Rubber bases can be removed for cleaning and replacement bristles are sometimes available.

Pneumatic brushes have a domed rubber base with bristles set in tufts. They can be plastic, natural bristle, or both.

Vent brushes have vented hollow centres that allow the air flow from the dryer to pass through them. Special bristle, or pin, patterns are designed to lift and disentangle even wet hair. Vents and tunnel brush heads enable the air to circulate freely through both the brush and the hair so the hair dries faster.

COMBS

Choose good quality combs with saw-cut teeth. This means that each individual tooth is cut into the comb, so there are no sharp edges. Avoid cheap plastic combs that are made in a mould and so form lines down the centre of every tooth. They are sharp, and gradually scrape away the cuticles layers of the hair, causing damage and often breakage.

Use a wide-toothed comb for disentangling and combing conditioner through the hair. Fine tail-combs are for styling; Afro combs for curly hair; and styling combs for grooming.

PINS AND CLIPS

These are indispensable for sectioning and securing hair during setting, and for putting hair up. Most pins are available with untipped, plain ends, or cushion tipped ends. Non-reflective finishes are available, so the pins are less noticeable in the hair, and most are made of metal, plastic, or stainless steel. Colours include brown, black, grey, blonde, white, and silver.

Double-pronged clips are most frequently used for making pin or barrel curls. Grips give security to curls, French pleats, and all upswept styles. In North America they are known as "Bobbi" pins, in Britain as "Blendrites" and "Kirbis". To avoid discomfort, position grips in the hair so that the flat edge rests towards the scalp.

Heavy hairpins are made of strong metal and come either waved or straight. They are ideal for securing rollers and when putting hair up.

Fine hairpins are used for dressing hair. They are quite delicate and prone to bend out of shape, so they should only be used to secure small amounts of hair. These pins are easily concealed, especially if you use a matching colour. They are sometimes used to secure pin curls during setting, rather than using heavier clips, which can leave a mark.

Sectioning clips are clips with a single prong, and are longer in length than other clips. They are most often used for holding hair while working on another section, or securing pin curls.

Twisted pins are fashioned like a screw and are used to secure chignons and French pleats.

ROLLERS

Rollers vary in diameter, length, and the material from which they are made.

Smooth rollers, that is, those without spikes or brushes, will give the sleekest finish, but are more difficult to put in. More popular are brush rollers, especially the self-fixing variety that do not need pins or clips.

SHAPERS

Shapers were inspired by the principle of rag-rolling hair. Soft 'twist tie' shapers are made from pliable rubber, plastic, or cotton fabric and provide one of the more natural ways to curl hair. In the centre of each shaper is a tempered wire, which enables it to be bent into shape. The waves or curls that are produced are soft and bouncy and the technique is gentle enough for permed or tinted hair.

To use, section clean, dry hair and pull to a firm tension, 'trapping' the end in a shaper that you have previously doubled over. Roll down to the roots of the hair and fold over to secure. Leave in for 30-60 minutes without heat, or for 10-15 minutes if you apply heat. If you twist the hair before curling you will achieve a more voluminous style.

STYLE EASY

The combination of practice and the right styling product enables you to achieve a salon finish at home. The products listed below enable you to do it in style.

GELS

Gels come in varying degrees of viscosity, from a thick jelly to a liquid spray. They are sometimes called sculpting lotions and are used for precise styling. Use them to lift roots, tame wisps, create tendrils, calm static, heat set, and give structure to curls. Wet gel can be used for sculpting styles.

> **TIP**
> A gel can be revitalized the following day by running wet fingers through the hair, against the direction of the finished look.

HAIRSPRAY

Traditionally, hairspray was used to hold a style in place; today varying degrees of stiffness are available to suit all needs. Use hairspray to keep the hair in place, get curl definition when scrunching, and mist over rollers when setting.

Hairsprays are available in a variety of formulations, including light and firm holds. Photography by Silvikrin

> **TIPS**
> ○ A light application of spray on a hair brush can be used to tame flyaway ends.
> ○ Use hairspray at the roots and tong or blow-dry the area to get immediate lift.

MOUSSE

Mousse is the most versatile styling product. It comes as a foam and can be used on wet or dry hair. Mousses contain conditioning agents and proteins to nurture and protect the hair. They are available in different strengths, designed to give soft to maximum holding power, and can be used to lift flat roots or smooth frizz. Use when blow-drying, scrunching, and diffuser drying.

> **TIPS**
> ○ Make sure you apply mousse from the roots to the ends, not just in a blob on the crown.
> ○ Choose the right type for your hair. Normal is good for a great many styles, but if you want more holding power, don't just use more mousse as it can make hair dull; instead, choose a firm or maximum-hold product.

SERUMS

Serums, glossers, polishes, and shine sprays are made from oils or silicones, which improve shine and softness by forming a microscopic film on the surface of the hair. Formulations can vary from light and silky to heavier ones with a distinct oily feel. They also contain substances designed to smooth the cuticle, encouraging the tiny scales to lie flat and thus reflect the light and make the hair appear shiny. Use these products to improve the feel of the hair, to combat static, de-frizz, add shine and gloss, and temporarily repair split ends.

> **TIP**
> Don't use too much serum or you will make your hair greasy.

STYLING OR SETTING LOTIONS

Styling lotions contain flexible resins that form a film on the hair and aid setting, and protect the hair from heat damage. There are formulations for dry, coloured or sensitized hair; others give volume and additional shine. Use for roller-setting, scrunching, blow-drying, and natural drying.

> **TIP**
> If using a styling lotion for heat setting look out for formulations that offer thermal protection.

WAXES, POMADES, AND CREAMS

These products are made from natural waxes, such as carnauba (produced by a Brazilian palm tree), which are softened with other ingredients such as mineral oils and lanolin to make them pliable. Both soft and hard formulations are available. Some pomades contain vegetable wax and oil to give gloss and sheen. Other formulations produce foam and are water soluble, and leave no residue. Use for dressing the hair and for controlling frizz and static.

When applying mousse use a "handful", and make sure you distribute it evenly. By Clynol.

APPLIANCES

Heated styling appliances allow you to style your hair quickly, efficiently, and easily. A wide range of heated appliances is available.

AIR STYLERS

Airstylers combine the versatility of a hairdryer with the convenience of a styling wand. They operate on the same principle as a hairdryer, blowing warm air though the styler. Many stylers are available with a variety of clip-on options, including brushes, prongs, and tongs, some with retractable teeth. Use for creating soft waves and volume at the roots.

TIP

Apply a styling spray or lotion before air styling and style the hair while it is still damp.

CRIMPERS

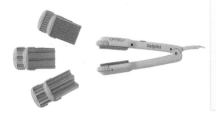

Crimpers consist of two ridged metal plates that produce uniform patterned crimps in straight lines in the hair. The hair must be straightened first, either by blow-drying or using flat irons. The crimper is then used to give waves or ripples. Some crimpers have reversible or dual-effect styling plates to give different effects. Use for special styling effects or to increase volume.

TIPS

❍ Do not use on damaged, bleached, or over-stressed hair.
❍ Brushing crimped hair gives a softer result.

HAIRDRYERS

Choose a dryer that has a range of heat, speed settings so that the hair can be power-dried on high heat, finished on a lower heat, and then used with cool air to set the style. The life expectancy of a hairdryer averages between 200-300 hours. Use for blow-drying.

TIPS

❍ Always point the airflow down the hair shaft to smooth the cuticle and encourage shine.
❍ Take care not to hold the dryer too near the scalp; it can cause burns.
❍ When you have finished blow-drying allow the hair to cool thoroughly, then check that the hair is completely dry. Warm hair often gives the illusion of dryness while it is, in fact, still damp.
❍ Never use a dryer without its filter in place – hair can easily be drawn into the machine.

The hairdryer is an essential piece of equipment, particularly when you need to dry your hair in a hurry. Photograph courtesy of BaByliss.

DIFFUSERS AND NOZZLES

Originally, diffusers were intended for drying curly hair slowly, in this way encouraging curl formation for scrunched styles. The diffuser serves to spread the airflow over the hair so the curls are not literally blown away. The prongs on the diffuser head also help to increase volume at the root and give lift. Diffusers with flat heads are designed for gentle drying without ruffling, and are more suitable for shorter styles. The

newest type of diffuser has long, straight prongs which are designed to inject volume into straight hair while giving a smooth finish. Nozzles fit over the end of the barrel of the hairdryer and are used to give precise direction when styling.

HEATED ROLLERS

HOT BRUSHES

Heated rollers are available in sets and normally comprise a selection of around 20 small, medium, and large rollers, with colour-coded clips to match. The early models came with spikes, which many women prefer because they have a good grip. New developments include ribbed rubber surfaces, which are designed to be kinder to the hair; curved barrel shapes that follow the form of the head, and clip fasteners are more recent innovations

The speed at which the rollers heat up varies, depending on the type of roller. PTC (positive temperature co-efficient) element rollers heat up fastest because they have an element inside each roller, and the heat is transferred directly from the base to the roller. Wax-filled rollers take longer, around 15 minutes, but they retain their temperature over a longer period. All rollers cool down completely in 30 minutes. Use heated rollers for quick sets, to give curl and body. They are ideal for preparing long hair for dressing.

Hot brushes are easier to handle than tongs, and come in varying sizes for creating curls of different sizes. Wind down the length of the hair, hold for a few seconds until the heat has penetrated through the hair, then gently remove. Cordless hot brushes, which use butane cartridges or batteries to produce heat, are also available. Use for root lift, curl, and movement.

When using a hot brush make certain you follow the manufacturer's instructions carefully. Photograph courtesy BaByliss.

STRAIGHTENERS

Straighteners, or flat irons, are based on the same principle as crimpers but have flat plates to iron out frizz or curl. Use for "pressing" really curly hair.

TIPS

○ Use a styling spray before heat straightening.
○ Straighteners are designed for occasional, not daily, use, as they work at a high temperature, which can cause damage to the hair.

TONGS

Tongs consist of a barrel, or prong, and a depressor groove. The barrel is round: the depressor is curved to fit around the barrel when the tong is closed. The thickness of the barrel varies, and the size of the tong that is used depends on whether small, medium, or large curls are required.

TIPS

○ Be careful when tonging white or bleached hair as it can discolour.
○ Always use tongs on dry, not wet, hair.
○ If curling right up to the roots, place a comb between the tongs and the scalp so the comb forms a barrier against the heat.
○ Leave tonged curls to cool before styling.

TRAVEL DRYERS

Travel dryers are ideal for taking on holiday. They are usually miniature versions of standard dryers, and some are even available with their own small diffusers. Check that the dryer you buy has dual voltage and a travel case.

Keep holiday haircare to a minimum by making use of dual-purpose heated appliances. Don't forget to pack a universal plug when travelling to other countries. Photograph courtesy of Silvikrin.

SAFETY TIPS

○ Equipment should be unplugged when not in use.
○ Never use electric equipment with wet hands, and don't use near water.
○ Only use one appliance for each socket outlet – adaptors may cause overload.
○ The cord should not be wrapped tightly around the equipment; coil it loosely before storing.
○ Tongs can be cleaned by wiping with a damp cloth; if necessary use a little methylated spirits to remove dirt.
○ All electrical equipment should be checked periodically to ensure that leads and connections are in good order.
○ Untwist the cord on the dryer from time to time.
○ Clean filters regularly – a blocked filter means the dryer has to work harder and will eventually overheat and cut out. If the element overheats it can distort the dryer casing.

BLOW-DRYING

By following our step-by-step
you can achieve the
smoothest, sleekest
blow-dry ever.

1 Shampoo and condition your hair.

5 Using your other hand, spread the
mousse through the hair, distributing
it evenly from the tips to the ends.

STYLING CHECKLIST

You will need:
✔ styling comb
✔ dryer
✔ mousse
✔ clip
✔ styling brush
✔ serum

2 Comb through with a wide-toothed comb to remove any tangles.

3 Partially dry your hair to remove excess moisture.

4 Apply a handful of mousse to the palm of your hand.

6 Divide your hair into two main sections by clipping the top and sides out of the way. Then, working on the hair that is left free and taking one small section at a time, hold the dryer in one hand and a styling brush in the other. Place the brush underneath the first section of hair, positioning it at the roots. Keeping the tension on the hair taut (but without undue stress), move the brush down towards the ends, directing the air flow from the dryer so that it follows the downwards movement of the brush.

7 Curve the brush under at the ends to achieve a slight bend. Concentrate on drying the root area first, repeatedly introducing the brush to the roots once it has moved down the length of the hair. Continue the movement until the first section of the hair is dry. Repeat step 6 until the whole of the back section is completely dry.

8 Release a section of hair from the top and dry it in the same manner. Continue in this way until you have dried all your hair. Finish by smoothing a few drops of serum through the hair to flatten any flyaway ends.

TIPS

○ Use the highest heat or speed setting to remove excess moisture, then switch to medium to finish drying.
○ Point the air flow downwards. This smoothes the cuticles and makes the hair shine.
○ When blow-drying, make sure each section is completely dry before going on to the next.

FINGER DRYING

This is a quick method of drying and styling your hair. It relies on the heat released from your hands rather than the heat from a dryer. Finger drying is suitable for short to mid-length hair.

1 Shampoo and condition your hair, then spray with gel and comb through.

2 Run your fingers rapidly upwards and forwards, from the roots to the ends.

> **TIP**
> Finger-drying is the best way to dry damaged hair, or to encourage waves in naturally curly, short hair.

> STYLING CHECKLIST
>
> *You will need:*
> ✔ spray gel
> ✔ styling comb

3 Lift up the hair at the crown to get height at the roots.

4 Continue lifting as the hair dries. Use your fingertips to flatten the hair at the sides.

BARREL CURLS

One of the simplest sets is achieved by curling the hair around the fingers and then pinning the curl in place. Barrel curls create a soft set.

1 Shampoo and condition your hair; apply setting lotion and comb through from the roots to the ends. Take a small section of hair (about 25 mm/l in) and smooth it upwards.

2 Loop the hair into a large curl.

3 Clip in place.

4 Continue to curl the rest of the hair in the same way.

5 Dry the hair with a hood dryer or allow it to dry naturally. Remove the clips. To achieve a tousled look rake your fingers through your hair. For a smoother finish use a hair brush.

ROLL-UP

A roller set forms the basis of many styles; it can be used to smooth hair, add waves or soft curls, or provide a foundation for an upswept style.

STYLING CHECKLIST

You will need:
✔ styling spray
✔ tail comb
✔ self-fixing rollers or brush rollers and pins
✔ hand or hood dryer (optional)
✔ hairspray

TIPS

❍ Use large diameter rollers for sleek, wavy looks, smaller rollers for curlier styles.
❍ Always use sections of equal width when setting the hair or you will get an uneven result.
❍ For maximum volume and control, let the hair cool completely before brushing through.
❍ A bristle brush will give a smoother finish to the style.
❍ If the finished set is too curly after brushing through, loosen the curl with a brush used with a hand dryer.
❍ To create extra volume and height use a fine-toothed comb to backcomb the roots.

1 Shampoo and condition your hair, then partially dry to remove excess moisture. Mist with a styling spray.

2 For a basic set, take a 50 mm/2 in section of hair (or a section the same width as your roller) from the centre front and comb it straight up, smoothing out any tangles.

3 Wrap the ends of the sectioned hair around the roller, taking care not to buckle the hair. Then wind the roller down firmly, towards the scalp, keeping the tension even.

4 Keep winding until the roller sits on the roots of the hair. Self-fixing rollers will stay in place on their own but if you are using brush rollers you will have to fasten them with a pin.

5 Continue around the whole head, always taking the same width of hair. Re-mist the hair with styling spray if it begins to dry out.

6 Leave the finished set to dry naturally, or dry it with a diffuser attachment on your hand dryer, or with a hood dryer. When using artificial heat sources allow the completely dry hair to become quite cool before you remove the rollers. Brush through the hair following the direction of the set. Mist the brush with hairspray and use to smooth any stray hairs.

SOFT SETTING

Fabric rollers are the modern version of old-fashioned rags. Apart from being very easy to use they are kind to the hair and give a highly effective set.

1 Dampen the hair with styling spray, making sure you distribute it evenly from the roots to the ends.

5 Leave the completed set to dry naturally.

TIP
For even more volume, twist each section of hair lengthwise before winding it on to the fabric roller.

3 Continue winding the roller right down to the roots.

2 Using sections of hair about 25 mm/1 in wide, curl the end of the hair around a fabric roller and wind the roller down towards the scalp, taking care not to buckle the ends of the hair.

6 When the hair is dry, remove the rollers by unbending the ends and unwinding the hair.

7 When all the rollers have been removed the hair falls into firm corkscrew curls.

4 To fasten, simply bend each end of the fabric roller towards the centre. This grips the hair and holds it in place.

8 Working on one curl at a time, rake your fingers through the hair, teasing out each curl. The result will be a full, voluminous finish.

STYLE AND GO

Heated gas stylers with tong and brush attachments enable you to create lots of styles. Here we show you two different techniques, which give two different looks.

2 Take a section of hair about 50 mm/2 in square and apply some styling lotion. Using the brush attachment on the styler gently smooth the hair from the roots to the ends. Place the styler near the roots, twist the hair around the brush, and hold for a few seconds. Gently unravel the hair and hold without pulling.

STYLING CHECKLIST

You will need:
✔ heated gas styler with brush and tong attachment
✔ styling lotion

1 Shampoo, condition, and dry your hair.

3 Place the ends of the hair into the styler and wind halfway down the hair length.

4 Unwind and loop the hair into a barrel curl, securing with a clip. Repeat steps 2 to 4 until you have done the whole head. Remove the pins. Comb.

1 Shampoo, condition, and dry your hair.

3 Continue wrapping the hair down the length of the barrel, taking care not to buckle the ends of the hair. Hold for a few seconds to allow the curl to form.

4 Release the depressor and allow the spiral curl to spring out. Repeat steps 2 to 3 until you have curled the whole head, then rake through the hair with your fingers for a softly tousled look.

Use the tong attachment for a tousled look.

2 Take a section of hair about 12 mm/ ½ in long and apply some styling lotion. Using the tong attachment on the styler, lift the depressor and keep it open. Slide the tongs on to the hair, just up from the roots. Holding the depressor open, wind the hair around the barrel, towards the face, ensuring the ends are smooth.

TIP
After tonging the hair, don't be tempted to brush your hair or you will lose the curl.

STYLING TRICKS
○ Always use heated gas stylers on dry hair, never on wet hair.
○ Don't use mousse or gel when heat styling. Instead, try special heat-activated styling lotions and sprays. These are designed to help curls hold their shape without making the hair sticky or frizzy.
○ Bobbed styles can be smoothed down and the ends of the hair tipped under using a heated gas styler. Just section the hair and smooth the tongs down the length, curving the ends. It is important to keep the tongs moving with a gentle sliding action, twisting the wrist and turning the barrel of the tongs under.
○ Unruly fringes can be tamed by gently winding the fringe around the tong or styler and holding for a few seconds.

Hair by Keith Harris
using Braun styling appliances,
photography Iain Philpott

TONG AND TWIST

Tongs can also be used to
smooth the hair and add just
the right amount of movement.

1 Shampoo, condition, and dry your
hair. Apply a mist of styling lotion.
Never use mousse as it will stick to the
tongs and bake into the hair. Divide off a
small section of hair.

2 Press the depressor to open the tongs.

3 Wind the section of hair around the
barrel of the tongs.

4 Release the depressor to hold the hair
in place and wait a few seconds for
the curl to form. Remove the tongs and
leave the hair to cool while you work on
the rest of the hair. Style by raking
through with your fingers.

STYLING CHECKLIST

You will need:
✔ styling lotion
✔ tongs

TIP
Never use tongs on bleached hair.
The high heat can damage the hair,
causing brittleness and breakage.

AIRWAVES

Air styling makes use of gentle heat and combines it with the moisture in your hair to give a long lasting curl.

1 Shampoo and condition your hair. Mist with styling lotion.

2 Using the brush attachment on the styler, start drying the hair. Lift each section to allow the heat to dry the roots.

3 Clip on the tong attachment and continue shaping the hair by wrapping it around the tongs.

4 Repeat steps 2 and 3 until the whole head is curled and waved. When the hair is completely dry rake your fingers through it.

STYLING CHECKLIST

You will need:
✔ styling lotion
✔ air styler with brush and tong attachment

TIP
Switch your air styler to low speed for more controlled styling and finishing.

CURL CREATION

A perm that is past its best can be revived using this diffuser drying technique.

1 The hair has the remains of a perm and is therefore flat at the roots with some curl from the mid-lengths to the ends.

2 Wash, condition, and towel dry your hair, then apply curl revitalizer to the damp hair.

3 Use a wide-toothed comb and work from the roots to the ends to ensure the curl revitalizer is distributed evenly.

4 Attach the diffuser to the dryer and dry the hair, allowing the hair to sit on the prongs of the diffuser. This action enables the warm air to circulate around the strands of hair, which encourages the formation of curls. To maximize the amount of curl, use your hands to "scrunch" up handfuls of hair.

TIP
This technique works equally well on naturally wavy or curly hair, giving separation and definition to curls and waves.

5 Tip your head forwards, allowing the hair to sit in the diffuser cup. Do not pull the hair, simply squeeze curls gently into shape.

6 Repeat steps 4 and 5 until all the hair is dry.

Hair by Trevor Sorbie, London.

SMOOTH AND STRAIGHT

STYLING CHECKLIST

You will need:
✔ comb
✔ dryer with diffuser attachment with long straight prongs

Volume can be added to long straight hair by using a dryer with a diffuser attachment that has long straight prongs.

1 Long thick hair often tangles easily and it is difficult to add volume and control.

2 Shampoo and condition your hair, then part it down the centre. Attach a diffuser with long prongs to your dryer and, as the hair dries, comb the prongs down the hair in a stroking movement. This will direct the airflow downwards, smoothing and separating the hair.

3 To create volume at the top and sides, slide the prongs through the hair to the roots at the crown, then gently rotate the diffuser. Repeat until you have achieved maximum volume.

Photograph courtesy of Braun. Appliance, Braun Supervolume.

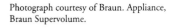

INSTANT SET

Hair can be given lift, bounce, and movement with a quick set using heated rollers.

1 Shampoo and condition your hair. Apply mousse and blow-dry smooth. Heat the rollers according to the manufacturer's directions.

3 Wind the rollers down towards the root, making sure that the ends are tucked under smoothly. Keep the tension even. Secure each roller with the clip supplied. Mist your set hair with a styling lotion. Allow the rollers to cool completely and then remove them, taking care not to disturb the curl too much. To finish, loosen the curls by raking your fingers through them.

2 Wind sections of hair (about 50 mm/2 in wide) on to a roller, taking care not to buckle the ends of the hair. Use medium and small rollers at the front and sides, larger rollers on the crown.

STYLING CHECKLIST

You will need:
✔ mousse
✔ styling lotion
✔ heated rollers with clips

TIP
A heated roller set forms the foundation for many styles and is a simple way to restyle the hair

Hair by Trevor Sorbie, London.

DOUBLE-STRANDED BRAIDS

These clever braids have a fishbone pattern, which gives an unusual look.

STYLING CHECKLIST

Time: 10 minutes
Ease/difficulty: Needs practice
Hair type: Long and straight

You will need:
✔ styling comb
✔ covered bands
✔ coloured feathers
✔ two short lengths of fine leather

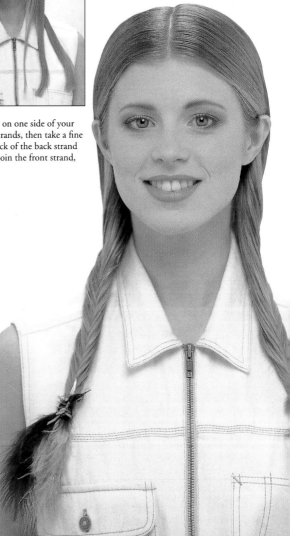

1 Part your hair in the centre and comb it straight.

2 Divide the hair on one side of your hair into two strands, then take a fine section from the back of the back strand and take it over to join the front strand, as shown.

3 Now take a fine section from the front of the front strand and cross it over to the back strand. Take a fine section from the back strand again and bring it over to join the front strand. Continue in this way; you will soon see the fishbone effect appear. Secure the ends with covered bands and add feathers, tying in place with fine leather. Repeat these three steps on the other side.

DRAGGED SIDE BRAIDS

Curly hair can be controlled, yet still allowed to flow free, by braiding at the sides and allowing the hair at the back to fall in a mass of curls.

1 Part your hair in the centre and divide off a large section at the side, combing it as flat as possible to the head.

2 Divide the section into three equal strands and hold them apart.

3 Begin to make a dragged braid by pulling the strands of hair towards your face and then braiding in the normal way, that is, taking the right strand over the centre strand, the left strand over the centre, and the right over the centre again, keeping the braid in the position shown.

4 Continue braiding to the end and secure the end with a covered band. Tuck the braid behind your ear and grip it in place, then make a second braid on the other side.

TIP

Encourage curls to form by spraying the hair with water and then scrunching with your hands.

STYLING CHECKLIST

Time: 5 minutes
Ease/difficulty: Easy
Hair type: Long and naturally curly or permed

You will need:
✔ styling comb
✔ covered bands
✔ hair grips

PONYTAIL STYLER

A simple ponytail can be transformed easily and quickly using this clever styler.

TIP
To smooth any flyaway ends rub a few drops of serum between the palms of your hands and smooth over the hair.

1 Clasp the hair into a ponytail and secure it with a covered band. Insert the styler as shown.

2 Thread the ponytail through the styler.

3 Begin to pull the styler down…

4 …continue pulling…

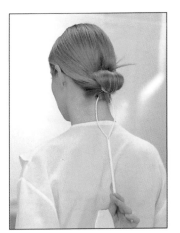

5 …so the ponytail pulls through…

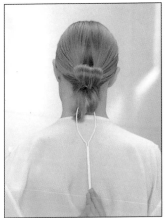

6 …and emerges underneath.

TIP
The same technique can be used on wet hair as long as you apply gel first, combing it through evenly before styling.

7 Smooth the hair with your hand and insert the styler again, repeating steps 2 to 6 once more to give a neat and smooth, chignon loop.

CURLY STYLER

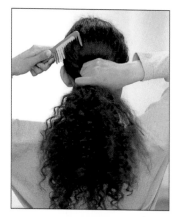

The ponytail styler can also be used to tame a mass of curls, creating a ponytail with a simple double twist.

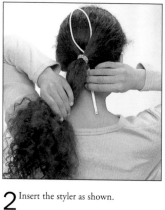

1 Use a comb with widely spaced teeth to smooth the hair back and into a ponytail. Secure with a covered band.

2 Insert the styler as shown.

3 Thread the ponytail through the styler.

Side view of finished style.

4 Begin to pull the styler down...

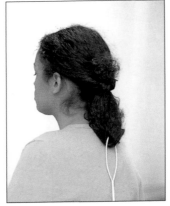

5 ...continue pulling...

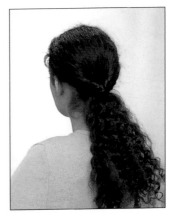

6 ...so that the ponytail pulls through.

7 Repeat steps 3 to 6.

8 Apply a little mousse to your hands and use it to re-form the curls, scrunching to achieve a good shape.

STYLING CHECKLIST

Time: 5 minutes
Ease/difficulty: Easy
Hair type: Long and naturally curly or permed

You will need:
✔ widely spaced tooth comb
✔ covered band
✔ ponytail styler
✔ mousse

TIP
When inserting the styler through a pony tail, carefully move it from side to side in order to create enough room to pull the looped end of the styler through more easily.

TOP KNOT

Ring the changes on finely braided locks by adding bright cord and tying the hair in a top knot.

1 Bind the end of each braid with cord, tying in a knot to secure.

2 Cross the braids over one another. Pick up and hold the braids from the crown section in either hand, as shown

3 Tie in a knot.

4 Repeat step 3 so you have a double knot. Secure the knot with a decorative hair pin.

STYLING CHECKLIST

Time: 15 -20 minutes
Ease/difficulty: Easy
Hair type: Long, finely braided or braided hair extensions

You will need:
✔ length of colourful cord about 5 m/5 yd long
✔ decorative hair pin

CROWN BRAIDS

By braiding the crown hair and allowing the remaining hair to frame the face you can achieve an interesting contrast of textures.

1 Clip up the top hair on one side of your head, leaving the back hair free. Take a small section of hair at ear level and comb it straight.

TIP
The volume of the curls can be increased by tipping your head forwards, then applying styling spray and scrunching the hair lying underneath.

2 Start braiding quite tightly, doing one cross (right strand over centre, left over centre), and gradually bring more hair into the outside strands.

3 Continue in this way, taking the braid towards the back of the head.

4 Make another parting about 25 mm/1 in parallel to and above the previous braid, and repeat the process. Continue in this way until all the front hair has been braided. Scrunch the remaining hair into fulsome curls to increase the volume. Finally, add a decorative Alice band.

STYLING CHECKLIST

Time: 15 minutes
Ease/difficulty: Needs practice
Hair type: Mid-length to long and naturally curly or permed

You will need:
✔ large clip
✔ small covered bands
✔ Alice band

TWIST AND COIL

This style starts with a simple ponytail, is easy to do, and looks stunning.

1 Smooth the hair back and secure in a ponytail using a covered band.

3 Holding the ends of a section, twist the hair until it rolls back on itself to form a coil.

2 Divide off a small section of hair and mist with shine spray for added gloss.

4 Position the coil in a loop as shown and secure in place using hair pins. Continue in this manner until all the hair has been coiled. Decorate by intertwining with a strip of sequins.

STYLING CHECKLIST

Time: 10 minutes
Ease/difficulty: Easy
Hair type: Long, one length, straight hair

You will need:
✔ covered band
✔ pins
✔ hair pins
✔ shine spray
✔ 1 m/1 yd strip of sequins

CAMEO BRAID

A classic bun is given extra panache by encircling with a braid.

1 Smooth the hair into a ponytail, leaving one section of the hair free.

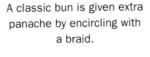

2 Place a bun ring over the ponytail.

3 Take approximately one third of the hair from the ponytail and wrap it around the bun ring, securing with pins. Repeat with the other two-thirds of hair.

4 Braid the section of hair that was left out of the ponytail, right strand over centre strand, left over centre and so on, and wrap the braid around the base of the bun, then secure with pins.

STYLING CHECKLIST

Time: 10 minutes.
Ease/difficulty: Needs practice
Hair type: Long and straight

You will need:
✔ covered band
✔ bun ring
✔ hair pins

BAND BRAID

A plain ponytail can be transformed by simply covering the band with a tiny braid.

1 Brush the hair back into a smooth, low ponytail, leaving a small section free for braiding. Smooth the reserved section with a little styling wax. Secure in place with a covered band.

2 Divide this section into three equal strands. Now, braid the hair in the normal way.

3 Take the braid and wrap it around the covered band . . .

4 . . . as many times as it goes. Finally, secure with a grip.

CLIP UP

Long, curly hair can sometimes be unruly. Here's an easy way to tame tresses but still keep the beauty of the length.

1 Rub a little wax between the palms of your hands, then work into the curls with the fingertips. This helps give the curl separation and shine.

2 Take two interlocking large curved combs and use them to push the crown hair up towards the centre.

3 Push the teeth of the combs together to fasten.

TIP

It's easier to disentangle curly hair if you use a comb with widely spaced teeth.

4 Repeat with two more combs at ear level to secure the back hair.

STYLING CHECKLIST

Time: 2 minutes
Ease/difficulty: Easy
Hair type: Mid-length to long, curly or straight

You will need:
✔ wax
✔ two sets of interlocking curved combs

DRAPED CHIGNON

This elegant style is perfect for that special evening out.

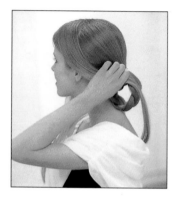

1 Part the hair in the centre from the forehead to the middle of the crown. Comb the side hair and scoop the back hair into a low ponytail using a covered band.

2 Loosely braid the ponytail – take the right strand over the centre strand, the left over the right, the right over the centre, and so on, continuing to the end. Secure the end with a small band, then tuck the end under and around in a loop and secure with grips.

3 Pick up the hair on the left side and comb it in a curve back to the ponytail loop.

4 Swirl this hair over and under the loop and secure with grips. Repeat steps 3 and 4 on the right side.

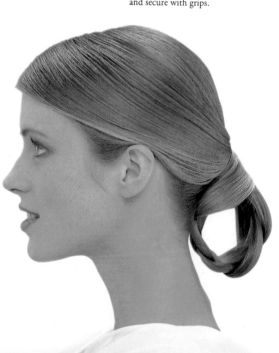

STYLING CHECKLIST

Time: 5-10 minutes
Ease/difficulty: Quite easy
Hair type: Long and straight

You will need:
✔ comb
✔ covered bands
✔ grips

TIP
Even long hair should be trimmed regularly, at least every two months, to keep it in good condition

CITY SLICKER

Transform your hair in minutes using gel to slick it into shape and add sheen.

1 Take a generous amount of gel and apply it to the hair from the roots to the ends.

2 Use a vent brush, a comb, or your fingers to distribute the gel evenly through the hair.

3 Comb the hair into shape using a styling comb to encourage movement.

TIP
Make sure you distribute the gel evenly all over your hair before styling.

4 Shape to form a quiff and sleek down the sides and back.

STYLING CHECKLIST

Time: 5 minutes
Ease/difficulty: Easy
Hair type: Short crops

You need:
✔ gel
✔ small vent brush
✔ styling comb

SIMPLE PLEAT

Curly hair that is neatly pleated gives a sophisticated style. The front is left full to soften the effect.

1 Divide off a section of hair at the front and leave it free. Smooth with a little serum. Take the remaining hair into one hand, as if you were going to make a ponytail.

2 Twist the hair tightly from left to right.

3 When the twist is taut, turn the hair upwards as shown to form a pleat. Use your other hand to help smooth the pleat and at the same time neaten the top by tucking in the ends.

4 Secure the pleat with hair scroos or pins. Take the reserved front section, bring it back and secure it at the top of the pleat, allowing the ends to fall free.

STYLING CHECKLIST

Time: 5 minutes
Ease/difficulty: Quite easy
Hair type: Shoulder length or longer, curly or straight

You will need:
✔ serum
✔ hair scroos or pins

LOOPED CURLS

Two ponytails form the basis
of this elegant style.

3 Place the remaining hair in a lower ponytail.

1 Apply setting lotion to the ends of the hair only. This will give just the right amount of body and bounce to help form the curls. Set the hair on heated rollers. When the rollers are quite cool – about 10 minutes after completing the set – take them out and allow the hair to fall free.

2 Divide off the crown hair and secure it with hair pins in a high ponytail. Apply a few drops of serum to add gloss, and brush the hair through.

4 Divide each ponytail into sections about 25 mm/1 in wide, then comb and smooth each section into a looped curl and pin in place. Set with hairspray.

STYLING CHECKLIST

Time: 10-15 minutes.
Ease/difficulty: Needs practice.
Hair type: Mid-length to long

You will need:
✔ setting lotion
✔ heated rollers
✔ serum
✔ covered bands, hair pins

FRENCH PLEAT

1 Backcomb the hair all over.

Mid-length to long hair can be transformed into a classic, elegant French pleat in a matter of minutes.

2 Smooth your hair across to the centre back and form the centre of the pleat by criss-crossing hair grips in a row from the crown downwards, as shown.

3 Gently smooth the hair around from the other side, leaving the front section free, and tuck the ends under.

4 Secure with pins, then lightly comb the front section up and around to merge with the top of the pleat. Mist with hairspray to hold.

STYLING CHECKLIST

Time: 5-10 minutes.
Ease/difficulty: Quite easy
Hair type: Mid-length to long

You will need:
✔ comb
✔ hair grips
✔ pins
✔ hairspray

SHORT AND SPIKY

Short hair can be quickly styled using gel and wax to create a cheeky, fun look.

1 Work a generous amount of gel through your hair from the roots to the ends.

2 Dry your hair using a directional nozzle on your dryer; as you dry, lift sections of the hair to create height at the roots.

3 When the hair is dry, backcomb the crown to give additional height.

TIP
Gel can be re-activated by misting the hair with water and shaping it into style again.

4 To finish, rub a little wax between the palms of your hands, then apply it to the hair to give definition.

STYLING CHECKLIST

Time: 10 minutes
Ease/difficulty: Easy
Hair type: Short, layered and straight

You will need:
✔ gel
✔ hairdryer
✔ comb
✔ wax

EXERCISE
AND DIET

ARE YOU UNFIT AND OUT OF SHAPE? YOU COULD
BLAME YOUR LIFESTYLE FOR THE STATE YOU ARE IN.
TODAY, EVERYTHING IS GEARED TO MAKE LIFE AS EASY
AS POSSIBLE. WE DO NOT HAVE TO WALK UP STAIRS
BECAUSE THERE IS USUALLY A LIFT TO CARRY US,
AND WE DO NOT HAVE TO WASH CLOTHES BY HAND
BECAUSE MOST OF US OWN A WASHING MACHINE TO DO
THE WORK FOR US. THOSE OF US WHO ARE OFFICE
WORKERS ARE AMAZINGLY INACTIVE; WE SIT ALL DAY —
IN A CAR, BUS, OR TRAIN, OR AT A DESK — AND SLUMP
ON A FAVOURITE CHAIR IN THE EVENING. DO YOU WANT
TO IMPROVE YOUR FITNESS BUT FEEL IT WOULD BE TOO
DIFFICULT? GETTING IN SHAPE APPEARS TO BE HARD
WORK AND TIME-CONSUMING, BUT IT DOES NOT NEED
TO BE. SO, IF YOU WANT A FITTER, FIRMER AND
HEALTHIER BODY, FOLLOW THE EXERCISES AND DIET
GUIDELINES IN THIS SECTION — AND GET FIT.

FITNESS AND EXERCISE

Fitness is the key to a healthy mind and body. It is based on stamina, strength, and suppleness – the three "S's"; better shape and self-esteem are two extra "S" bonuses. Being fit does not merely improve your physical prowess and grace, it also makes you feel better over-all. Most of us know that if we were fitter, we would have more confidence and greater zest for life. But although we are more health-conscious about our diet nowadays, regular exercise is still not a part of most people's daily lives. Surveys always draw the same conclusions as to the reasons for this: lack of time, energy, interest, and confidence. Becoming fit is neither as difficult nor as time-consuming as it may appear to be: you can get fit – and get a better body into the bargain – more quickly, easily and enjoyably than you may think.

HOW FIT DO YOU NEED TO BE?

There is no such thing as a standard fitness gauge – it all depends on your personal make-up and why you want to be fit: being robust enough to run a marathon, for example, is very different from honing the three "S's" to gain improved physical shape and health. For exercise to be of any help to you, though, it should boost your metabolism and improve your cardiovascular (heart and circulation) and respiratory (breathing) systems.

GOALS AND RECORD RESULTS

Finding a goal that will inspire you is one of the secrets of success. To achieve that goal, you must have a motive that matters enough to give you an iron will, such as improving your figure for a special event (for example, your wedding and honeymoon), buying yourself a longed-for figure-hugging dress, or simply boosting your fitness levels generally. Set the dead-

Swimming is an excellent way of keeping the whole body in good physical condition when done regularly and conscientiously.

WHY BOTHER WITH FITNESS?

Why are you reading this book? Are you fed up with having low self-confidence? Are you tired of running out of puff, being out of shape (obese, even) or always feeling under the weather? Do you often get colds, or suffer from bad pre-menstrual syndrome (PMS), stress, or sleepless nights? These are just a handful of the signs that could manifest themselves when you are unfit. So exercise is worth the effort, because when you are fitter, recurring problems such as these may ease or disappear.

Women are increasingly attracted to strenuous sports such as boxing that until recently were considered to be solely a male preserve.

Competitive team sports such as volleyball not only provide an opportunity to improve physical fitness, they are also highly enjoyable.

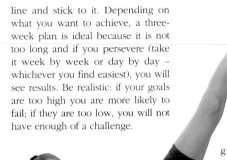

line and stick to it. Depending on what you want to achieve, a three-week plan is ideal because it is not too long and if you persevere (take it week by week or day by day – whichever you find easiest), you will see results. Be realistic: if your goals are too high you are more likely to fail; if they are too low, you will not have enough of a challenge.

Goals will inspire you, but speedy results are the key to keeping up regular exercise – it is natural to want to see rewards for all your hard work – although it is advisable to build up a pattern gradually. The minimum amount of exercise you need to do to improve your

personal fitness is 20 minutes 3 times a week – the "3 x 20" maxim. This means three bouts of exercise vigorous enough to make you fairly breathless (but not gasping for breath). So if you do the general fitness exercises outlined in this book 3 times a week for 20 minutes you will get fitter. If you want to see fast results, though, you need to add extra activities – such as a couple of games of tennis, swimming, or brisk walking – to your exercise quota, so that you are actually exercising six days a week.

Taking part in a team sport once a week is a good idea: not only will it make you fitter, slimmer, and happier, the competitive spirit will

also strengthen your resolve. Some sports need special skills but you do not have to be an athlete to do most of them.

CONTRA-INDICATIONS

Before taking up any form of rigorous exercise or training, you should consult your doctor – especially if any of the following conditions apply to you:

○ diabetes or epilepsy
○ over 35 years of age with a long history of inactivity
○ cardiovascular or respiratory problems
○ severe illness and ensuing medication
○ chronic joint or back problems
○ obesity
○ pregnancy
○ heavy drinking or smoking

WARMING UP AND COOLING DOWN

Warm-up activities are important as they prime you for exercise: they ease your muscles into action so that your muscles react more readily to activity; they also prepare you for a rise in heart rate and body temperature. Warm ups should be done slowly and rhythmically for 5–10 minutes (depending on age and personal fitness).

Be sure also to set time aside to cool down after exercising: keep walking or moving around slowly for 5 minutes. The cool-down period is important because it allows you to decrease gradually the amount of exercise. This avoids feelings of faintness that may be caused by the pooling of blood below the waist that occurs during vigorous exercise.

YOUR PULSE RATE

Monitoring your pulse rate allows you to keep a check on whether you are exercising adequately. The maximum heart rate for an adult is roughly 220 beats per minute minus your age in years. The ideal heart rate during exercise is in a target zone of 65-80 per cent of this figure. The aim of exercise is to get your heart rate to within a certain range. These are the ideal exercise heart rate ranges for the different ages:

Age	Pulse Range
20+	130–160
30+	124–152
40+	117–144

To find out your active pulse rate per minute, rest two fingers lightly on your pulse immediately after exercising, count the beats for 10 seconds and multiply by 6.

Hockey is a demanding sport that strengthens the legs, is beneficial to the heart and lungs, and significantly improves co-ordination.

A good many water sports demand strength, stamina, and a fine sense of balance. Wind surfing is no exception to the rule.

EXERCISES FOR GENERAL FITNESS

This exercise routine helps to improve over-all fitness and should take you roughly 30 minutes to complete. Aim to do it three times a week and try to do extra aerobic exercise – such as swimming, walking or cycling – on the other days (aerobic exercises include any activity that can be done rhythmically and continually and that boosts the efficient uptake of oxygen). To warm up your muscles before exercising, either spend two minutes running up and down the stairs, walking briskly, cycling, or doing the special warm-up exercises outlined below.

Think of warm-up exercises as a way of easing your body into increased activity. The movements should be slow and rhythmical, not sharp and jerky.

Warm-up Exercise A

1 Stand upright with your feet apart and in line with your shoulders, with your arms hanging loosely at your sides and your shoulders down.

WARM-UP EXERCISES

2 Bring your shoulders forwards.

IMPORTANT NOTE

If you feel any pain – or experience anything other than the normal sensation of muscle fatigue – stop exercising. Quit if you feel dizzy too. Always work out at your own pace; and skip exercise if you are ill, have a virus or a raised temperature.

3 Then raise them as high as you can.

4 Now move your shoulders back as far as possible. Finally, bring them back to the start position.

REPETITION GUIDE FOR GENERAL FITNESS EXERCISES

Toning Exercises	Repeats/Time Allowance
Warm-ups	5 minutes
Press-ups	10 repeats
Lying Flies	10 repeats
Reverse Curls	10 repeats
Sit-ups	10 repeats
Squats	10 repeats
Cool Downs	3–5 minutes
Aerobic Exercise	20–30 minutes

The recommended 10 repeats are for beginners – you should aim to repeat each exercise (from Warm-ups to Cool Downs) 15 times, or as often as is comfortable. Start by doing this set of exercises twice a week, work up to three times a week and combine it with some other form of exercise – ideally aerobics – for the time suggested above.

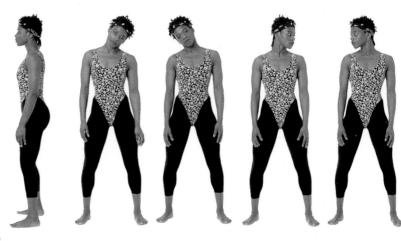

Warm-up Exercise B

1 Maintain an upright posture as in Exercise A. Tip your head forwards so that your chin is almost resting on your chest.

2 Raise your head, stretching and lengthening your neck as you return to the upright position. Repeat 4 times.

3 Now tip your head to the left, keeping your shoulders down. Bring it back to the centre and then stretch and lengthen your neck.

4 Repeat Step 3 but tip your head to the right side. Repeat 4 times on each side, remembering not to raise your shoulders.

5 Keep your head upright and turn so that you are looking over your left shoulder. Then face forwards again and stretch and lengthen your neck.

6 Now turn and look over your right shoulder. Face forwards again and stretch and lengthen your neck. Repeat Steps 5 and 6 four times, then do the whole sequence again twice.

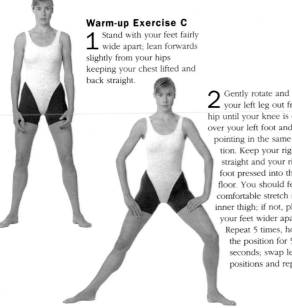

Warm-up Exercise C

1 Stand with your feet fairly wide apart; lean forwards slightly from your hips keeping your chest lifted and back straight.

2 Gently rotate and bend your left leg out from the hip until your knee is directly over your left foot and pointing in the same direction. Keep your right leg straight and your right foot pressed into the floor. You should feel a comfortable stretch in the inner thigh; if not, place your feet wider apart. Repeat 5 times, holding the position for 5 seconds; swap leg positions and repeat.

THE GENERAL EXERCISES

Chest Muscles:Press-ups

1 Place yourself on all fours with your knees directly under your hips, your hands beneath your shoulders with your fingers pointing forwards, your palms flat. Make sure your back is straight – that is, parallel with the ceiling – all the time. Achieve this by pulling your stomach in and tucking your pelvis under.

2 Steadily lower yourself – nose first – towards the floor . . .

3 . . . then raise yourself back to the starting position, breathing in as you go.

Upper Back Muscles:Lying Flies

1 Lie on your front on the floor with your hips down, and keep your body relaxed. Rest your forehead on the floor, your arms out on each side at right angles to your body, elbows bent.

2 Keeping your elbow bent, steadily lift both arms, making sure they are parallel to the floor.

3 Lower your arms once again. Make sure you don't pull your elbows back; keep them in line with your shoulders and keep your hips and feet in contact with the floor all the time.

ABDOMINAL MUSCLES

When you do these exercises, keep your lower back pressed into the floor throughout and work slowly, with total control. In the Upper Abdominals exercise, lift your head and shoulders as one unit, never separately; roll up from the top of your head; imagine you are holding a peach between your chin and your chest and keep this gap constant throughout. Make sure your face muscles are relaxed all the time.

Lower Abdominals:Reverse Curls

1 Lie flat on your back on the floor, arms by your sides, palms flat on the floor beside you.

2 While keeping your arms and hands flat on the floor, bring your knees in towards your chest one at a time, and once there, keep both knees together in the bent position.

3 Breathe in and, keeping your spine firmly pressed into the floor, pull in your abdominal muscles while at the same time curling up your coxyx (tail bone) to bring your knees closer to your chest. Keep your feet relaxed throughout. Lower your body to the starting position, exhaling as you go down.

Upper Abdominals:Sit Ups

1 Lying flat on the floor with your arms by your side, palms flat on the floor, bend your knees and keep your feet flat on the floor a little distance apart in line with your hips.

2 Lift your head and shoulders – inhaling as you move up – and push your fingertips towards your knees keeping your arms straight.

3 Lower your body back to the starting position, exhaling as you go down; repeat the movement.

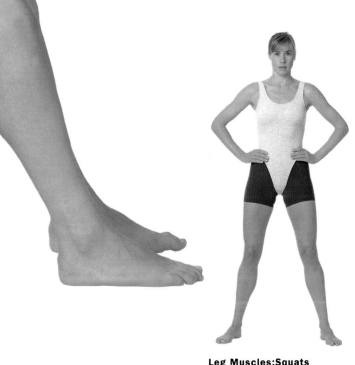

Leg Muscles:Squats

1 Stand up straight with your feet a little wider than shoulder-width apart. If you stand on tiptoe, this exercise tones your calf muscles and your quadriceps, the muscles on the front of your thighs; if you angle your toes slightly outwards while on tiptoe, it benefits your inner thighs.

2 Resting your hands on the front of your thighs and keeping your arms straight, steadily bend your legs to a squatting position, exhaling as you go down.

3 Then, inhale as you rise steadily back to the starting position. When you do this exercise, it is important to keep your back straight and your knees flexible. Don't let your knees bend further forward than your toes.

SPORTS ACTIVITIES

Team sports and work-outs at the gym are not only fun, they also give you the chance to add to your exercise quota for the week, and therefore reach your self-improvement goals that much faster. The benefits of taking part in specific sports and of working out are given here.

Badminton: aerobic; improves joint flexibility, stamina, leg and shoulder tone and strength; 30-40 minutes continuous play burns up around 200-800 calories.

Golf: improves arm, shoulder and leg tone, and strength (you walk four to five miles when you do a round of golf).

Jogging: aerobic; improves stamina, leg strength and tone; an hour's jogging burns up 200-350 calories. If you think that jogging or running will suit your new active way of life, take the standard precautions before you start: check with your doctor and, as with all aerobic exercise, increase the pace gradually; always wear the right trainers (and support bandages if your joints are weak).

HOUSEWORK TIME NEEDED TO BURN UP 100 CALORIES:

○ Ironing: 50 minutes
○ Sweeping the floor: 30 minutes
○ Washing-up: 28 minutes
○ Vacuuming: 40 minutes
○ Polishing furniture: 52 minutes

DIETING COMBINED WITH EXERCISE

You will lose weight if you limit your food intake, but not as quickly or as evenly as you would if you combined a balanced weight-loss diet with regular exercise. Exercise increases your metabolism, and, if you want to lose weight more quickly, you need to exercise in conjunction with dieting.

MAKE EXERCISE EASY TO DO

Your body cannot "store" fitness, so once you have started, you have to keep exercising regularly. Make your routine flexible: if you think it is going to be hard to maintain, don't choose an activity that requires good weather or a long detour from your office or home.

Tennis: aerobic; boosts stamina and suppleness; strengthens and tones your shoulders, forearms, calves and thighs; play energetically (ideally twice a week) for an hour and you will burn up around 300-400 calories.

Brisk walking: aerobic; strengthens and tones your legs.

Cycling: aerobic; builds stamina; tones your legs.

Skipping: aerobic; boosts stamina, strength and leg tone. Start by doing 3 skipping sets for 30 seconds a time with a 5-minute

Golf is a sport that particularly benefits shoulders, arms, and legs. Playing a round involves a good deal of walking.

Judo is a body contact sport and one of the major martial arts. It requires a good deal of strength, agility, and physical courage.

GYM-BASED BENEFITS

Aerobics: specific aerobics classes combine exercise with constant movement for up to an hour; they are fast fat-burners and an ideal activity to do regularly if you are after speedy results.

Circuit, cross, resistance, or weight training: aerobic; increase stamina, strength and suppleness; an hour of circuit training burns up between 350-550 calories.

Step classes: aerobic; improves stamina; tones and strengthens your lower torso (bottom, thighs and calves); an hour-long class burns up between 500-800 calories.

Yoga: improves posture; tones, strengthens, and relaxes the body; loosens joints; an hour of yoga burns up about 200 calories.

Football: aerobic; improves stamina; strengthens and tones your legs; an hour's play burns up around 250-1000 calories.

Boxing: tones and strengthens your chest, shoulders, and arms; an hour's boxing burns up around 400-600 calories.

Volleyball: aerobic; improves stamina; tones and strengthens the whole body, especially your legs and arms; mobilizes joints; an hour's play burns up 200-600 calories.

Squash: as above; an hour's play burns up 400-1000 calories.

break after each set; build up to skipping for 2 minutes with a 10-minute break and also increase the repetitions.

Rebounding: aerobic; bounding on a mini trampoline is a fun way to get fit at home.

Swimming: aerobic; swimming is one of the fastest (and best) ways to boost overall fitness, muscle tone, joint flexibility, and relaxation. Do 4 lengths of a 25 m/25 yard pool, rest for a minute and build endurance by reducing rest time and increasing swim time; within a fortnight you will be noticeably fitter and firmer; an hour's breaststroke burns between 500-800 calories.

HELP FOR PMS

Exercise is the last thing you feel like doing when you are pre-menstrual. But if you do push yourself now, you will feel more relaxed and relieve the symptoms. If you cannot face an aerobics class, go for a swim: this will ease pre-menstrual cramp and put you in a better mood.

ARE EXPENSIVE TRAINERS A WASTE OF MONEY?

What you wear on your feet is crucial to your performance and to the benefits you will get from exercise. Good sports shops will give advice on the right trainers to wear for different activities, but cross-trainers – designed to be worn for most sports – are probably your best investment because they are good all-rounders. Bare feet (and something comfortable such as leggings and a T-shirt) are fine when you are doing the exercises outlined in this book.

BODY SHAPE

The shape of your body is unique; it is important to remember this because the basic skeletal and muscular form that you inherit is unchangeable. Features such as your height, foot size, shoulder width and the length and shape of your legs, nose, fingers and toes combine to produce a whole. Each person is an individual, with characteristics particular to their genetic make-up.

BODY BRACKETS

Although we come in a variety of shapes and sizes, the human body is cast from three basic moulds. Often, features from two or three of these body types are jumbled with our individual characteristics, but it is the more dominant features that slot us into one of the following groups: ectomorphs; mesomorphs, and endomorphs.

Ectomorphs are usually small- and slender-framed with long limbs, narrow shoulders, hips and joints. They have little muscle or body fat. Mesomorphs have medium to large – but compact – frames with broader shoulders, pelvic girdle and well-developed muscles. Endo-morphs are naturally curvaceous, with more body fat than muscle, wider hips, shorter limbs and a lower centre of gravity than the other two body types.

SELF-IMAGE

If you are a bit on the tubby side, it can be annoying to hear someone who you think is poker-thin whining about being overweight. But there is a logic behind this that stems from self-image. Very few of us actually see ourselves as we really are. We tend to misjudge our bodies with sweeping claims to fatness, even when we have only a spot of excess flab around our midriff to show for it. And although

it sounds amazing, the way we behave in every-day life (and think others see us) often tallies with our self-image. It's a vicious circle: we think that we don't measure up to the standard beauty ideal so our self-esteem dips, often so low that we feel that we will never have a better body. This in turn causes self-confidence to plummet further, we feel even worse, and so the vicious circle continues.

Taking control of your self-image brings enormous bonuses. And the faster you can do this, the greater the rewards, as speedy results boost your confidence more quickly. But before you undertake a scheme to get into better shape, you must work on your positive thinking: realize your potential by deciding on (and accepting) your body model, then use this as your goal. Forget conventional beauty ideals – you don't have to have mile-long legs to have a dynamite figure; what you already have – your basic shape – is great. It just needs per-fecting, and that is something that everyone can do.

GOOD POSTURE

Even though it sounds like some pointless exercise from your schooldays, there is real wisdom in the old dictum "head up, shoulders back, bottom in". The difference that good posture makes to the look of our bodies is enormous, mainly because when we are standing properly our abdominal muscles are in their correct supporting role and the whole body is aligned so it looks leaner and taller. Good posture is also helpful to our mental and physical health; some alternative therapies (such as the Alexander Technique) are based on the principle of correct posture because it can ease back pain, stress, and even headaches.

Posture Exercise Stand in front of a mirror, try these exercises and see what they do for the shape of your body:

1 Do this exercise facing yourself first, then turn so you are sideways on:

○ Lift your head up and lengthen your spine.

○ Tuck in your chin and your bottom.

○ Bring your shoulders back and down.

2 Now stand with your legs slightly apart.

○ Check whether your weight is evenly spread.

○ Keep your shoulders and hips level and your weight balanced between the heel and ball of each foot.

TROUBLE SPOTS

Very few people are able to say honestly that they are totally happy with their body. Everyone has at least one gripe – if it is not big feet, it is thin hair or knobbly knees. All these perceived "flaws" can be improved or disguised, but as anyone who has ever tried (and failed) to move the fat that sits on strategic points such as hips, thighs, stomachs, and buttocks knows, it is much easier to hide the flaws than to tackle them. Trouble spots such as these are notoriously stubborn to shift, but it is possible to alter your outline with a combination of diet and exercise.

COMMON PROBLEMS

Any of the following can be discouraging, but remember – each problem has a solution.

Slack stomachs Our stomachs become flabby when the abdominal muscles slacken; this usually happens through lack of exercise. Your abdomen extends from just under the bustline to the groin, and

The best way to assess your figure is to stand in front of a full-length mirror. Be honest with yourself, and look for areas that need improving.

FINDING AND IMPROVING YOUR TRUE FORM

Step 1: Confront Your Body
Go on, be brave. Strip to your underwear, stand in front of a mirror and have a good look at your body. Take your time and be tough but realistic. You may have disliked your thighs since you were 16 – and they will probably never be those of a supermodel – but if you look hard enough you might just find that they are not as bad as you have always thought they were, and that improving them is not going to be that hard after all.

Step 2: Put Your Complaints In Writing
Note down all the things that irk you (and that you can do something about) as well as those that you like or do not mind. Then go through your list of dislikes, ticking the things that you really want to do something about. Also, make a mental note to start appreciating your good points: the more you focus on them the less you will notice the not-so-good zones.

Step 3: Action Checklist
Now, add a set of action points under the problem zones you have listed. If you want to firm up your arms for that sleeveless sundress you have been unable to wear for a decade of summers, make notes like this:
Flabby Upper Arms
○ Do Basic Exercises.
○ Check Diet.
○ Exfoliate/Moisturize.
Finally, add your goal(s) and your deadline to the top of the list and put it somewhere where you are going to see it frequently.

TWO QUICK THIGH-TONERS

If you do not have time to do a full exercise routine, grab 10 minutes in the morning and evening to warm up and do these two exercises.

○ **Outer Thighs:** sit on the floor with your legs straight out in front and hold your arms out to the sides as shown left. Roll sideways on to your bottom – go right over on to your outer thigh and then roll right over on to the other thigh. Do this 20 times.

○ **Inner Thighs:** stand upright and consciously tighten – and hold – your buttock muscles for a slow count of five. Repeat with your thigh muscles and then your calf muscles. You can do this while you are waiting for your bath to run, standing at the bus stop, and so on.

it is packed with muscles that crisscross to form a wall to hold the abdominal contents in place – a bit like a corset. Exercise is not the only way to keep your stomach flat though: weight is also an important factor and the long-term answer is diet and exercise.

Thunder thighs Thighs – like bottoms and busts – are a great source of discontent, whether it is because they are too flabby, muscular, or skinny. You inherit the basic shape of your thighs, but that does not necessarily mean that you were born with the excess fat that may now be covering them. Thigh size and tone can certainly be altered with the right diet, correct body care and regular exercise. Sports such as cycling, skiing, tennis, squash, and riding (a great inner-muscle firmer) will tone your thighs, as will weight training for specific areas of the body.

Large bottoms There are three large muscles in our buttocks: *gluteus maximus, medius, and minimus.*

These create the shape, but not the size, of our rear ends. It is the tone of these muscles and the fatty tissue around them that gives us the bottoms we have. The good news is that buttock muscles respond well to exercise, which means that any

effort you put into bottom-toning exercises will be rewarded quite quickly. Locomotive exercises – such as fast walking, running upstairs, and jogging – are especially good bottom trimmers. Other exercises are given in the Basic Exercise Routines.

ANKLE EXERCISES

Whenever you remember – while sitting at your desk or relaxing in the evening – move your ankles around in a clockwise motion 10 times, then repeat anti-clockwise.

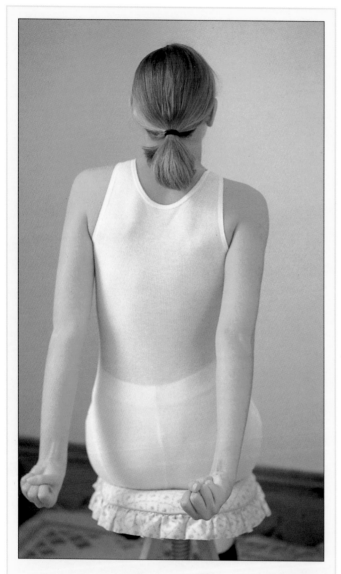

FLABBY ARM FIXER

To firm up flabby arms, add this exercise to your daily exercise routine, or spend five minutes doing it twice a day. Sit on a chair holding your hands in loose fists, and, with your arms extended out behind, make downwards punching movements backwards and forwards.

Slack upper arms Our arms do not really change shape much during our lives, unless we lose or gain a lot of weight. Muscle tone is the main problem, but, as in the case of thighs, exercise and specific weight training will tone up and re-shape flabby arms; very often, any changes in body shape that happen through exercise and diet are noticeable most quickly on your upper arms.

Droopy breasts Breast shape and size only really change when our weight swings dramatically, or during pregnancy, breast-feeding, menstruation, or if taking oral contraceptives. Gravity is the bust's worst enemy, especially if the breasts are not given proper support, because it literally drags the breasts down and slackens their tone. Although the breasts are supported by suspensory ligaments, they do not contain any muscle (the milk glands are buffered by protective fatty tissue) so you cannot noticeably reverse lost tone. However, if you exercise the pectoral muscles beneath your armpits you will give your breasts a firmer base and more uplift.

Thick ankles Trim and slender ankles that seem set to snap with every step are a great asset. But if you are not blessed with these, or if your ankles tend to become stiff and puffy from fluid retention, you need to master the art of deception and brush up on some ankle improving exercises.

Assess the flexibility of your ankles by sitting on a chair or stool with your feet on the floor and, while keeping your heel down pull the rest of your foot up as far as it will go: if the distance between your foot and the floor measures 12-15 cm/5-6 in your joint flexibility is good; if it is between 10-12 cm/ 4-5 in it is fair; and if it is less than that, your joint flexibility is poor.

The following exercises will help to improve the muscles that support your breasts.

1 Stand erect and bend your arms at the elbows, holding your arms horizontally in front of your chest, with your fingertips touching. Move your elbows back as far as they will go, with a firm, quick movement. Remember to keep your lower arms level, as shown. Return to the starting position and repeat as many times as you wish.

2 Resume the position you took in Step 1, but this time, as you move your elbows back, straighten your arms, so that you fling them behind you. Repeat several times.

3 Stand erect and hold your arms in front of your chest, with elbows bent. Grasp your left arm just above the wrist with your right hand, and your right arm just above the wrist with your left hand, as shown. Now pull on each arm, as if you were trying to pull your hands apart, but maintain a tight grip. Hold for a few seconds. Relax your hands and then repeat again several times.

4 Now raise your arms and hold them out in front of your mouth; repeat Step 3 in this higher position. If you wish, you can also do the exercise holding your arms out just in front of your waistline.

BASIC EXERCISE ROUTINE

Add these basic exercises to your general fitness routine to give special problem areas extra work, or do them on their own as an isolated routine. If you do them on their own, use the abdominal muscle exercises from the general fitness plan for your stomach – and remember to warm up first and cool down afterwards.

THIGH MUSCLES
Exercise A

1 Lie on your back on the floor with your arms resting straight out at right angles to your body and your feet apart in line with your hips.

2 Hold a cushion between your knees and, keeping your back pressed into the floor, press your knees together 10 times quickly, and 10 times slowly, keeping the cushion in place throughout.

3 Now repeat the same sequence again, holding a tennis or golf ball between your knees.

Exercise B

1 Lie on your back on the floor with your legs straight, and your lower back pressed to the floor. Put your arms along your sides, palms to the floor.

2 Stretch your arms out at right angles to your body. Bend your legs and bring your knees up to your chest.

3 Keeping your legs together, steadily straighten them so that they are pointing up towards the ceiling. Keep your feet relaxed.

4 Slowly open your legs out sideways – as wide as you can – then close them again. Repeat the exercise (Steps 2-4) 4 times. When you get used to the exercise, you can do it with small weights tied to your ankles.

Exercise C

1 Stand sideways on to a chair or table (lightly holding the edge to maintain your balance) with your shoulders down and relaxed, and with your knees bent and your feet facing forwards.

2 Lift your left hip slightly and slowly move your leg out and up (no higher than 45 degrees), keeping your foot and knee facing forwards. Make sure you do not let your body tilt – keep it as straight as possible. Carefully lower your leg. Repeat the whole exercise 10 times, then turn and repeat with the other leg.

Exercise D

1 Lie on your right side on the floor with your legs out straight. Support your head with your right hand.

2 Bend your lower leg behind you to maintain balance and tilt your hips slightly towards the floor; your head, hips, knees, and feet should all be facing forwards. Balance yourself with your left hand on the floor in front of you.

3 Slowly lift your upper leg, then bring it down to touch the lower one; raise it again and repeat this action 6 times. Turn over and repeat Steps 1-3 on the other side.

ANKLES AND CALF MUSCLES
Exercise A

1 Sit up straight on a chair, with your knees together and heels on the floor and slightly apart, in line with your hips. Bring your big toes up (as high off the floor as possible) and roll your feet in towards each other.

2 Now tilt and move both feet down and outwards from the ankle, keeping your big toes raised as much as possible as you roll your feet on to their outer edges. Repeat 10 times.

Exercise B

1 Lie flat on your back on the floor with your legs straight.

2 Bring one leg up and hold it beneath the back of your thigh so that it is pulled towards your chest. Rotate your foot 10 times in a clockwise direction and 10 times anti-clockwise. Repeat with the other leg. Increase the number of repeats to 20 for each foot, working alternately in groups of 7.

BUTTOCK MUSCLES
Exercise A

1 Stand upright and lightly hold the back of a chair or the edge of a table with both hands to maintain your balance. Put your weight on your right leg and turn your left leg out from the hip.

2 Keeping your foot flexed, take your left leg back as far as you can without bending it at the knee, forcing the movement or over-arching your back. Repeat with the other leg. Repeat 5 times for each leg and gradually build up to 20 repetitions.

Exercise B

1 Lie on your back with your knees bent and your feet slightly apart, in line with your hips. Place your arms by your sides, palms flat on the floor.

2 Place your weight on your shoulders and upper back (not your neck), raise your bottom to a comfortable height and tighten your buttock muscles, keeping your feet flat on the floor and your arms by your sides. Hold for several seconds. Lower your bottom to the floor. Repeat 5 times, building up to 20 repetitions.

Exercise C

1 Kneel on all fours with your knees slightly apart, in line with your hips, but keeping them tucked right under your hips. Place your hands in front of you, a shoulder-width apart and facing forwards. Bend your elbows so that you are leaning on your forearms.

2 Keeping your foot flexed, push your left leg out straight behind you, keeping your back and hips parallel.

3 Bring your leg and foot down to the floor, keeping your foot flexed and your leg straight. Repeat Steps 2 and 3 twelve times. Return to the original position, then repeat the exercise with your other leg. Build up to 20 repetitions.

UPPER ARM MUSCLES

1 Stand upright with your feet slightly apart and your hands hanging loosely by your sides.

2 Lift your arms and make 5 small circles forwards and then backwards with both arms moving simultaneously. Aim to build up to 20 circles, and when you are used to the exercise, hold a can of beans in each hand and repeat. You can vary the exercise by bringing your arms around to the front and tracing the circles there as well.

BUST (PECTORAL) MUSCLES
Exercise A

1 Stand upright with your feet slightly apart in line with your shoulders. Keep your shoulders up, your back straight, and your bottom and stomach tucked in. Keep your legs slightly bent. Let your arms hang loosely by your sides.

2 Make a scissor movement across the front of your body (at waist-level) by crossing one hand over the other while holding your arms straight out in front.

3 Raise your arms to chest level and repeat the action.

4 Then repeat the action holding your arms at head level. Keep the scissor movements controlled as you swing; do 20 repetitions at each level.

Exercise B

1 Kneel on all fours as if you are about to do press-ups, with your legs raised at the back and your feet crossed. Your arms should be straight.

2 Bend your arms as you lower your body to the floor. Do this 10 times to begin with, and build up to 30 repetitions.

EXERCISE AND STRESS

We push ourselves at such a cracking pace these days that feeling stressed can, at times, almost become the normal way to feel. A bit of stress is quite useful because it helps to keep us on the ball, but being under prolonged pressure, and ignoring physical signs such as shaky hands, hyperventilation, and a fast heartbeat is not at all healthy. So if any of these sensations sound familiar to you, resolve to make time every day to relax your body and free your mind of problems.

HOW EXERCISE HELPS YOU TO RELAX

Exercise does not just tone your muscles, it also eases the muscular aches and pains that go hand-in-hand with stress; it also distracts your mind from the worries that make you tense. Regular exercise – and especially yoga – lifts your mood (remember how good you felt the last time you did some invigorating exercise?) and soothes your mind. As you become fitter, you will find that your ability to cope with mundane problems that crop up improves.

YOGA – A GOOD ROUTE TO RELAXATION

Yoga is an exercise technique and ancient doctrine based on achieving mind, body, and spiritual harmony. The belief is that when all these elements are in tune with each other, mental and physical health is at a peak. As well as improving joint mobility, suppleness, shape and self-image, yoga can dispel the headaches and tiredness brought on by stress and nervous tension. The practice involves many active principles, but the most popular ones that are used in Western teaching are as follows.

○ **Asana, or postures:** These are held for several minutes at a time and, together with the correct breathing, perfected to give certain physical, spiritual, and emotional benefits before each new step is learned.

○ **Pranayama:** This is deep, slow breathing which is done while sitting – either in a lotus position, or on a chair that allows your spine to stay straight.

○ **Relaxation:** Up to 15 minutes is spent resting (usually lying flat on

---

DAILY RELAXATION TECHNIQUE

○ Lie flat on the floor and shut your eyes. Take a deep breath and exhale twice, then breathe normally.
○ Slacken your feet: let them go floppy, then relax your ankles, knees and thighs.
○ Push your tummy out as far as you can, hold it there and then relax it completely, letting it move in and out freely while you breathe easily.
○ Relax your shoulders, and then feel them drop back to the floor.
○ Relax your facial muscles completely, then move the focus to your mind: force yourself to clear it – blank out and forget the day's problems – and enjoy emptying your head. All you should be thinking about now is whether your body is completely at ease; if you become aware of a tense muscle in your body, release it.
○ Rest like this – blissfully relaxed – for a minimum of 10 minutes; when you have had enough, open your eyes and get up slowly.

INSTANT RELAXATION

Stand by an open window and take deep, steady breaths for a slow count of 10 or 12. Then hold your breath for about 10 seconds, releasing it with a long, low "aaah". (Do not try this more than twice or it might make you feel a bit dizzy or faint.)

Right: Complete relaxation is fundamental to yoga teaching
Opposite: Two yoga asanas.

the floor) after yoga to help your mind and body unwind and recharge. Yoga principles and postures are best learned with a teacher, rather than out of a book.

NECK AND SHOULDERS – TENSION FOCUS

Anyone who has ever been tied to their desk or hunched over a computer keyboard or typewriter for long periods without a break knows all about the discomfort that a stiff neck, back, and shoulder "knots" can cause. Our upper torso is usually the focal point for mental and physical stress, and the stiffness this causes can lead to headaches and back pain. One of the best ways to avoid and relieve this type of physical stress is to get up and walk around the room regularly, stretching and loosening your shoulders by circling them backwards and forwards as you go.

IMPROVING YOUR RESPIRATORY AWARENESS

Our emotional state is reflected by our breathing patterns. When we are under strain or nervous, we tend to either hyperventilate (over-breath) or inhale short, shallow breaths – a habit that you can only break when your attention is drawn to it. Take stock and examine the way you are breathing now: is your breathing pattern regular and steady? If not, take a couple of deep breaths and start again, this time making a conscious effort to breathe steady, equal, calm breaths.

RELAXATION CHECKLIST

If you find yourself becoming tense, grab 10 minutes at the end of each day to run through this progressive relaxation checklist.

O Check your body: tense every little bit of it, then consciously relax every part. Bunch your toes, then free them; clench your thigh and buttock muscles, then let them relax; pull in your stomach muscles and let them go; hunch your shoulders, then relax them; clench and relax your hands several times.

O Check your breathing pattern: inhale deeply and slowly, hold your breath for a couple of seconds, then release it again, letting your body flop as you exhale.

O Check your posture: sitting, standing and walking badly can also produce knots and tightness in the muscles in your back, neck, and shoulders.

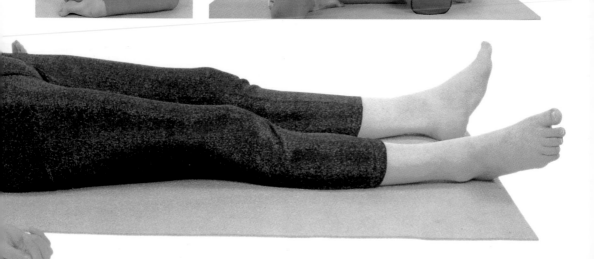

FACIAL EXERCISES: A QUICK FRESHENER AND TONER

Tension shows in your face when your features look drawn and your expressions frozen and rather set. A good laugh is the best way to relax a tense face, but this exercise routine also helps to liberate and tone the key muscles quickly; try it when you are sitting in the bath – not at the traffic lights.

1 Scrunch up your whole face for a few seconds so that your nose is wrinkled, your forehead furrowed, and your eyes and mouth are tightly closed.

2 Do the opposite: open your mouth and eyes as wide as you can (as if you are silently screaming) to release your throat muscles.

3 Close your mouth again, purse your lips, and push your mouth up to the left, then to the right.

4 Grin – as if from ear to ear – and open your eyes wide again.

5 Hold and repeat the grin, but this time, tuck in your chin to tighten your neck muscles.

DIET FOR LIFE

Eat monounsaturated fats such as olive oil, and polyunsaturates such as sunflower oil, in preference to butter and other saturated fats.

Starchy carbohydrates should make up about 50 per cent of the daily diet.

Balance is important to a healthy diet. The way we eat affects our well-being, so knowing how to choose a healthy combination of foods is the first step towards improving our eating habits and lifestyle.

FAT – FRIEND AND FOE

Eggs, butter, milk, and meat are a good source of energy, but we tend to eat too much fat which is why many of us are overweight: fat produces fat. Cut down on fat in your diet but do not cut it out completely: eat less fatty red meat and more fish and poultry; grill, bake, or stir-fry (using polyunsaturated and monounsaturated oils), eat eggs in moderation, and use semi-skimmed or skimmed milk instead of full-fat milk. Try to use margarine, or try switching to a reduced fat olive-oil spread instead of butter; if you like butter, reserve it for special occasions.

Saturated fats come mainly from animal products (milk, butter, cheese, and meat) and in excess are thought to contribute to raised cholesterol levels.

Polyunsaturated fats are found in vegetable oils such as sunflower, safflower, corn, and soya bean oils; they are also found in some fish oils and some nuts, and are said to help lower cholesterol levels.

Monounsaturated fats are found in olive and rapeseed oils; they are also said to lower cholesterol levels.

GRAINS, FRUIT, AND VEGETABLES

Eat plenty of wholegrain foods such as brown rice, wholemeal bread, wholemeal flour, and wholemeal pasta; they should form the bulk of a healthy diet. Also concentrate on eating lots of fresh fruit and vegetables: these are rich in carbohydrates, minerals, and vitamins. To obtain all of these nutrients, try to eat as many raw vegetables as possible.

SUGAR SWEET

Many of us tend to eat too much sugar so try cutting added sugar out of your diet completely for 21 days (your body will still obtain it naturally from certain vegetables and fruit) and see how you feel: even if you are not actively dieting you will probably find that you lose some weight. Craving sugary foods such as doughnuts and pastries when you are pre-menstrual is common in some women. One way of combating this is to eat little and often; snack on fruit with a high water content, such as watermelon and strawberries.

SALTY ISSUES

Even if you are not dieting you should eat less salt as it may lead to high blood pressure. There are some good low-sodium salts available, so use these instead of the real thing if you do need to season food with salt. Do not buy salted butter, avoid processed and smoked cheeses, add the barest minimum of salt (or none at all) to cooking water, and avoid processed foods.

FLUID INTAKE

Drink plenty of water: your body loses between 2-3 litres/3-5 pints of fluid every day, so drink no less than 1.5 litres/2½ pints of water daily. Once you get into the swing of it, consciously drinking water is an easy habit to maintain. Just keep some to hand and sip it slowly throughout the day.

HEALTHY DIET CHECKLIST

The healthy eating guidelines summarized here are not difficult to apply to a daily diet. Once you

FIBRE FACTS

Fibre is important to a healthy diet. Your body cannot digest it, so, in rather basic terms, it goes in and comes out, taking other waste with it. Fibrous foods include bread, rice, cereals, vegetables, fruit, and nuts. We should aim for about 30 g (just over 1 oz) of fibre a day. These are some examples of good fibre sources:

Good Sources	Average Portion	Grams of Fibre
wholemeal pasta	75 g/3 oz (uncooked)	9
baked beans	125 g/4 oz	8
frozen peas	75 g/3 oz	8
bran flakes	50 g/2 oz	7
muesli	50 g/2 oz	4-5
raspberries	100 g/3½ oz	6
blackberries	100 g/3½ oz	6
banana	average fruit	3.5
baked jacket potato	150 g/ 5 oz	3.5
brown rice	50 g/2 oz	3
cabbage	100 g/3½ oz	3
red kidney beans	40 g/1½ oz	3
wholemeal bread	1 large slice	3
high-fibre white bread	1 large slice	2
stewed prunes	6 fruit	2

Dairy products such as egg yolks, hard cheeses, and full fat milk contain high levels of fat. Choose low fat milks, cheeses, and yogurts.

Ideally, you should eat at least two portions of vegetables – fresh, frozen, or tinned – with your main meal.

have adopted them, they will become part of your daily routine so there is no reason why you cannot follow a healthy diet for the rest of your life.

○ Eat lots of fresh fruit and vegetables, ideally five portions, or about 398 g/14 oz a day.

○ Be wary of the amount of fat you eat.

○ Try to eat half your daily food in the form of starchy carbohydrates such as potatoes, bread, pasta and rice.

○ Replace refined flour with wholemeal flour.

○ Eat more fibre-rich foods such as wholemeal bread and pasta, brown rice and pulses.

○ Cut down on sugar.

○ Cut down on salt.

○ Drink lots of water; reduce coffee and tea. The caffeine they

VITAMIN VALUES

Vitamin	Sources include	Benefits
Vitamin A	liver (especially fish livers), egg yolk, fortified margarine, oily fish, oranges, apricots, carrots, tomatoes, melons, dark green leafy vegetables	eye sight; skin; may protect against cancer
Vitamin B_1	most foods – including wheatgerm and pulses, whole grains, brewer's yeast, nuts, fortified breakfast cereals	helps break down carbohydrates; nervous system
Vitamin B_2	brewer's yeast, liver, kidney, dairy produce, wheat bran, wheatgerm, eggs	repairs body tissues
Vitamin B_3	wheatgerm, whole grain cereals, meat, fish	essential for tissue chemical reactions
Vitamin B_6	avocados, liver, whole grains, egg yolk, lean meat, bananas, fish, potatoes	nervous system; skin; red blood cells
Vitamin B_{12}	liver, kidney, some fish (including shellfish), eggs, milk	healthy blood and nerves
Vitamin C	citrus fruits, potatoes, tomatoes, leafy greens	helps heal wounds, may fight colds, 'flu and infections; protects gums, keeps joints and ligaments in good working order
Vitamin D	fish liver oils, fatty fish, eggs, fortified margarine also synthesized by ultraviolet light	calcium deposits in bones
Vitamin E	vegetable oils, some vegetables, wheatgerm	cell growth; antioxidant
Vitamin K	most vegetables – especially leafy greens ones, liver	essential in production of some proteins

contain is stimulating, so try swapping them for herbal teas. If you cannot give up coffee switch to organic Arabica beans, which can be brewed instead of instant granular coffee – and limit yourself to two cups a day.

○ Cut down on sugary canned drinks and particularly on alcohol intake. It is very important to cut down on alcohol if you drink more than 14 units a week (for a woman); 14 units is equivalent to 2 glasses of wine a day.

IDEAL WEEKLY FOOD QUOTA

Eat food from each of the four main food groups each day.

○ Starchy foods, including bread, cereals, pasta, potatoes and rice.

○ Dairy products (preferably low fat).

○ Meat, fish, poultry, beans and lentils, nuts, and eggs.

○ Vegetables and fruit.

Some authorities, such as the World Health Organization, recommend eating 5 portions a day from this group; this is thought to help prevent cancer.

Fresh fruit makes a healthy, low calorie snack food that is filling as well as delicious.

VALUABLE MINERALS

As well as vitamins, a wide variety of minerals are essential for good health, growth, and body functioning. Some, such as calcium and iron, are needed in quite large amounts, and for some people there is a real risk of deficiency if they do not eat a healthy diet.

Calcium: A regular supply of calcium is vital because bone tissue is constantly being broken down and rebuilt. A calcium-rich diet is particularly important during adolescence, pregnancy, breast-feeding, the menopause, and for the elderly. Smoking, lack of exercise, too much alcohol, high protein and high salt intakes all encourage calcium losses.

Iron: Only a fraction of the iron present in food is absorbed, although it is much more readily absorbed from red meat than from vegetable sources. Vitamin C also helps with absorption. Pregnant women, women who have heavy periods, and vegetarians should all be particularly careful about ensuring an adequate intake.

Trace elements: These include other essential minerals such as zinc, iodine, magnesium, and potassium. Although important, they are only needed in minute quantities. They are found in a wide variety of foods and deficiency is very rare.

Mineral	Sources	Essential for
Calcium	cheese, milk, yogurt, eggs, bread, nuts, pulses, fish with soft bones such as whitebait and tinned sardines, leafy green vegetables	healthy bones, teeth and nails; muscle and nerve function; blood clotting; milk production in nursing mothers
Iron	liver, red meat, oily fish, whole grain cereals, leafy green vegetables	makes haemoglobin, the pigment in red bloods cells that helps transport oxygen around the body

EATING FOR ENERGY

How often do you feel tired and lethargic? Does your energy dip dramatically in the afternoons making you feel dozy (even if you have not washed down a three-course lunch with a bottle of wine) and in need of 40 winks? If you life is regularly disrupted by fatigue and you want to take action, one of the wisest things to do is to look at your diet and, if necessary, change what you eat and how you eat it.

OFF TO A GOOD START
There is logic behind the saying "breakfast like a king, lunch like a prince and dine like a pauper." If you start the day with a substantial breakfast your body will be getting all the energy it needs early on.

CHANGING YOUR EATING HABITS
You are most likely to succeed in changing your diet if you eat regularly, in moderation, and slowly – and savour every mouthful. Although the bonuses of eating in a balanced way do not come instantly, if you take stock now and concentrate on eating the fresh foods suggested below, as well as avoiding high-fat, sugar-rich foods such as cakes, pastries, and salty snacks, you will probably notice a marked difference in your energy levels within a couple of weeks.

VITALITY FOODS FOR EXTRA ENERGY
A diet that makes you feel more energetic is based on natural, wholesome foods that are nutritious, rather than fatty and fast foods. If you want to boost your energy levels, stock up on fresh and dried fruits that are high in natural sugars such as pears, kiwi fruit, and apricots, vegetables such as peas, spinach, cabbage, and

Nutritionists and other health professionals recommend eating fresh fruit every day.

onions, and oily fish, poultry, and red meats such as game and lean beef. Eat nuts, brown rice, seeds, pulses, wheatgerm, whole-grains, and foods that contain minerals such as magnesium, phosphorus, and zinc, and water-soluble vitamins B and C. Use cold-pressed oils such as grapeseed, olive, sesame, sunflower, hazelnut, and walnut to dress salads; do not skip dairy foods but use milk and natural yogurt (preferably low fat); replace sliced white loaves with bread made from wholemeal flour.

SUPER SQUEEZES AND SHAKES
Home-made fruit juices and milk- or yogurt-based drinks are energy-boosting alternatives to commercially prepared drinks, and are easy

to prepare. Choose sweet fruits such as mango, banana, and apricots – these have a naturally high sugar content – switch on the juicer or liquidizer and drink them chilled. Here are two sparkling shakes to try:

1 mango
2 slices pineapple
1 banana
150 ml/5 fl oz semi-skimmed or skimmed milk or a small carton of natural low fat yogurt
2.5 ml/1/2 tsp honey (optional)
or:
a handful of raspberries and strawberries
2 apricots
100 ml/4 fl oz milk or natural low fat yogurt

DIET AND WEIGHT LOSS

People tackle weight loss in ways that suit their lifestyles. But the safest and best way to shift excess pounds is to combine regular exercise with a balanced calorie-controlled diet. What you eat when you are trying to take off weight should not be that different from a normal eating plan – except for the amount you consume. If you only have a small amount to lose and you cut your calorie intake by 1000 from the recommended 2300 calories per day, you will lose weight; if you are aiming to lose a significant amount, stick to 1200 calories a day and you will get there. Your basic weight loss ethos is less sugar and saturated fats, more fibre and starch; the calories you eat should come from foods that supply you with the right number of nutrients to keep your body functioning properly.

MIND OVER MATTER

Quick weight loss is inspiring, but it is important to think ahead too: you need to retrain your palate and eating habits and reassess your physical activity so that you can lose weight and stay slim. You cannot expect to achieve miracles in a few days, but you will see a difference within three or four weeks if you eat properly and exercise regularly. Losing weight successfully is like getting fitter: you need a horizon – or goal – ahead of you to help spur you on.

ABSOLUTELY AVOID

Chocolate, biscuits, doughnuts, fizzy drinks, cakes, ice cream, sugared cereals – in fact anything that contains refined sugar, it's just empty calories: a confectionary bar, for instance, has 230 calories and has absolutely no food value.

SLIMMERS' TIPS

○ If you can, eat more at the start of the day to give you energy and time to burn off the calories.
○ Eat little and often to stop hunger pangs.
○ Drink lots of water.
○ If you want to snack, keep a supply of raw fruit, vegetables, and raisins nearby.
○ Don't be tempted to take slimming pills, diuretics, or laxatives to speed up weight loss; they upset the body's natural equilibrium – something that can take considerable time to rebalance.
○ Exercise regularly; extra activity uses up calories, and this is essential to weight loss.
○ Don't give up if you lapse: it is quite normal to veer off track every so often, and as long as you get back on course as soon as you can, all your hard work will not be ruined.

HOW MUCH WEIGHT CAN I LOSE?

To lose weight you have to eat fewer calories than your body burns up every day, but the amount varies from person to person. The exact amount depends on your personal composition – how much fat your body has, your metabolism, and the amount you weigh to begin with. As a rule of thumb though, the heavier you are when you start slimming, the more weight you are likely to lose within 21 days or a month. When you lose weight it comes off all areas of your body, but it can take longer to shift from certain areas, such as your arms and legs. This is where exercise is particularly helpful: working on specific trouble spots will encourage the weight to come off more quickly.

Left: Don't be tempted to weigh yourself too often – once every 10 days is enough.

MYTH-BREAKER:
If I Stop Smoking Will I Gain Weight?

You may well put on a small amount of weight at first but if you are serious about getting fitter you have absolutely no choice but to kick smoking. Tobacco is toxic. If you are a smoker, stopping is the biggest leap you can make towards living a healthier lifestyle; if you are following a straightforward weight-loss diet and think that kicking the habit will make you pick at food all day, keep lots of raw vegetables and raisins on hand to munch on.

EATING OUT – AND STAYING ON COURSE

The problem of what to do when dieting and eating out is a tricky one. At the height of the 1980s' slimming boom, some restaurants offered specific diet options on their menus, but few give this kind of service now that dieting is less fashionable. The best way to get around the problem of dining out without lapsing – without drawing attention to yourself and still being able to enjoy yourself – is as follows:

○ Order a salad starter.
○ Skip bread or breadsticks, or eat a piece of bread without butter - it can be just as delicious.

MYTH-BREAKER:
If I Skip Meals Will I Lose Weight More Quickly?

Do not be tempted to skip meals. Skipping meals makes you crave, overeat at the next meal, and it slows down your metabolism, which ultimately hinders weight loss.

Left: Keeping an accurate record of your measurements is one way of calculating weight loss.

○ Drink one glass of wine, and lots of water.
○ Choose a simple main course, something like grilled fish or chicken; avoid anything that is drenched in a rich sauce or in lots of butter.
○ Choose a simple low fat dessert: a sorbet is ideal.
○ Finish with herbal tea (peppermint is very refreshing and settles your stomach after eating); or, if you have to have a coffee, choose espresso or black coffee, not cappuccino.

GAUGING WEIGHT LOSS

You may choose to weigh yourself once a week first thing in the morning. Drawing up a goal chart to record any weight losses (and gains) may help to keep you inspired. Or, if you prefer, ignore the scales and just focus on how you feel by keeping a check on how your clothes feel. When tight clothes become more comfortable

A sandwich with fresh ingredients makes a healthy lunch – even for weight watchers.

this is a sure sign that you are losing weight. Alternatively, you may prefer to keep a record of your measurements (bust, waist, and hips) and see how they alter over the 21-day period. Do whatever works for you, and when you have lost a little weight reward yourself with a special calorie-free treat such as a new lipstick, eyeshadow, or a manicure.

Nutritious, starchy foods such as pasta are not fattening if eaten with low fat sauces.

INDEX

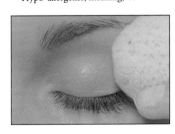

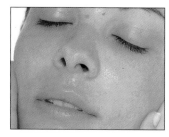

NOTES

NOTES

NOTES

NOTES